I0211488

BRIGHT ALLIANCE

EVOLUTION'S ALLY

EVOLUTION'S ALLY

Our World's Religious Traditions
as Conveyor Belts of Transformation

Dustin DiPerna

Foreword by Ken Wilber

BRIGHT
ALLIANCE

Evolution's Ally

Copyright © 2018 by Dustin DiPerna
All rights reserved.

Published by Bright Alliance

Paperback Edition

Cover Design by James Redenbaugh

Author photo taken by David Vergne

Second edition design: Brad Reynolds
integralartandstudies.com

BrightAlliance.org

ISBN 978-1-7321579-0-3

Printed and Bound in the United States

For My Family

Table of Contents

Figures and Illustrations

Foreword
By Ken Wilber

Integral Theory, as it shows up in Integral Spirituality (and Integral Religious Studies) is based on a few fundamental ideas, some of them quite novel. One, every event has at least four perspectives (called quadrants—namely, the interior and exterior of the individual and the collective, or "I," "We," "It," and "Its"—or, again, art, morals, and science, or first-person, second-person, and third-person modes, counting the two exterior modes as one). These quadrants show development—namely, through developmental lines or streams that grow and evolve through developmental levels or waves (e.g., multiple intelligences, such as cognitive intelligence, moral intelligence, self intelligence, spiritual intelligence, kinesthetic intelligence, emotional intelligence—with all of these streams growing through essentially similar waves or levels of complexity). The "deep structures or patterns of these levels are basically similar wherever they appear, although their "surface features" or patterns vary considerably from culture to culture. In addition to these lines and levels or structures of consciousness, there are states of consciousness (e.g., waking, dreaming, deep sleep, meditative). Finally, rounding out this Integral outline, there are types, which are patterns that continue to appear at each level of development (such as masculine/feminine, or Enneagram types, etc.). All in all, that gives us five major elements that every human being in the world possesses (indeed, every sentient being), and the point about an integral approach is that if you want to have a truly comprehensive and inclusive picture of any event, you need to include all five elements.

This is as true for religion and spirituality as for anything else. (Although the word "spirituality" is usually used to refer to the more interior aspects of religion, and "religion" to the more exterior, institutional aspects, I will use them synonymously unless otherwise indicated.) Religion has all five dimensions or elements: quadrants, levels, lines, states, and types. Virtually all five of those assertions are novel, they—and especially their connectivity—is what makes the Integral Theory approach to religion so new and creative, capable of handling some very difficult questions that have eluded humankind virtually from the start (see Integral Spirituality for a further discussion of this). This book, *Evolution's Ally*, focuses on three of the five elements in particular: quadrants, levels, and lines. Namely, when we focus on the interior quadrants, every major religion has a developmental component or developmental line that progresses through the same five major levels. What does that mean?

Although when presenting Integral Theory I often use 10 or so levels, in this book, Dustin wisely focuses on five major levels: magic, mythic, rational, pluralistic, and integral. What this means is that every major religious tradition—its main theories, dogmas, or dharmas, as well as its major practices—grow and develop through at least these five major levels of consciousness or levels of complexity. Magic is egocentric, and focused on the individual himself, often with magical practices. Mythic is ethnocentric, or group oriented ("chosen people"), and often prayer focused. Rational is a "de-mythologized" stage, where ultimate reality, even if itself trans-rational, is conceptualized or at least explained in rational terms (e.g., Deism). Pluralistic is egalitarian or relativistic, with its teachings maintained to be relative and changing from culture to culture (since Spirit will itself appear differently to different cultures), with none of them ultimately more true than the others (and all of them capable of delivering "salvation" if adequately followed).

Each of those junior stages (magic, mythic, rational, pluralistic) have at least one thing in common: they each believe their views and beliefs are the only true ones in the entire lot. What makes the integral stage so novel is that it is the first stage in history (phylogenetic or ontogenetic) that believes there is some degree of truth in all the previous levels ("everybody is right," even if some are "more right" than others).

Dustin's wonderful contribution has been to supply details for all of these stages in four of the world's major religions—Christianity, Islam, Buddhism, and Hinduism. This is a major accomplishment. First, it shows the general correctness of Integral Theory applied to religion on a worldwide basis. But just as important, it fundamentally alters the way in which religion or spirituality can (and should) be taught and practiced. Namely, since individual human beings progress through the same major stages in their own lives, they should be taught the religion corresponding to their stage of development—magic individuals should be taught the magic form of their religion; mythic should be taught mythic; rational taught rational; pluralistic taught pluralistic; and integral taught integral. Better yet, individuals would begin learning religious inquiry in their childhood years by interacting with the magic version of their religion, move to the mythic version in later childhood, move to rational in adolescence, move again, this time to pluralistic, if and when they reach that stage, and likewise for integral.

In this way, each of the world's great religions can act as a "conveyor belt" of development, helping individuals move, develop, grow, and mature along the entire spectrum of development, thus acting as a "pacer of transformation" (or conveyor belt), instead of— as they do now—attempting to halt individual development at the mythic/fundamentalist level (where Moses really did part the Red Sea, Lao Tzu really was 900 years old when he was born, the Lord really did rain down locusts on the Egyptians, etc.).

The first thing that an integral approach to religion would do is stop the silly, boring, absolutely needless battles between religion (which is usually mythic) and science (which is allowed to develop to rational and higher). As Integral Studies has amply demonstrated, there are forms of both religion and science on every level of development (one isn't "higher" than the other). But instead of seeing that there is, for example, mythic science and mythic religion, and rational science and rational religion, religion is frozen at mythic (and the "old gray-bearded gentleman in the sky," along with other concrete literal myths) and science is allowed to continue developing to rational and higher— thus creating a steel band around the world, separating science (with "objective truth") and religion (with "mythic nonsense"). This crushes human beings' spiritual intelligence at the mythic level, and makes religion in general look like childish twaddle to all the higher levels (which is what it basically is, when frozen at childhood mythic levels). Then the rational and higher levels throw religion out completely, and consequently we are frozen out of the higher levels of the development of spiritual wisdom, and thus also out of higher ways of answering the question, "What is of ultimate concern?" Only spiritual intelligence can address that question, and to freeze it at mythic (and thus essentially throw it out entirely) is to cripple a human being's fundamental capacity to face and address life's most pressing, compelling, and significant questions. Spiritual intelligence, frozen at mythic and thence discarded, is usually replaced with cognitive intelligence, thus arriving at "scientific materialism," which can't address the question of Spirit in any event (it is true that science cannot prove Spirit, but equally true that it cannot disprove it either, something the critics conveniently forget). Spiritual intelligence, on the other hand, can approach this task and this question with great success, which is why it evolved with a dozen or so other intelligences in the first place, each addressing a different domain—ethics, aesthetics, emotional, interpersonal, kinesthetic, musical, mathematical, etc.

With the integral approach to religion and spirituality, individuals would ideally begin their study with magic, then (around age 6 or 7 years old) move to mythic, then (around 11 or 12 years old) move to rational (if they choose to believe), then to pluralistic in their twenties and integral as they grow older. At each developmental stage of the individual, the individual's religion matches the rest of his or her truths and values, and doesn't stay arrested at mythic! Imagine the difference in the world scene if such a conveyor belt were in place for every major religion!

Now, according to Integral Theory, all religions also have access to another of the five major elements, namely, states of consciousness. Whereas the above-discussed structures or levels of consciousness determine how one will interpret one's experience (magically, mythically, rationally, etc.), states of consciousness determine the types of phenomena that will be experienced in the first place, based on the natural states of consciousness available (such as waking, dreaming, deep formless sleep, etc.). States of consciousness become extremely important in mystical spiritual experiences (such as nature mysticism with the waking state, deity mysticism with the dream state, and formless mysticism with the deep-sleep state). Structures of consciousness and states of consciousness are relatively independent, and thus, for example, one could be in a subtle dream state and interpret it magically, mythically, rationally, pluralistically, or integrally, depending upon one's structural development. Structures are how we grow up; states are how we wake up. States are obviously the most important in contemplative or meditative spiritual consciousness development, and both variables (structures and states) are necessary in order to determine a person's overall spiritual/religious development. Dustin's first volume to this series, *Streams of Wisdom*, focuses on the dynamic relationship between states and structures together. This second volume, that you hold in your hands now, narrows the scope with its emphasis on structures alone. All of these factors, along with the other elements of integral theory, make up the core of Integral Religious Studies.

The religious or spiritual dimension is arguably the most important dimension there is, and spiritual intelligence the most important intelligence available. Yet if we look at the bulk of the world's religions as they are most commonly practiced, we find two fundamental problems with them. The first is that they are mostly frozen at mythic levels (although each contains exceptions of higher-level saints and sages that are greatly revered—precisely because they are drawing on higher levels!). The second is that, although virtually all of the great traditions began in a series of mystical state experiences in their founders, and their basic teachings were methods for awakening higher states of unity consciousness (all the way to enlightenment or salvation, where "I and the All are One"), the practice of state development has often been forgotten or ignored, and these states of consciousness replaced mostly by the structures of consciousness in spiritual intelligence (and then often frozen at magic or mythic, representing the culture of the time, although rarely the highest level found or allowed in the founder's teachings). Overcoming these two major "problems" with today's religions would amount, quite literally, in a massive world transformation—starting with opening spiritual intelligence to levels higher than ethnocentric (70% of the world's population is at ethnocentric or lower levels, and most of them are kept their by their religious dogmas). Reintroducing meditation or contemplation (state training) would complete the transformation, and taken together, these two "corrections" in the world's religions would indeed act as pacers of transformation for the entire world, drawing it into worldcentric levels of morals, beliefs, values, and truths that would change the face of humanity forever.

Dustin's articulation here in *Evolution's Ally*, along with the other insights he offers in his series of books on Integral Religion and Spirituality, are a brilliantly important part of that first step, showing how a truly integral spirituality can lead to an integral humanity. The value of this simply cannot be overstated...

Ken Wilber
author of *Integral Spirituality*

Acknowledgements

American philosopher Ken Wilber offers a simple yet effective way to organize knowledge using what he calls the "integral lens."[1] With its capacity to organize vast amounts of information, the integral lens provides a comprehensive framework to start making sense of our complex world. In his many books, Wilber uses the integral approach to point out connections between fields of inquiry that might otherwise be left unnoticed. Weaving a tapestry of synthesis from diverse fields such as biology, psychology, cultural studies, and systems theory, Wilber's insights provide intellectual outlines waiting to be expanded by future generations of scholars.

The realm of spirituality and religious studies is one area in which Wilber's intellectual outline is particularly ripe and ready to be elaborated in serious academic fashion. Building upon many ideas offered throughout decades of scholarship, but most importantly, the work assembled in Wilber's *Integral Spirituality*, this book (in combination with volume 1 of the series) brings shape to a new discipline called Integral Religious Studies.[2] With the aim of honoring Wilber's legacy, *Evolution's Ally* is a direct response to his call to action to "make available and better known the [rational] (and higher) levels of development of spiritual intelligence."[3]

Just as Wilber stood on the shoulders of the many scholars to precede him, I have the honor and privilege of standing on Wilber's platform, striving to push Integral Theory into new realms of understanding and application. In doing so, the first few chapters begin by using several of Wilber's insights as foundation, while later chapters develop the notions into more fully fleshed-out concepts. At times, points already explained in Wilber's work are reiterated in order to bring the reader up-to-date with Integral Theory. In other situations, the book moves beyond Wilber's initial ideas, examining how the integral lens can be applied in an analysis of four specific religious traditions. In both instances, the presentation does its very best to clarify which ideas are reiterations of Wilber's work and which ideas represent novel expressions of integral scholarship.

In addition to the intellectual framework and support Wilber's work offers, further acknowledgement must be extended to the many others who made this book's publication possible. I'd like to thank Clint Fuhs who, at Wilber's request, checked this entire manuscript for its consistency with AQAL (Integral Theory). Along with Clint, gratitude must be extended to Rob Smith, Colin Bigelow, Brian Berger, and an entire family at Integral Life and Integral Institute who helped make the publication of this book a reality.

For the beautiful graphics and figures, I thank Mathias Weitbrecht. Mathias, from Visual Facilitators, was responsible for the graphics and for coming up with the general style and aesthetic. Mathias' supports change and facilitates the unfolding of potential through visualization. Both by hand work (being one of the top graphic facilitators) as well as in digital format (process visualization, info graphics, etc.) his work contributes to the evolution of consciousness in a rapidly changing world -- visualfacilitators.com and IntegralInformationArchitecture. com.

A special acknowledgement also needs to be extended to those individuals who engaged this book in its early draft form, at that time the text was titled *Infinite Ladder*. This book would not be the same were it not for the hours of support and conversation I received from Kate Wilson during the composition of that first draft. Other thoughtful editors of this first draft include Keith Borden, Rolf Buerkle, Janet O'Keeffe, Elijah Petersen, Paul Lonely, Michael Garfield, and Frank Visser (among others). I thank you all for the hours of editing (and translating, i.e., Visser) that you devoted to this piece. Your recommendations gave me the reinforcement necessary to continue with this enormous project.

My debt continues to overflow to the hundreds of you who were eager and willing to offer feedback and suggestions on one of the two drafts of this book as they circulated in electronic format for several years. Finally, my deep thanks Ben Williams and Mark Schmanko, for their feedback on the final version of this book before its publication.

The current edition would not have been possible had I not received so much positive support. I am honored that so many of you were willing to offer your time, insight, and energy. Thank you.

Dustin DiPerna
California, 2014

Introduction

This book, *Evolution's Ally*, serves as volume 2 in a series dedicated to Integral Religion and Spirituality. Whereas volume 1, *Streams of Wisdom*, gave a more general outline of spiritual development as it unfolds through three of four key elements (state-stages, structure-stages, and states), this book focuses specifically on the dimensions of structures and structure-stages. In addition to building upon the insights articulated in volume 1 of the larger series, this book offers additional support for a new paradigm of inquiry called *Integral Religious Studies*.[4] As with all integral endeavors, the theories outlined herein are not intended to be the final word on the subject. Instead, this book represents one of the first attempts to describe the contours of a territory only now beginning to emerge. It is my hope that the publication of this work continues to generate enough interest that others will feel propelled to build upon or even correct these initial arguments with further clarification and research.

Initial Inquiry

This book was inspired by several questions relevant to the collective well-being of humanity:

1. If accessed and influenced appropriately, what are leverage points in society and culture that might lead to the most effective forms of human evolution and development?

2. How might humanity create a global culture that promotes the flourishing of Earth and all of its inhabitants?

3. What are the major blockades standing in the way of accessing higher degrees of our collective human potential?

There are, of course, many acceptable answers to each of these questions. However, throughout the course of my own research and finally culminating in my experience of attending the inaugural event at the Integral Spiritual Center in June of 2005, a single response seemed to keep reappearing again and again, "the key is religion."

As soon as I accepted the fact that religion might very well be the critical sociocultural acupuncture point for which I was searching, things immediately fell into place. If the power of religion was properly tapped, it could serve as a colossal leverage point to influence billions. In some circumstances, when its power and potential is harnessed properly, religion holds the capacity to promote flourishing and well-being across the globe. Yet even with these initial insights, I could also see, simultaneously, that when used for selfish or ethnocentric means, religion serves as one of the largest blockades to positive global transformation, with the potential to instigate conflict, violence, and terrorism.

As the hours and hours of research unfolded and the scope of the book narrowed, new questions materialized. I began to ask: How could it be that this single structure we call religion wields such force in the world for both tremendous good and unprecedented negativity? Is it possible to make sense of this rich tapestry of perspectives and interpretation so that we might intentionally cultivate and propagate those forms of religion that are healthy and aligned with our evolutionary growth and development? Can we consciously learn to propagate and promote positive expressions of religion while simultaneously curtailing the spread of those forms of religion in each tradition that create turmoil?

As the analysis and initial inquiry deepened, several important insights emerged:

- The contemplative practices offered in our world's religious traditions offer important technologies designed to cultivate human happiness, interconnectivity, and well-being that we, as a collective species, cannot afford to lose.
- Religion, as is commonly understood, interpreted, and practiced, through its lower and often fundamentalist levels of expression, has the capacity to create cultural, ideological, and often ethnocentric boundaries that prevent the emergence of a mutually supportive global worldview.

- Humanity desperately needs a clear explanation of how and why religion plays such a disparate role in the world. Collectively, we need a more comprehensive understanding of how the psychological infrastructure of those practicing religion influences their interpretation and action. Such an understanding will allow us to map and highlight which forms of religion serve as a boon to human growth and which do not. Ultimately, we must come to understand that when religion is allowed to express itself through more complex lenses of interpretation, practice, and care, many of its negative influences fade leaving only those elements that align with positive growth and development for all of mankind.

I was clear about the book's intention: the cultivation and propagation of particular forms of religion as a force for good is not only possible but is a moral imperative for all those concerned with our shared future.

Objectives

This book seeks to:
- Describe why religion can play such varying roles in the world
- Articulate which forms of religion are useful for global well-being
- Provide a map of developmental possibility within each of our world's religious traditions
- Promote the healthy expression of religion at every level of psychological development
- Offer a lens and a metric with which we might successfully promote those forms of religion that serve greater progress and prosperity, while minimizing the negative impact of those forms of religion that do not

Each of these objectives is accomplished as this book expands its central thesis. In sum, this book suggests that within each of our world's religious traditions there exists a multitude of religious perspectives. Each of these varying perspectives result from both the cultural and psychological level of maturity of the adherent and not, as is sometimes erroneously assumed, from the religion itself. The varying levels of religious maturity not only offer a glimpse into the evolving nature of humanity's relationship to religion but also evidence as to how every unique level of psychological development influences the way human beings interpret and practice particular religious traditions. Acquiring a deeper understanding of the varying levels of religious expression that stem from the multitudes of cultural variation and psychological stages allows us to tease apart why in some circumstances religion can contribute to the betterment of all, while in others it can be detrimental to global welfare.

The following four-part argument helps to further clarify this book's main proposal:

1. Cross-cultural studies in the field of developmental psychology demonstrate that human beings (regardless of race, class, creed, religion, or geographical region) all develop through a common core of psychological stages with each higher stage increasing in complexity and care.[5]

2. Human beings, with their dynamic and varying degrees of psychological capacities, are the entities who endorse, interpret, and practice religious traditions.

3. Due to the fact that the stages of psychological development exist within the human psyche cross-culturally and because humans are the entities endorsing, interpreting, and practicing religion, there is a direct correlation between the stages of human psychological maturity and the varying levels of endorsement, interpretation, and practice in each of our world's great religious traditions.

4. Finally, the higher levels of complexity and care that unfold as human beings mature psychologically, provide a direct metric by which we can measure the potential for religion to be a positive force in the world.[6] The more individuals shift their religious views away from fundamentalist and ethnocentric beliefs at lower stages to frameworks of universal care at higher stages, the more we will find religious actors as leaders of a thriving global culture.

To deepen its thesis, this book outlines five broad stages of psychological maturity that act to influence the way individuals practice and interpret religion. Rather than coercing the reader into learning a new and complicated academic lexicon, this book uses simple vocabulary to describe and categorize each developmental stage. Moving from the stage of least complexity and care to the stage of the highest complexity and care, the reader is introduced to the following basic terms: (1) magic, (2) mythic, (3) rational, (4) pluralistic, and (5) integral.[7] This five-stage developmental rubric, also referred to as the "stages of religious orientation,"[8] allows one to translate every expression and interpretation of religion into a holarcy of greater inclusivity and depth.

In addition to supporting its central thesis, this book also does its very best to develop and address potential counter arguments. For instance, in light of the fact that most postmodern scholars hesitate to employ hierarchical models due to the arrogant and Western-centric proposals of the past, this presentation clearly and directly answers the postmodern call for cultural sensitivity. Once postmodern concerns about hierarchy and the fear of social Darwinism are laid to rest, the result is a startling post-postmodern model of religious analysis that sheds light on elements of society and culture heretofore unrealized.

For ease of organization and readability, this book is divided into three parts. Part 1 helps to clarify the academic and theoretical basis for the proposal. The reader will find references to many of the most prominent developmental psychologists of the past several decades, an introduction to the stages of religious orientation, and a brief overview of the model of developmental religious pluralism. Next, using the ideas uncovered in Part 1, Part 2 provides practical examples of each stage of developmental complexity as it is expressed in Christianity, Hinduism, Islam, and Buddhism. This part is full of concrete evidence that reinforces the book's thesis. Finally, Part 3 takes the reader beyond both the *theory* offered in Part 1 and the *evidence* offered in Part 2, to recommend several immediate courses of action.

Methodological Caveats

Five caveats help to better frame some of the potential shortcomings of the general methodology used to construct this book:

1. Simplification of two complex disciplines. As this book has already hinted at but has yet to state explicitly, there is a nexus between the two disciplines of developmental psychology and religious studies that needs to be examined. To be sure, one could spend a lifetime immersed in the nuances and intricacies of either one of these disciplines and still only scratch the surface of available knowledge. How, then, is this book to adequately offer a synopsis of the relationship between these two fields, while simultaneously doing justice to the mountains of research and scholarship already in existence? Although it may not be possible to offer a *complete* description of both of these areas enough to satisfy the thirst of religious and developmental specialists, I am confident that the meta-systemic approach[9] applied herein does provide a broad, accurate, and, most importantly, digestible set of "orienting generalizations."[10]

2. Outlines of the many theories within each discipline may seem overly simplistic. The methodology employed attempts to offer a balance between radical inclusivity and practical efficiency. The use of broad brush strokes may cause some readers to take issue with what appears to be an oversimplification of the ideas proposed by key researchers and theorists. Although such alarm is understandable, the concern is unwarranted once this book's intention and methodology are properly understood. One brief example helps to illustrate the point.

Exploring the ways in which values unfold over time, this book draws upon the work of Clare Graves. Graves' work is in itself a complete bio-psychosocial approach to human emergence. However, using a generalist framing of his work, this book only incorporates those aspects of Graves' research directly relevant to our particular field of inquiry. Rather than explaining all the richness that Graves has to offer in all realms of psychology, biology, and sociology, this book narrows its presentation to only the individual and his or her personal psychological development.

In circumstances like this, it is not my intention to reduce the work of any theorist to fit neatly into a particular model. Rather over the course of writing and research, deliberate choices were made as to how to include the relevant features of each theorist in a fair and honest way, while simultaneously providing the ideas to the reader in a manageable format. To correct for any oversimplification that does occur, I'd like to urge readers interested in further details to consult the primary source texts of each theorist as cited in the book's footnotes and bibliography.

3. Limitation of addressing only four traditions. Part 2 of this book provides examples of developmental religious interpretation from within four major traditions (Christianity, Hinduism, Islam, and Buddhism). The decision to use only four traditions rather than some greater number was made in the interest of keeping the presentation as concise as possible whilst still delivering a potent message. The same type of developmental evidence provided in this book for Christianity, Hinduism, Islam, and Buddhism, can be easily reproduced for any number of traditions. In no way should the selection of these traditions be misconstrued as privileging one set of traditions over another. The four traditions used for evidence were chosen simply based on the fact that they are traditions with the highest populations of religious adherents in our world today. It is my hope that future research will take this initial proposal further to analyze the stages of development within other traditions such as Judaism, Sikhism, Taoism, Baha'i, and indigenous traditions, among others.

4. The fluid nature of development. Part 2 brings up a second important point that should be acknowledged. The dynamic and fluid nature of human beings propels individuals to demonstrate a range of religious expression depending on both the setting and the context in which they act. To this end, it is important that all readers allow room for fluctuations in human psychological development in each of the examples provided.

The body of evidence offered is indeed intended to accurately signify the various developmental expressions that exist within each tradition, and therefore has the capacity to offer a roadmap for potential growth and development. However, as chapter 3 articulates, it is not the intention of this book to box each exemplar into a particular level of psychological maturity. As my integrally informed colleague Zak Stein correctly points out:

> There is overwhelming evidence showing that our metrics are limited and that we can't touch the true complexity of human development. In this light, the idea that a holistic assessment could tell us about the essence of a person is absurd and flagrantly ideological. Developmental assessments at their best can only paint pictures of the differential distribution of capabilities within persons. We can't assess people as a whole, we can only assess their performances along particular lines in particular contexts.[11]

Furthermore, this book takes into account that narrative, shadow, unconscious motivations, and inter-subjective dynamics all play deeply into religious interpretation in general and faith development in particular. All of which were key features missing in earlier iterations of faith development theory.[12]

In step with many other integral theorists, it is my intention that the categorizations provided are used to promote both horizontal and vertical transformation for the betterment and well-being of all of humanity. That is to say, as a first step, this book seeks to help each level of interpretation to be as healthy as possible, just as it is (horizontal translation). Second, it also helps create the conditions for positive growth from one level of development to the next (vertical transformation). If my intentions are properly assimilated, the categories and evidence provided herein should never be used for the selfish promotion of any one particular individual, group, or level of religious orientation at the exclusion of others but rather to help individuals guide themselves along the vertical spectrum while simultaneously allowing each level to express itself through healthy forms.

5. Postmodern allergy to hierarchy. Finally, this book offers a note to those currently involved in related work at the university level or other areas of academic inquiry. As many interested in this type of work are already well aware, postmodern scholarship has brought with it a visceral reaction to hierarchy. As one professor kindly pointed out during my graduate studies, "any theory that uses the terms evolution or development sends red flags up immediately." Most scholars, all with the best of intentions, are very sensitive to the way that ideas like evolution and development were used over the past century for colonial and often Western-centric motivations.[13] For example, academic inquiry in humanities in general and religious studies in particular is ultrasensitive to the works of modern scholars like E. B. Tylor and others who often characterize religions as moving in an evolutionary direction from animistic, to polytheistic, to monotheistic. Placing the Christian tradition above and against all other religious systems of the world (especially the so-called "savage" traditions of indigenous cultures), this type of intellectual maneuver represents an irresponsible form of scholarship now viewed as brazenly ignorant. The authentic and honest attempt at clarification offered in this book comes to terms with these types of critiques from the very beginning, adjusting its thesis appropriately.

Even if hierarchy was used irresponsibly in the past, we cannot afford to abandon it altogether. In fact, when hierarchical descriptions are used responsibly in conjunction with postmodern sensitivity, they bring a type of clarity yet to be seen in postmodern scholarship. Not only is the responsible implementation of hierarchy useful on an individual scale but it also offers an accurate tool to describe the larger evolutionary process that we find ourselves in collectively as we move toward a world of more complexity and care.[14]

Properly differentiating this book's use of hierarchy from previous uses requires one further delineation. Unlike some scholars of the past, this book does not contend that monotheists or Western values are at the top of some arbitrary hierarchy with all others below. Instead of comparing apples to oranges (i.e., Christians to Hindus or Western values to Eastern values), this book looks within each tradition itself to compare apples to apples (Christians to Christians, Muslims to Muslims, Buddhists to Buddhist, Hindus to Hindus) avoiding cross-cultural or cross-religious comparison where doing so would prove inaccurate. The explicitly integral approach taken herein yokes the cultural sensitivity of the postmodernists with the most recent developmental insights to form a type of post-postmodern scholarship.

Throughout the presentation I do my best to continue highlighting the contexts in which the aforementioned caveats arise and where the particular methodology presented may be limited.

What's in it for You?

Although this book began with an intention to offer solutions for broad systemic change, it quickly became clear that it also serves a complementary purpose for all those interested in their own personal well-being. Because religions are designed to address ideas of ultimate concern, understanding one's own relationship to religion serves as a fundamental catalyst to finding direction and meaning in everyday life. When viewed from a psychological perspective, religions serve as a type of technology for human happiness, offering direction and meaning to our behavior and conduct in their exoteric forms, and insights into the nature of human consciousness and even Ultimate Reality in their esoteric forms. Sadly, both of these benefits are often lost in today's world because religion has become exclusively identified with immature levels of expression and interpretation. The stages outlined in this book demonstrate how our world's varying religious systems might be adapted to meet the needs of a diverse array of intelligence levels so that they can once again be enacted as technologies for personal happiness and transformation.

Ultimately, the articulations of higher stages of religious expression described herein are designed to touch even those who have abandoned religion altogether (especially those who assumed it was infantile or out of sync with their modern beliefs). The levels of expression explained in the following chapters offer a way for religion to rest inline with the very best of today's modern, postmodern, and integral sensibilities. It is my deepest hope that all of this helps to demonstrate the important role of religion in the Great Human Tradition.

Definitions

Before diving into the core of this book and elaborating how one's interpretation of religion and even religious studies itself might evolve to a new more comprehensive stage of analysis, several sets of terms need to be defined.

First, the words "spirituality" and "religion" are used repeatedly. When used by itself, the word spirituality refers to beliefs that have been personalized. Simply put, spirituality is the sacred framework one uses to create meaning in his or her life, a meaning-making system or worldview framing one's ultimate concern. The word religion, on the other hand, refers to what we call "institutionalized spirituality." That is to say, religion is a form of spirituality that has been collected into a common core of beliefs, values, and understanding about the world, assembled—whether orally, visually, or written—and passed along to others. Individuals practicing and contemplating without a community tend to have a personal spirituality. Groups of people who subscribe to similar meaning-making systems, organize their beliefs in a systematic way, and pass their ideologies along to others, we will consider to be part of a religion.

Secondly, the terms "spiritual development" and "spiritual intelligence" are used interchangeably.[15] As will be made clear along the way in general, and in chapter 2 in particular, both terms refer to a specific line of development related to James Fowler's *Stages of Faith*.

Thirdly, this book oscillates between the two terms "spiritual orientation" and "religious orientation." Both of these terms describe the unique structural perspective through which one views, practices, and interprets a religious tradition. Each perspective varies according to an individual's psychological makeup. As discussed in detail in chapter 3, a religious orientation is a composite of several distinct areas of intelligence (faith, cognitive, ego, values, and moral).

Finally, the terms "traditional," "modern," and "postmodern" refer to three major intellectual movements in Western thought. As we shall explore in appendix 2, each of these terms roughly correlate to the stages of religious orientation called mythic, rational, and pluralistic, respectively.

All of these terms and definitions are made delightfully clear in the pages and chapters to follow.

The Big Picture

Although the specific focus of this book is limited to an analysis of our world's great religious traditions, this book's conception and publication was launched in collaboration with a global meshwork of integral thinkers. This trans-national community of integral pioneers (some self-consciously integral, others not) are working in countless other disciplines with the common goal of unlocking humanity's full potential. Stunning new releases on Integral Ecology, Integral Psychotherapy, and Integral Education are paving the way.[16] As human consciousness continues to evolve, other areas of human knowledge will spring forth in the form of trans-disciplinary breakthroughs similar to the efforts already being expressed by others. It is my deepest intention that the ideas offered here will help nourish the greater integral vision for the benefit of all.

PART 1: THEORY

Chapter 1
Adding Altitude to Religious Pluralism

This first chapter serves two basic ends. First, it begins to set the context for Integral Religious Studies in general and more specifically developmental religious pluralism. Second, it provides a brief survey of some of the various approaches to religious pluralism most commonly employed today. This survey of common practices sets the foundation to show how the integral lens can correct for the inherent limitations of many postmodern methodologies and how a new developmental approach to religious pluralism is emerging.

The postmodern paradigm of religious studies initiated an unprecedented degree of nuance and sophistication in the study of religion and religious phenomena. This is a fantastic leap that ought to be fully honored. The postmodern worldview revealed the fact that the interpretation of various religious traditions is broadly based upon social, cultural, and linguistic influences. Among the various positive outcomes that came from this sort of sensitivity was a massive reorientation that encouraged scholars to reevaluate the colonialist and often ethnocentric tendencies of modern Western scholarship. Meeting each culture and each tradition on its own terms became a central and important way of approaching the study of religion. The implications of these postmodern discoveries reached far and wide. Not only were culturally sensitive insights flourishing in the ivory towers of universities. Many of these important pluralistic notions were also internalized by the culture at large.[17] Ultimately, these shifts have led many in mainstream culture to conclude no single perspective ought to be given preference over any other. A sort of cultural relativism emerged generally around the Western world that asserted: "Everybody is right when understood within his or her particular context."

Harvard Professor Diana Eck explains this relativistic position as follows:

What we speak of as truth is relative to our cultural and historical standpoint as well as the frame of reference through which we see it. What is true is always "true for" someone, for there is always a point of view—conditioned in multiple ways by whether one is Christian or Muslim, American or Asian, male or female, rich or poor, a prosperous farmer or a homeless refugee. Matters of truth and value are relative to our conceptual framework and world-view, even those matters of truth that we speak of as divinely ordained.[18]

The repercussions of the relativistic view deeply affected the consciousness of the postmodern West. A society whose worldview was once broadly based on the bias attitude of white Christian males suddenly found itself open to the fact that perhaps its particular orientation wasn't the only valuable window on reality. As women gained greater freedom in the workplace, as ethnic and racial minorities gained greater equality within the broader social structure, and as spiritual and religious leaders from outside of the Christian tradition began traveling and teaching in the West from abroad, many individuals found themselves taking an open-minded approach to a diverse array of perspectives like never before.

It was at this time, in mid to late 1960s, that a form of postmodern social pluralism was born in full strength.[19] This socially oriented pluralism fed into notions of religion and spirituality almost immediately. "If all religious traditions and their subsequent interpretations are culturally, contextually, and linguistically conditioned," claimed the new religious pluralists, "then each tradition must, in some way, represent a different but equally valid interpretation of ultimate reality." In a dynamic feedback loop between culture and academia, notions around the concept of religious pluralism began to multiply.

Although a relativistic approach to religion and a pluralistic approach to religion are close in meaning, one term cannot be reduced to the other. In fact sometimes the two terms work antithetically. As Diana Eck astutely points out, there are at least two different "shades of relativism" that work in opposition to pluralism:

> The first is nihilistic relativism, which denies the very heart of religious truth. One of the common strategies for diffusing the challenge of religious and ideological difference is to insist that there is no ultimate centering value, no one-life-completing truth....The second shade of relativism that must clearly be distinguished from pluralism is a relativism that lacks commitment.... Pluralism can only generate a strong social fabric through the interweaving of

commitments. If people perceive pluralism as entailing the relinquishing of their particular religious commitments they are not interested....The pluralist, on the other hand, stands in a particular community and is willing to be committed to the struggles of that community, even as restless critic.[20]

To say it another way, whereas a relativistic stance toward religion may result in a tentative commitment to a tradition, easily abandoned, and often overly malleable, a pluralistic position allows one to stand strong in a particular belief structure even in the most challenging of times. The term religious pluralism, as I will use it most often in this book, does not require that an individual be any less Christian or Muslim or Buddhist, it simply implies a willingness to engage the religious "other" in serious conversation. As Eck states: "Pluralism is not, then, the kind of radical openness to anything and everything that drains meaning from particularity. It is, however, radical openness to Truth—to God— that seeks to enlarge understanding through dialogue."[21] Rather than erasing differences religious pluralism makes even more room for the diversity within each of our world's faiths. "Religious pluralism is not primarily about common ground," says Eck. "Pluralism takes the reality of difference as its starting point. The challenge of pluralism is not to obliterate or erase difference, nor to smooth out differences under a universalizing canopy, but rather to discover ways of living, connecting, relating, arguing, and disagreeing in a society of differences." [22]

With the distinction between relativism and pluralism clear, let's dive into some of the various models of religious pluralism that have emerged in the past few decades.

A Variety of Approaches to Religious Pluralism

Approaches to religious pluralism are as complex as they are diverse.[23] Nonetheless, a few orientating generalizations are useful to start.

Theologians and historians of religion such as John Cobb, John Hick, Wilfred Cantwell Smith, Karl Rahner, and Karl Barth have all confronted and addressed issues of religious pluralism. Some in approval while others firmly rejecting the idea. A general survey of the existing scholarship reveals that there are at least three diverse orientations used to address religious pluralism.

1. The first category of approaches to religious pluralism gives primary emphasis to the ontological and epistemological truth-claims that exist between religious systems. Approaches

to religious pluralism that fall within this first category focus most of their attention on the philosophical and theological implications of religious diversity using a comparative lens to examine the doctrines and teachings of multiple traditions.

2. In a second broad category of approaches to religious pluralism, scholars examine the ways in which diverse religious traditions function and interact as complex systems within a common social space. These socially oriented approaches tend to examine how we can live together in shared space even when our values and religious beliefs might be quite different.

3. A third approach to religious pluralism gives greatest emphasis to the individual practitioner rather than to the claims and beliefs themselves. When using a lens that focuses on the individual, scholars tend to point to the general spectrum of attitudes people hold toward the religious "other." In this context we usually hear phrases like "religious extremist" and "religious moderate".

Below I expand upon several of the most common approaches to religious pluralism within each of the three broad frames outlined above.[24] This general introduction will help to further set the context for Integral Religious Studies as well as set the background for the second half of the chapter where I introduce a two-axis model of religious development.

Competing Truth-Claims about Ultimate Reality

Religious pluralism is a common response to the fact that there exists a multitude of various religious traditions, each of which lay some claim to know the nature of ultimate reality.[25] This great diversity has stimulated much debate as to the nature of religious truth claims and how they ought to be considered.[26] Issues of religious diversity and how to handle their respective truth claims arise in Christian, Muslim, Jewish, Buddhist, and Hindu traditions alike, all presenting their own unique dilemmas and issues of further study and contemplation.[27]

In a theological context, use of the term religious pluralism usually suggests some sort of "harmony, convergence, or compatibility across religious traditions."[28] It is not uncommon for some religious scholars and theologians to begin with an approach to pluralism that affirms the fact that no single religious tradition can be held superior to another. John Hick, for instance, affirms that the salvific quality that exists within Christianity, leading away from self-centeredness to a form of "Reality-centeredness," is available within all traditions "to a more or less equal extent."[29] Consequently, Hick views all religions as equally valid approaches to a single ultimate reality.[30] [31]

Other religious scholars like John Cobb and Mark Heim take a dramatically different approach.[32] Both Cobb and Heim criticize Hick's approach, claiming instead that the different traditions all lead to different goals.[33] If John Hick's perspective was explained using a metaphor of a mountain, that all religious paths lead up different sides of the mountain only to meet at a single peak, Cobb and Heim's perspective might be explained by saying that instead of all religious paths being on the same mountain, each path is on its own separate mountain leading to its own unique peak.

Although Heim rejects pluralism altogether Cobb develops what he describes as a "fuller and more genuine pluralism"[34] that avoids the pitfalls he attributes to Hick's universalist claims.[35] Rather than arguing that the various perspectives all lead to the same truth, Cobb argues that the inherent diversity and very different goals within each tradition might actually be able to complement the perspective of the religious other. For example, an even fuller version of Christianity might emerge when it has been properly exposed to the teachings of Buddhism. Conversely, deeper meaning within Buddhism might be revealed if it is exposed to Christian teachings. These forms of "Christianized Buddhism" and "Buddhized Christianity" will "remain what they are but at the same time be thoroughly different."[36]

One novel contribution to religious pluralism over the past few years from within this first particular frame (and a source of pluralism related, in certain ways, to the ideas set forth in this book) can be found in the collection of essays edited by David Ray Griffin. In his book *Deep Religious Pluralism*, Griffin calls upon scholars to examine religious pluralism through the lens of Alfred North Whitehead's process philosophy.[37] One of the essays titled "Toward an Integrative Religious Pluralism," by Chung-ying Cheng, deserves further mention.

In his article, Cheng aspires to what he calls an "integrative" approach, developing three categories of religious pluralism. The first type of pluralism he calls "differential pluralism," a type of pluralism "set on recognizing the differences between religions." The second type of pluralism he calls "complementary pluralism." Complementary pluralism "is set on seeing all religions as complementary forms of religious practice and belief." And the third type of pluralism he calls "integrative pluralism," which is "intent on showing that all religions are to be regarded as integral parts of a holistic developmental process of humanity as its understanding of the world."[38]

Although there are significant differences,[39] Cheng's approach can be appropriately compared to the form of developmental religious pluralism I outline in this book in several ways. For starters, both Cheng and I set out to transcend and include other approaches to religious pluralism using a process-oriented approach. Cheng points out that he "wholeheartedly appreciates John Cobb's and David Griffin's work in developing complementary pluralism." I too appreciate Cobb's and Griffins work as far as it goes. However, both Cheng and I contend that this form of pluralism must also go "one step further" toward something more integrative.[40] I agree with Cheng that this sort of step will allow us to "avoid relativism while preserving uniqueness." It will allow us "to embrace the whole while achieving the part." And it will help us "to realize the global while enjoying the local."[41] In so far as the integrative pluralism Cheng proposes meets these specific ends, then it has the potential to work brilliantly as a complementary approach to the model of developmental religious pluralism introduced in this book.

Social and Systemic Approaches to Religious Pluralism

Some of the most well-known approaches to religious pluralism come less from theologians and more from those who are concerned with religion's influence on social dynamics. These scholars find deepest interest in examining how we ought to live side by side in harmony despite the radically different religious views that we all might hold.

Often this type of concern for collective well-being leads scholars to consider an approach to religious pluralism that emphasizes religion's relationship to politics, economics, and other similar social systems. Such was the case for John Rawls, Jacques Maritain, and Alasdair MacIntyre among many others.[42] When used in its social context, Thomas Banchoff defines religious pluralism as "the interaction of religious actors with one another and with society and the state around concrete cultural, social, economic, and political agendas."[43]

Banchoff further exemplifies how theories from within this frame often involve an inquiry into social causes and conditions. According to his socially oriented analysis, "the new religious pluralism is, in part, an outgrowth of a more fluid demographic and cultural landscape. Migration flows generate greater demographic diversity, while modernization tends to loosen social attachments and generate more fluid and multiple possibilities for religious identification and belonging." Banchoff continues: "Pluralism is about the responses of minorities to majorities and vice versa. Only by viewing the interaction among religious groups on an uneven playing field can one specify distinctive contours of the new religious pluralism."[44] [45] To a similar end, other socially minded scholars look at religious pluralism from the view of religious actors who find themselves as minorities in a larger social system. Kumar's *Religious Pluralism in Diaspora*, for instance, gives a chance for Muslims in the United States after September 11, and Hindus in England still functioning within a form of a caste system.[46]

Still, other social and systemic approaches to religious pluralism look to find the historical roots of pluralism in the traditions themselves. Although many usually attribute pluralistic ideals to Western Enlightenment thinkers, scholars like Alyssa Gabbay provide evidence for early forms of pluralism that flourished within premodern Muslim communities.[47] Others like William Hutchinson examine the roots of pluralism in America.[48] Highlighting many of the setbacks along the way, Hutchison recounts America's own struggles with religious diversity and explains how Muslims, Hindus, Jews, Mormons, and Catholics have all helped to shape the type of pluralism enjoyed in the United States today.

Later in this book, we pick up on many of these social themes in relation to religious pluralism. In chapter 6, we explore some of the historical roots of pluralism within Islam. In chapters 8 and 9 we examine pluralism in its relation to how the new perspectives offered with an integral lens might influence social, economic, and political dynamics on a global scale.

Individually Oriented Approaches to Religious Pluralism

Individually oriented approaches to religious pluralism emphasize the attitude of the individual as their primary focus, only to address the broader social and theological dynamics of interaction as secondary concerns. In the postmodern West, our shared values dictate that each individual has a right to pursue their own religious truth. This social contract usually leads individuals to treat religions with equal value within the public sphere. It is rare, for example, to hear someone declare publicly that one tradition is better than another.[49] Alongside this politically correct view of equality, however, it is fully acceptable to say that within a single tradition individual expression varies to a large degree.

One of the most popular approaches used to describe individual variance employs a model of "health" that classifies individuals as either extremists or moderates. Figure 1 below provides a pictorial representation of extremist and moderate degrees of health.

Figure 1

The use of this horizontal spectrum of health has become so widespread that the terms "religious moderate" or "religious extremist" are used frequently in magazines, newspapers, and other forms of international journalism. Usually, these terms are used in a normative context implying that religious extremism is "bad" while religious moderation is "good." Despite the ubiquity of its use, this particular approach to religious typology is often clumsy and overly simplified.[50] As a result we are left with approaches to pluralism that could be far more intelligent. In the next section, we shall see why a single horizontal spectrum of classification lacks the sophistication and nuance needed to understand religion in the twenty-first century.

A second popular approach to individually oriented pluralism employs what Diana Eck calls an "attitudinal continuum."[51] This spectrum ranges from exclusivism to inclusivism to pluralism. The terms themselves are fairly accurate descriptions of the attitudes to which they point. Speaking generally, exclusivists relate to the religious "other" as an outsider. Inclusivists begin to open their perspectives to allow at least some inclusion of other religious views. Pluralists openly embrace the religious "other" in a process of dialogue and exchange.

According to Eck, the difference between the various attitudes can be determined by the degree of "self-consciousness of one's understanding of the world and God." She continues: "If we are inclusivists, we include others in a world-view we already know and on the terms we have already set. If we are pluralists, we recognize the limits of the world we already know and we seek to understand others in their own terms, not just on ours."[52]

Jorge Ferrer explains the same categorizations in a different voice:

> The standard responses to religious diversity—exclusivism, inclusivism, and ecumenical pluralism—can be situated along a continuum ranging from more gross to more subtle forms of "spiritual narcissism," which elevate one's favored tradition or spiritual choice as superior. The religious superiority of one's preferred tradition is normally conceived in terms of its conveying a more complete or accurate picture of a purportedly single religion or "the way things really are." The dogmatically apologetic nature of these approaches arguably limits their effectiveness to facilitate a genuinely symmetrical, dialogical, and mutually

enriching encounter among religious traditions in which deep transformation and even the risk of conversion are real possibilities. [53]

Both Eck and Ferrer acknowledge the importance and prominence of such terms in current scholarship.

Although this book uses a comprehensive methodology that attempts to include the basic insights of the three categorical approaches to religious pluralism listed above (those that address [1] competing truth-claims, [2] social dynamics, and the [3] psychology of the individual), its core thesis focuses the majority of its attention on the psychologically oriented approach. In other words, instead of focusing on social implications of religious pluralism or how theological truth claims might be reconciled (although these are both certainly included and addressed in subsequent chapters), I instead use a physiological approach to focus primarily on how we might establish a more sophisticated methodology to address the diversity of religious attitudes in individuals.[54]

Limitations of a Single Spectrum Approach to Religious Pluralism

If only a single axis is used to describe differences in religious attitude, its effects are limited and at times even harmful.[55] A single horizontal classification, like one that distinguishes only rudimentary distinctions between extremists and moderates, forces social commentators to place all individuals on an overly simplistic playing field. As a result, most postmodern social theorists, media pundits, and policy makers conclude that if we are to fight religious extremism, a sensible goal is to help promote more moderate religious views.

Although such a goal has an initial thrust in the right direction, it is based on a pluralistic model that is now both outdated and partial. In the single spectrum model there is an implicit assumption that there are only two directions of possible movement: either religious adherents become more extreme or they grow into moderation. The integral religious scholar opens a new line of inquiry: What if there were multiple directions for a religious adherent to move and grow? What if we discovered that extreme religious views were the result of specific developmental deficiencies?[56] What if by tracing extremism to specific developmental capacities we could then target those capacities as part of educational reform? As it currently stands, because only a single horizontal spectrum is used, actions that stem from most models used today produce less than efficient results. As demonstrated in the following section, it is only when we use at least two axes (one representing development, the other degree of health), that we are able to obtain fuller understanding of religious attitudes.

Developmental Religious Pluralism

With varying temperaments and diverse degrees of intelligence, human beings require a more comprehensive model that is able to account for a broad range of psychological differences. The single axis of categorization offered by the majority of postmodern thinkers must be transcended. Is there a model that allows for multi-directional growth and movement beyond the common models of health that are usually employed?

Developmental religious pluralism suggests one example of a new and more comprehensive type of approach to religious pluralism, embracing the horizontal spectrum of health (ranging from extremist to moderate) and moving beyond it to include a new dimension of depth and development. (As we shall see together in the chapters that follow, the attitudinal continuum leading from exclusivist, to inclusivist, pluralists can be arranged along a vertical developmental spectrum.) Wilber has so often posited, we can begin with the postmodern impulse that "everybody is right". And we can add to it that "some are more right than others". That is, we can honor each view as a partial view of reality, while simultaneously honoring the fact that some views are more comprehensive. Said another way, some views are less partial than others.

The model of developmental religious pluralism uses the latest research in developmental studies to show that various expressions of religious orientation within a single tradition can be divided into a natural pattern of increasing complexity and care.[57] When the horizontal spectrum of health offered by the common pluralistic approach is combined with this vertical dimension of transformation discovered by developmental psychologists, a double-axis model emerges that includes both vertical "stages" and the horizontal "health" of religious orientation.[58]

Stages and Types of Religious Orientation

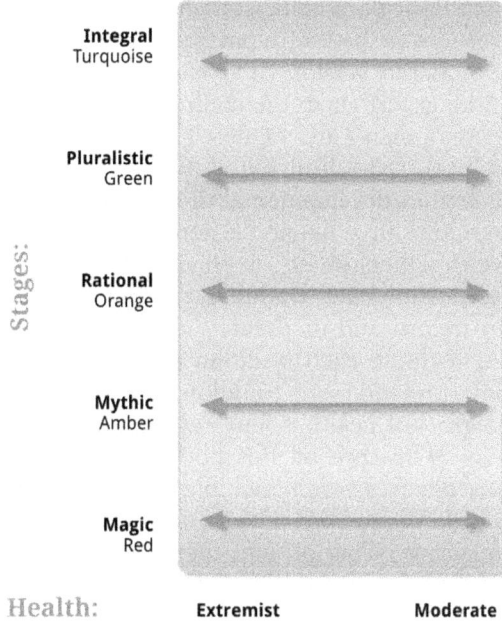

Figure 2

As shown in figure 2 above, the model of developmental religious pluralism allows us to maintain the horizontal spectrum of health (extremist versus moderate) yet add to it a vertical spectrum of development. In figure 2, the vertical y-axis takes into consideration developmental stages of increasing complexity and care. Wilber calls these stages "altitude" ranging from magic to mythic to rational to pluralistic to integral.[59] The horizontal x-axis at each of those stages charts the various degrees of health of religious expression ranging from extremist to moderate.

With the new model of developmental religious pluralism in place, individual differences within religious traditions can now be categorized using two very unique spectrums simultaneously.[60] Instead of simply suggesting that religious adherents embrace extremist views or moderate views, developmental religious pluralism demonstrates that individuals also take one of five vertical orientations, depending on their psychological stage of structural development. The integral scholar employing this model sees clearly that each religious tradition has not only two different expressions of health (extreme or moderate), but at least ten different religious orientations (a minimum of 2 different expressions of health x 5 stages = 10 orientations).

The last point is worth repeating, as its implications in our modern and postmodern world are monumental. In the older postmodern pluralistic paradigm, it is still commonly assumed that only two or three versions (at best) of a particular tradition exist: an extreme version and a moderate version, or an exclusivist, inclusivist, and pluralist variation. Adding further to the confusion, both of these spectrums (health and development) are conflated as if they were the same. Developmental religious pluralism uses a two-axis model. Demonstrating that there is both a developmental dimension to religious interpretation (y-axis) resulting in a magic version, a mythic version (extremist), a rational version (inclusivist), a pluralistic version (pluralist), and an integral version of each tradition, as well as a two-pole spectrum of health (extremist and moderate) within each of those developmental stages. As a result, each tradition contains at least ten different versions of interpretation (one tradition x five stages of religious orientation x two degrees of health = ten)—all real, all valid, and all in existence today.

The core of this book provides evidence from each of these perspectives across multiple traditions. Evidence shows that there are magic versions of Christianity expressed through an extremist lens, magic versions of Christianity expressed through a moderate lens, mythic versions of Christianity expressed through an extremist lens, mythic versions of Christianity expressed through a moderate lens, etc. Among the plethora of immediate implications, the most relevant one is that even if religion was once assumed to be a relic of the past, trapped at mythic versions of interpretation, there is an adequate and appropriate form of religion for every developmental stage no matter how complex or evolved an individual's perspective might become.

Religious Orientation in Brief

Because this new dimension of development is a basic requirement of any integral approach to religious studies, it is worth examining here in brief, before going into greater detail in chapters 2 and 3. Reading through the outline below, two important points should be considered:

1. Each stage of development described has its own unique set of defining characteristics. In other words, each stage of psychological development offers a bundle of orienting principles with a similar flavor.

2. Each stage represents a deep structure underlying human psychological development. Because the deep structures are present in all humans, each stage on the vertical spectrum of development can be found in every religious tradition.[61]

Although it is true, as most postmodern scholars will warn, that we must be careful when suggesting any sort of universal characteristics shared by all humans, it is equally important to recognize that interiority, or consciousness, does indeed move from levels of less complexity to more complexity regardless of culture or geographic location.[62] The following list examines the orienting characteristics of individuals at each stage of religious expression:

Magic:[63] power-driven, superstitious, ritualistic, literal interpretation of scripture, egocentric, exclusivist

Mythic: literal interpretation of stories, miracles, traditionally focused, conformist, absolutist, ethnocentric, exclusivism

Rational: logical, scientifically oriented, tolerant, focused on universal human rights, modern, worldcentric, inclusivism

Pluralistic: sensitive, egalitarian, multicultural, multi-perspectival, postmodern, global, pluralism

Integral: comprehensive, evolution-oriented, universalizing, holistic in vision, unitive, Kosmo-centric, developmental pluralism

The broad strokes listed above are directly related to the level of psychological maturity exhibited by the individual. As we will see as the book unfolds, each stage of development, as described above, leads to dramatically different interpretations of one's religious tradition. The higher stages of development (rational, pluralistic, and integral) offer far more efficient vehicles for positive transformation in the world and are less likely to cause social or political turmoil through violence and conflict.

In reading the remainder of part 1 keep in mind that the information's purpose is to help us analyze religion in entirely new ways. Consider the following as you read:

1. Psychological development affects the way individuals orient themselves towards religion.

2. If we are to move beyond the limited pluralistic models of religious analysis, we must use at least a two-axis model that understands the difference between developmental religious orientations (magical, mythical, rational, pluralistic, and integral) in addition to basic classifications of health (extremist and moderate).

3. A clear understanding of the developmental stages of religious orientation will have at least three important and immediate impacts. First, in the external world, we can begin making sense of why religious individuals are motivated to make the choices they do. Second, we can break the stronghold that our religious traditions currently have on mythic (exclusivist) levels of consciousness and transform them into "conveyor belts" of human potential and vertical growth. And third, this new understanding imparts to us the ability to turn the analysis inward. When shifting the lens to ourselves, we can begin to examine our own relationship to religion—if we apply the model of developmental religious pluralism to our own lives we can find which stage and which degree of health of religious orientation might serve us. Religions have the capacity to serve as technologies for everyday happiness. Knowing where we are on the developmental spectrum and matching our needs to an appropriate expression of a tradition could have massive benefit in our lives.

Chapter 2
Defining Religious Orientation

Through an exploration of current research in developmental psychology, this chapter helps to ground the book's presentation within current academic theories. I examine three questions in detail: (1) What do we mean by the phrase "psychological development"? (2) How can one determine an individual's developmental stage of religious orientation? (3) What specific areas of development might be significant to such an analysis?

A Closer Look at Psychological Development

Is there really any evidence to support the fact that we move through psychological stages of development? Before we answer that question, let's make sure we begin with a solid understanding of what the word "development" actually means. Put simply, development is the process by which predictable and patterned changes take place within a particular individual over the course of a lifetime. We might also characterize development as the degree to which levels of "maturity and complexity" unfold in human beings. The textbook *Developmental Psychology Today* describes the process of change as "continuous, cumulative, directional, differentiated, organized, and holistic";[64] a complicated way of saying that development occurs over time, in a sequential order, each stage building on the previous.[65]

In his book *Integral Spirituality*, Wilber suggests that an individual's level of psychological development will change his or her interpretation of a religious tradition.[66] Elaborating on his vision and in support of his initial claims, this chapter explores the evidence for development in five specific areas of psychological growth. However, rather than relying solely on Wilber's interpretations of developmental research, this book will turn to primary sources of scholarship for each of the psychological models investigated.

First, and perhaps most significantly, this book hones in on the work of James Fowler and his detailed look at the development of faith. Although Fowler's work is indeed seminal to the field of religious studies (and our proposal in particular), it is not broad enough to include all of the various aspects of a human being that are crucial in determining one's religious orientation.[67] In order to expand Fowler's view of faith development, our analysis includes the work of several additional scholars. Moving forward together, we explore Jean Piaget's research into cognitive development and demonstrate how an individual's capacity for perspective taking increases with developmental maturity. We examine ego development, as researched by Jane Lovinger and later expanded upon by Susanne Cook-Greuter. We also look at the development of values as originally researched by Clare W. Graves.[68] And, finally, we examine stages of moral development as researched by Lawrence Kohlberg.

When considering ideas of religion and spirituality in the postmodern world, all of the above *lines* of development play a significant role in shaping the way an individual or group of individuals orient themselves to a particular tradition. The more details we understand about the psychological orientation of the individual(s), the more effective the analysis and intended action will be.

The Integral Psychograph

In 1983, Howard Gardner popularized the idea of multiple intelligences with his book *Frames of Mind*.[69] Gardner divided intelligence into domains instead of specific abilities. In doing so, he suggested seven different kinds of intelligence: linguistic; musical; logical-mathematical; spatial; bodily-kinesthetic; and two types of personal intelligence, intrapersonal (understanding oneself) and interpersonal (understanding others). Gardner's research demonstrated that levels of intelligence can and often do vary to great degrees in each line. For example, the psychological makeup pictured in the graph below (figure 3) shows that the individual has very high logical-mathematical intelligence but low musical and intrapersonal intelligence.

Gardner's Multiple Intelligences

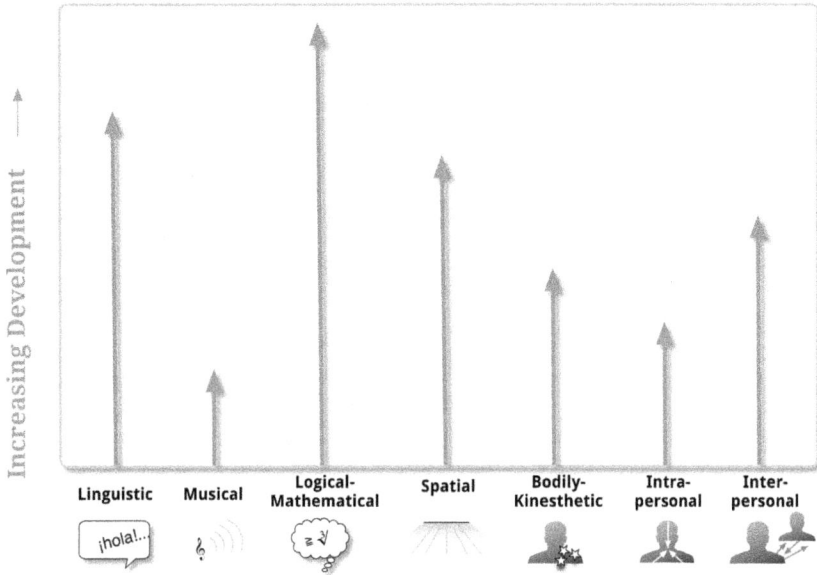

Figure 3

As he most poignantly outlines in the book *Integral Psychology*, Wilber used the theory of multiple intelligences as a foundation to design a tool called the Integral Psychograph.[70] Offering the reader a simple pictorial representation of religious orientation, the Integral Psychograph plays a critical role as we move forward.

The next graph (figure 4) elaborates further on the notion of the Integral Psychograph. Figure 4 depicts the five major lines of psychological development we consider necessary to determine an individual's stage of religious orientation. Although the graph may seem overwhelming at first, the unfolding of each line of development will be made clear as we proceed in the following chapters.

An Integral Psychograph

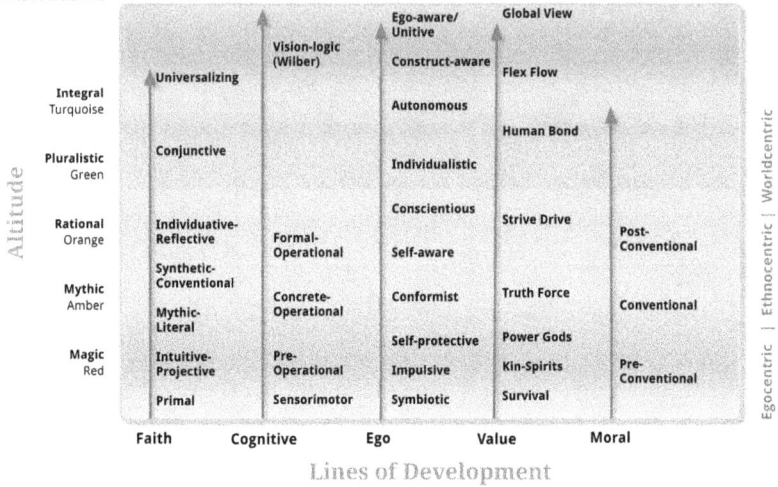

Stages of Religious Orientation

Altitude — Integral Turquoise / Pluralistic Green / Rational Orange / Mythic Amber / Magic Red

Altitude	Faith	Cognitive	Ego	Value	Moral
			Ego-aware/ Unitive	Global View	
		Vision-logic (Wilber)	Construct-aware	Flex Flow	
	Universalizing		Autonomous		
Integral Turquoise				Human Bond	
Pluralistic Green	Conjunctive		Individualistic		
			Conscientious		
Rational Orange	Individuative-Reflective	Formal-Operational	Self-aware	Strive Drive	Post-Conventional
	Synthetic-Conventional				
Mythic Amber	Mythic-Literal	Concrete-Operational	Conformist	Truth Force	Conventional
			Self-protective	Power Gods	
Magic Red	Intuitive-Projective	Pre-Operational	Impulsive	Kin-Spirits	Pre-Conventional
	Primal	Sensorimotor	Symbiotic	Survival	

Egocentric | Ethnocentric | Worldcentric

Lines of Development

Figure 4
(adapted from Wilber's *Integral Spirituality*)

Stretching along the y-axis of the graph a colored spectrum ranges from red to turquoise indicating "altitude," an increasing level of developmental complexity. In other words, the higher a particular skill reaches in altitude the further along it is in its hierarchical unfolding. As we briefly outlined in our last chapter, altitude ranges from magic[71] in its earlier forms to integral in its most developed, with further levels of complexity and care continuing to emerge as evolution unfolds.

Additionally, each line in the figure above develops relatively independent of all the other lines.[72] That is to say, just as Gardner originally discovered, some lines might be well-developed, while others underdeveloped. For example, explaining one's own Integral Psychograph, one might say, "I have high cognitive capacity but sometimes feel as if I have low moral standards." Once understood, the Integral Psychograph is entirely intuitive, for we all know that we are more skilled in certain domains of our life than in others.

The Integral Psychograph imparts several benefits to any type of analysis. First, it allows easy reference when comparing stages of development within a single line. For example, we could say that in any particular line of development, "green pluralistic" altitude is higher than "orange rational" altitude. That is, *pluralism* transcends the limitations of the *rational* level of development yet includes all of its important contributions. In turn, orange represents a higher level of complexity than red, and so on.

To give a second example, the psychograph is also useful if we desire to investigate a single altitude across various lines. Examining the graph at one particular altitude (or color) provides us with a general orientation of where a stage in one line rests in comparison to a stage in another. Although each researcher uses different criteria to determine development in each line, we can see by looking at the graph that Loevinger's "conformist," Fowler's "synthetic-conventional," and Piaget's "concrete-operational" all are contained within the amber altitude. So although we cannot say that all three of these levels are the same, we can indeed begin to intuit a similar flavor within the various stages. Both of these benefits (i.e., the ability to compare stages within a single line and the ability to investigate a single altitude across various lines) show us how a graphic representation of complex matters can allow us to make reference quick and easy.

Before moving on, it is useful to expand one brief example of development in order to give the reader a practical account of how development actually occurs. Notice that the labels egocentric, ethnocentric, and worldcentric appear on the right side of the graph (figure 4). With this in mind, one notices that the stages falling within the red (magic) altitude or lower are to be considered egocentric; those near amber (mythic) altitude are considered ethnocentric; and those orange (rational) and above are considered worldcentric.

As development unfolds, humans gain the ability to take the perspective of others and include more individuals in a circle of compassion and trust.[73] This is another way of saying that the higher an altitude is on the psychograph, the greater the capacity to be more inclusive and to offer a more compassionate worldview. Here again we reiterate some of Wilber's initial work to provide the reader with a proper foundation. A summary of the three worldviews of increasing development can be explained as follows:

Egocentric: Egocentric individuals have the least capacity to take on the perspective of others. Their realm of compassion and care does not extend beyond themselves. For example, this worldview is represented by a self-centered child who steals a toy from a sibling simply because he or she wants to play with it. The child has no ability to take the perspective of the sibling and has not yet learned how to share.

Ethnocentric: Ethnocentric individuals allow their care and concern to extend beyond the boundaries of the self to embrace and include those whom they identify as their own group. This may include family, tribe, group, race, religious community, etc. Ethnocentric individuals do indeed have the capacity to take the perspective of the "other" within their own group but fail to place any real value on those outside of their group. This category might include a fundamentalist Christian who believes that all those who do not believe in Jesus will go to hell or a Muslim extremist who is willing to bomb innocent bystanders who do not subscribe to his or her particular set of beliefs. According to Wilber's research, it is estimated today that 70 percent of the world's population is ethnocentric or lower.[74]

Worldcentric: Worldcentric individuals have learned to look deeper into the human condition than individuals in the first two categories. They have learned to see all human beings as existing on an even playing field. Compassion and care extends to all humans regardless of race, color, or creed. A classic example of this worldview is represented by Martin Luther King Jr. King's famous quote, "Injustice anywhere is a threat to justice everywhere," reverberates a worldcentric perspective that understands the broad interconnectedness of humanity. Depending on one's research agenda, this category can be extended beyond humans to include all potential sentient beings in the universe, culminating in what is called Kosmo-centric worldview.

As one learns to interpret and read the psychograph, one is able to see a clearer snapshot of an individual's development. When including religion into the fold, one begins to intuit how each line of intelligence and each worldview might drastically affect the way an individual interprets a particular tradition. For example, an ethnocentric interpretation of Hinduism is much different from a worldcentric Hinduism.

Although the culturally dominant worldview may change over time, today we find individuals distributed across every available level of religious orientation precisely because all individuals are born at the lowest levels of development and work their way up the spiral.[75] In short, every individual begins at the first and most simple stage and, depending on social, economic, educational, and cultural (among other) influences, develops through the stages at varying speeds, resting in stagnation at any one along the way. Each stage of development becomes a valid station in life.[76] When fully expanded up the spectrum, religious traditions can become what Wilber calls a conveyor belt, helping to usher adherents up the ladder of transformation.[77]

Assessing Religious Orientation

Assessment of religious orientation is always a complex issue.[78] With this in mind there are multiple ways to determine an individual's level of development. Each method is context-dependent and should be adjusted to take into account the available data. The ideal and most accurate way to determine one's stage of religious orientation is to conduct a series of psychometric assessment tests[79] that directly inquire into all relevant lines of development (faith, cognitive, ego, values, moral). When such tests are administered in a controlled environment and properly scored, they offer direct results that can be plotted onto an Integral Psychograph. If not all lines are available for testing then it is appropriate to use faith-development testing as an alternative. In this case, if the testing results are obtained without major error, religious orientation can be determined by correlating an individual's level of faith development to its corresponding altitude (magic, mythic, rational, pluralistic, or integral). If direct assessment of faith development is not obtained through testing but additional data related to other lines is secured via a proper assessment, one can speculate about the level of psychological maturity by determining the individual's average level of functioning (or what Wilber calls "center of gravity") across the given lines.

Although a scenario in which developmental tests are conducted is preferred, it is seldom possible to obtain a detailed analysis of an individual's psychological makeup in circumstances that fall outside of a controlled setting. Consequently, if we are to have a theory of religious orientation that remains not only accurate but also pragmatic, we must also have a simpler and complementary methodology with which to speculate about religious orientation in those situations where developmental assessment tests are not possible. For example, in cases where we might want to analyze a religious terrorist from afar or to better communicate to a religious leader who might otherwise be hard to reach, developmental assessment tests are not a plausible option.

In these circumstances, we must infer religious orientation indirectly using the available information that we do have (signs, expressions, and behavior). Although these observable signs can never truly replace psychometric tests, they can and do offer the best alternative to understanding an individual's general level of psychological maturity. Despite the fact that inferring through observation is at times less accurate than direct testing, it does indeed still offer a useful reference point for action. Both of these methods of assessment (direct and inferred) are explained below.

A Bundle of Lines

Religious orientation, whether assessed through direct testing or inferred through observation, is determined using two types of input:

a primary line of development (faith) and four secondary lines of development (cognitive, ego, values, and moral).

If the level of the primary indicator (faith development) is clearly established, it can often, on its own accord, provide sufficient evidence to estimate an individual's level of religious orientation.[80] In other cases, when faith development is uncertain, secondary indicators (cognitive, ego, values, and moral) are used to help one make an educated and careful speculation. It is important to remember that because of the fact that lines of development progress at uneven rates, secondary indicators are merely sign posts of a general altitude. To this end, we must never confuse external signs and expressions with *definite* representations of one's interior level of development.[81] Despite its limitations, observational analysis of secondary indicators proves useful in settings when an estimate of an individual's level of religious orientation is better than nothing at all.

Below, I (1) offer the reader a brief synopsis of both the primary and secondary lines of intelligence included in this book's analysis and (2) explain why each of these lines can aide in determining one's religious orientation. For all those eager for an in-depth analysis of each line beyond the scope of this book, I recommend consulting the work of each researcher directly (see the footnotes and bibliography). Each of the brief outlines provided in this chapter are expanded upon in chapter 3 where we describe the details of each stage along the rainbow of religious orientation.

Faith Development

Faith development, as researched and first formally presented by James Fowler, is the primary indicator when determining an individual's level of religious orientation. Figure 5 below shows the correlation between Fowler's stages of faith development (center of the graph) and the stages of religious orientation (left-hand column of the graph). Fowler's "primal" and "intuitive-projective" stages of faith development correlate to a magic level of religious orientation. Fowler's "mythic-literal" and "synthetic-conventional" stages of faith align with the mythic level of religious orientation. Fowler's "individuate-reflective" stage of faith correlates to the rational level of religious orientation; Fowler's "conjunctive" to this book's pluralistic; and Fowler's "universalizing" to this book's integral.

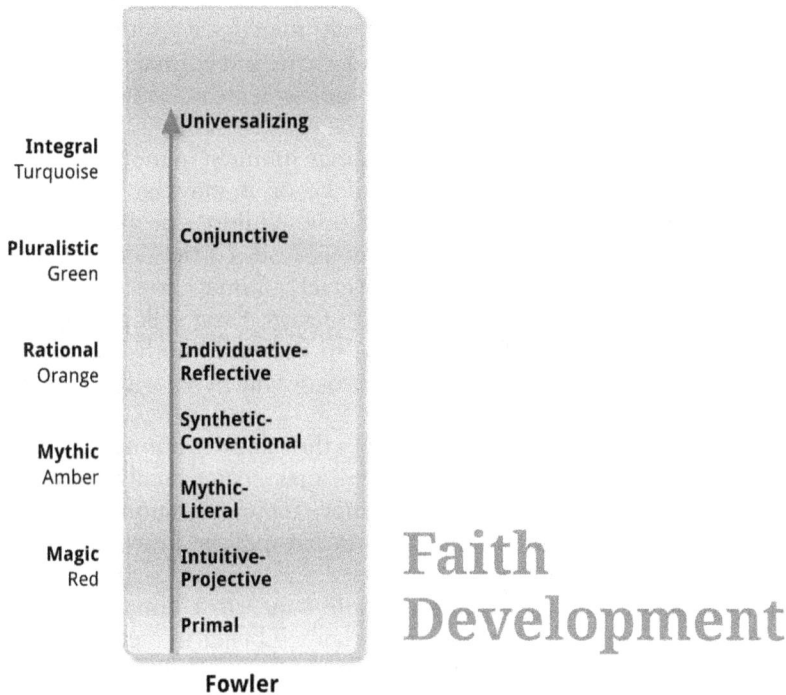

Integral Turquoise	Universalizing
Pluralistic Green	Conjunctive
Rational Orange	Individuative- Reflective
Mythic Amber	Synthetic- Conventional Mythic- Literal
Magic Red	Intuitive- Projective Primal

Fowler

Faith
Development

Figure 5

The following introduction to faith development is three-fold. First, we explore *what* Fowler's research actually measures. Second, we articulate some of the details that characterize each of his stages. Finally, we briefly address some of the criticism around Fowler's work and show how the model presented here resolves potential problems.

In a short but powerful book called the *Dynamics of Faith*, theologian Paul Tillich defined faith as "that which is of ultimate concern." Taking Tillich's lead, Fowler built upon this initial definition and began systematically interviewing a wide range of individuals asking each of them to answer the question "What is your ultimate concern?". Some of the answers he received were spiritual in content; others were not. Over an extended period of time at Harvard University, Fowler was able to organize the data into a progressive ladder of increasing complexity.

Before going into the details of each stage, it is useful to take a closer look at what both Fowler and Tillich meant when they defined faith as "that which is of ultimate concern." At least in its initial stages of development, "ultimate concern" has at least two sides. First, it involves a focus of attention; it becomes the center around which one structures his or her life. As the reader can surely imagine the list of ideas, concepts, and items that one might indicate as his or her ultimate concern is multifarious.

One's ultimate concern may change moment to moment, focused on immediate surroundings and safety, or it may be long-term in nature, attuned to the well-being of one's children or grandchildren. One's ultimate concern may be centered on a strict commitment to communion with the Divine or conversely ultimate concern might be driven solely by wealth and material success. Even still, perhaps one's ultimate concern has found a way to reconcile both material and spiritual concerns into a deeper and broader harmony without negative tension.

In his own words, Fowler clarifies the inclusive nature of the term "ultimate concern": "ultimate concern may center finally on our own ego and its extensions—work, prestige and recognition, power and influence, wealth. One's ultimate concern may be invested in family, university, nation, or church. Love, sex and a loved partner might be the passionate center of one's ultimate concern. Ultimate concern is a much more powerful matter than claimed belief in a creed or set of doctrinal propositions."[82] The wide range of possibilities leaves room for almost anything to be one's ultimate focus in life.

On the other side of the coin the "focus of attention" translates into a hope for "ultimate fulfillment."[83] That is to say, whatever it is that an individual decides to elevate to the role of greatest importance in his or her life is assumed to be that which will also bring the deepest satisfaction.[84] In a similar vein, an individual's ultimate concern directly represents the specific technology that he or she most deeply trusts to bring happiness and satisfaction in life. The spectrum of faith development, as uncovered by Fowler, can be seen as a ladder of increasing complexity, wherein each rung points to a new way one might be able to navigate, interpret, and practice a religion (or any other meaning-making system) to secure ultimate fulfillment.

Fowler's Stages of Faith[85]

If we are to more deeply understand the relationship between faith development and the ways in which individuals interpret, practice, and express religion in the modern and postmodern world, then it is crucial to understand the stages of faith Fowler uncovered during his years of rigorous academic research.[86] Below, we begin with the stage of faith that requires the least amount of psychological capacity and proceed to describe each further stage as they increase in their requisite level of complexity. The following explanations are paraphrased from Fowler's work, most notably his book *Stages of Faith*.

Primal: Life begins here. Oscillating between trust and panic, this stage centers on emotion. Ultimate concern often revolves around one's caretaker, bottle, nipple, or any other basic mode of survival.

Intuitive-Projective: This stage involves an intense merging of fantasy and reality. Not yet constrained by logic, those at this stage are inspired by tales and legends. Ultimate concern is usually related to safety, protection, and avoidance of threats. If ideas of God exist they are often anthropomorphic and magical.

Mythic-Literal: Preoccupied with miracles and literal interpretations of scripture or oral tradition, an individual at this stage begins to differentiate real from fantasy and egoic projections. Ultimate concern is often rooted in narrative stories regarding reality.

Synthetic-Conventional: Personal identity, role, and relationships become important to an individual at this stage. Ultimate concern resides in a personal relationship with the Divine (whatever "divine" might be). The individual is aware of the faith of others and is often defined by the beliefs of one's group. The unquestioning emphasis on role and identity at this stage can lead to blind faith in tradition or external authority and a lack of empathy for those outside of one's group.

Individuative-Reflective: At this stage, the individual "questions, examines, and reclaims" their relationship to both spirituality and ultimate concern. No longer does this stage confine an individual to embracing literal interpretations of ideas and scripture. In fact, at this stage, one begins to interpret scripture and make decisions based on one's own authority. A new ultimate concern emerges at this stage, wherein the individual finds himself committed to truth. If ultimate concern remains religious in nature, it revolves around logic and reason.

Conjunctive: At this stage of faith, the individual takes multiple perspectives and can see many sides of an issue simultaneously. Other religious traditions become important and even complementary to one's own. With a deep desire for wholeness, ultimate concern leads one to embrace and integrate internal polarities.

Universalizing: This stage is marked by a constant relationship with the Divine. Ultimate concern revolves around a moment-to-moment communion with or identification as the Divine. In summary, Fowler concludes:

> [Those at this stage] have identified with or they have come to participate in the perspective of God. They begin to see and value *through* God rather than from the self. This does not mean that the self is not valued: the self is included in God's loving and valuing of all creation. But the self is no longer the center from which one's valuing is done; it's done from an identification with God [Buddha-Nature, the Self, Allah, Jehovah].[87]

Faith-development theory has had a massive influence in academia over the past thirty years. According to published numbers, over 100 dissertations have used Fowler's work as a central theme since the early 1980s.[88] [89] The next few paragraphs will note some of the criticisms that Fowler's work attracted, and show how the model in this book is careful to correct for any potential problems.

Perhaps the strongest critique of Fowler's work comes from Heinz Streib. Streib's fundamental argument rests on his assertion that Fowler's work has grown too intimately intertwined with the Piagetian cognitive paradigm and as a result ignored other critical areas of importance. Streib writes:

The shift of emphasis to, even the overburdening of, cognitive development is one face of the coin, the other is the disregard for dimensions which are just as crucial for the constitution development of religion such as: the psychodynamical-interpersonal dimension (the psychodynamic of the self-other relationship); the interpretive, hermeneutic dimension (the dynamic of the self-tradition relationship); and the life-world dimension (the dynamic of the self-social world relationship). [90]

Despite his critiques, Streib does not think we should throw out Piagetian structures altogether, acknowledging that "there is enough indispensable genius with the cognitive-developmental perspective that makes it worthwhile to rethink and revise the Piagetian legacy." Rather than suggesting we get rid of the developmental model altogether, Streib thinks that the narrative and life world, rather than cognition "should move into focus of the developmental perspective on religion."[91] He more fully states his suggestion for a more balanced and integrative approach elsewhere, where he writes: "Inclusion of narrative approaches and the accounting for content dimensions hold the greatest promise for a significant innovation.... However, these creative new research designs tend toward throwing out the baby with the bathwater by favoring narrative or content analysis at the cost of the structural dimension. A decidedly integrative and consistent approach is desirable."[92]

Other critiques of Fowler's work were launched and subsequently defended at a 1999 academic gathering in Boston titled Symposium on Faith Development Theory and the Modern Paradigm. The core purpose of the conference was to examine Fowler's work using a critical postmodern lens to see if any of his work has fallen victim to modern paradigmatic assumptions (the deficiencies of the modern paradigm are discussed in detail in appendix 2) and how in fact we might ensure a comprehensive study of religious development beyond the modern paradigm. Critiques from authors brought brilliant insight that this book tries to incorporate both explicitly and implicitly wherever possible. For instance, scholars like Ana-María Rizzuto added a psychoanalytic perspective to faith development and raised questions of conscious and unconscious motivations and constructions of faith.[93] Others, like James Day, described the problems of a strictly structuralist approach to religious development and further explained how the networks and influence of speech and narrative need to be included into future models of faith development. Still others, like John McDargh, took a careful look at the postmodern problem of foundations and whether or not it was truly possible to decipher a universal human religious orientation.[94]

Although all of the critical comments and suggestions were welcomed to ensure that Fowler's work is aligned with the currents of postmodern thought, at times the critiques took the fundamental elements of the postmodern worldview too far. Day, for example ultimately claims that "what developmentalists hold to be hierarchical may be more a matter of personal style (and the communicative networks of which we are part), influenced by factors of stress, content specific to the question of the moment, and to personal history than to the participant's relative cognitive sophistication and capacity for advanced reasoning."[95] Clearly, from an integral perspective, Day's move to flatten all development into horizontal typologies or styles (proposed elsewhere in a more nuanced way by Streib in his model of religious styles) is seen as a postmodern fallacy that this book is careful to avoid.[96]

With its combination of both horizontal degrees of health and vertical stages of development this book recognizes that there is indeed strength to adding a typological perspective at each stage. However, developmental pluralism holds strong to not allow developmental perspectives to vanish all together. The arguments set forth in this book regarding faith development theory are reinforced by Fowler's latest comments on the subject that warn against a flattened postmodern variation of religious orientation.

To be sure, both Fowler's most recent iterations on faith development theory and the model of developmental religious pluralism set forth in this book agree on certain aspects of the postmodern critiques. For one we both agree that "the formal structuring of the stages is, at best, only half the story as regards the shaping and maintaining of a person's (or a group's) worldview."[97] Consequently, this book acknowledges that "there is both structuring and deconstructing power in the cultural environment with its social and media 'surround.'" That is to say, this book fully acknowledges a version of postmodern cultural sensitivity and takes into consideration the ways in which cultural and regional values are sure to influence the flavor and development of each stage of religious orientation. Similarly, developmental pluralism is careful to acknowledge unconscious motivations and life stories and how such elements might influence interpretation whenever such evaluations are context appropriate.

Even with these agreements in place, the model in this book is careful not to fall into any sort of postmodern anti-hierarchical extreme. Because development is still so poorly accounted for in religious interpretation, our model still gives emphasis to the structural dimensions of faith development in hopes of generating more awareness around its importance. As a whole, the approach taken in this book agrees with Fowler's rebuttal to the strictly typological models offered at the 1999 symposium. Fowler concludes that what the field truly needs is "a theory of types that can crosscut stages but not replace them."[98] An integral approach to religious studies attempts to do just that.

Cognitive Development

Although faith development is the primary indicator in determining one's religious orientation, other lines of development are necessary if we are to obtain a well-rounded snapshot of a particular individual. As described thus far, secondary indicators like cognitive development offer signs that may help to point to an individual's average level of psychological maturity or "center of gravity," especially in those cases where faith development is unknown and direct testing is unavailable.

Cognitive development is often erroneously taken to mean a measure of one's IQ or logical capacity. In actuality, research into cognitive development asks two basic questions: (1) "What am I aware of?" and (2) "Of that which I am aware, how many perspectives can I take?"[99] We examine these questions and frame the use of the cognitive line using the work of Jean Piaget, Ken Wilber, and Robert Kegan. The introduction below shows (1) the basic stages of cognitive development and (2) how cognitive development directly interplays with faith development.

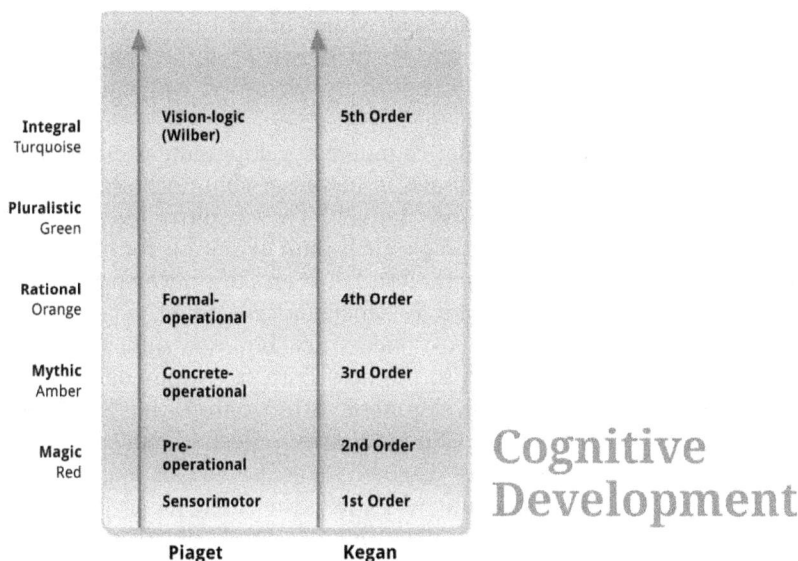

	Piaget	Kegan	
Integral Turquoise	**Vision-logic (Wilber)**	**5th Order**	
Pluralistic Green			
Rational Orange	**Formal-operational**	**4th Order**	
Mythic Amber	**Concrete-operational**	**3rd Order**	
Magic Red	**Pre-operational**	**2nd Order**	**Cognitive**
	Sensorimotor	**1st Order**	**Development**

Figure 6

Humans all begin at a stage in cognitive development wherein they are only aware of their own sense perceptions (Sensorimotor/1st order consciousness).[100] Thinking, to the extent that it takes place, is a mixture of instincts and reactionary impulses to one's immediate environment. In both this first stage and its immediate predecessor (pre-operational/2nd order consciousness) individuals still lack the ability to take the perspectives of others. As cognitive capacities mature, individuals gain the ability to empathize and speculate about orientations to life different from their own. Eventually, this increased level of perspective-taking and the speculative capacities that come with it sets the foundation for the next level of psychological complexity to unfold. Building on the capacity to think beyond the immediate moment, human beings begin to develop the ability to think linearly and logically (concrete operational/3rd order of consciousness).[101] If this capacity of "hierarchical complexity"[102] is sufficiently stabilized, an individual will have the building blocks in place to move beyond simple logical/linear thought. In the next and "4th order" of consciousness, an individual gains the capacity to step back and examine his or her own logical thought processes (formal operational).[103] In those human beings who are particularly well equipped to push cognitive capacities to an even higher level, a "5ᵗʰ order" of consciousness can evolve similar to what Wilber calls vision-logic. This fifth order is most notably recognized by signs of an "aperspectival awareness"—one is no longer trapped to a single perspective held within linear time, instead he or she can rapidly switch back and forth between various perspectives simultaneously without being exclusively identified with any one in particular.

Wilber often contends that cognitive development, as outlined by Kegan and Piaget in figure 6 above, is "necessary but not sufficient" for the further development in other lines.[104], The cognitive line, in other words, is like a trailblazer, burning a clear path in altitude for other lines to follow. Let's look at the interaction between faith development and cognitive development to obtain a deeper understanding.

If we take the notion of "necessary but not sufficient" and examine it in detail we begin to see how faith development is in fact dependent upon cognitive development. A move from the "synthetic-conventional" stage of faith to "individuative-reflexive" can only occur if cognitive development has reached Piaget's "formal operational" level of cognition. Let's examine why this is the case.

With Piaget's "formal operational" level of development, individuals can for the first time step back to reflect upon their own morals, religious thoughts, and values. Cognitive development is "necessary" for types of faith development that require similar reflective skills. An individual at the previous stage of cognitive development ("concrete operational") lacks the psychological capacity to question his/her own beliefs; one has the cognitive capacity to think logically (concrete operational) but does not yet "think about thinking" (formal operational).

The cognitive line is however "not sufficient" for the change in stage of faith. In other words, just because an individual has the capacity to reflect on his own religious beliefs (formal operational), it does not automatically signify that he or she has developed to a corresponding altitude in the faith line (individuative-reflexive). Even if one has the capacity for a higher stage of faith, this does not mean that he or she will necessarily develop to embrace his or her highest potential in all other lines.

Moving forward we find that the later example provided above is one of the most prevalent phenomena in Western psychological development today. In countless cases, individuals with highly developed cognitive intelligence have an arrested spiritual intelligence. In part, this is a direct result of the fact that, until this book, religion has yet to be clearly articulated in higher forms of complexity and expression beyond its standard mythical or traditional packaging. It is my deep hope that all those with complex cognitive development can find a particular expression of faith that is both adequate and appropriate to meet his or her particular set of advanced developmental needs.

Ego Development

The work of researcher Jane Loevinger and Susanne Cook-Greuter determines how an individual might answer the question, "Who am I?".

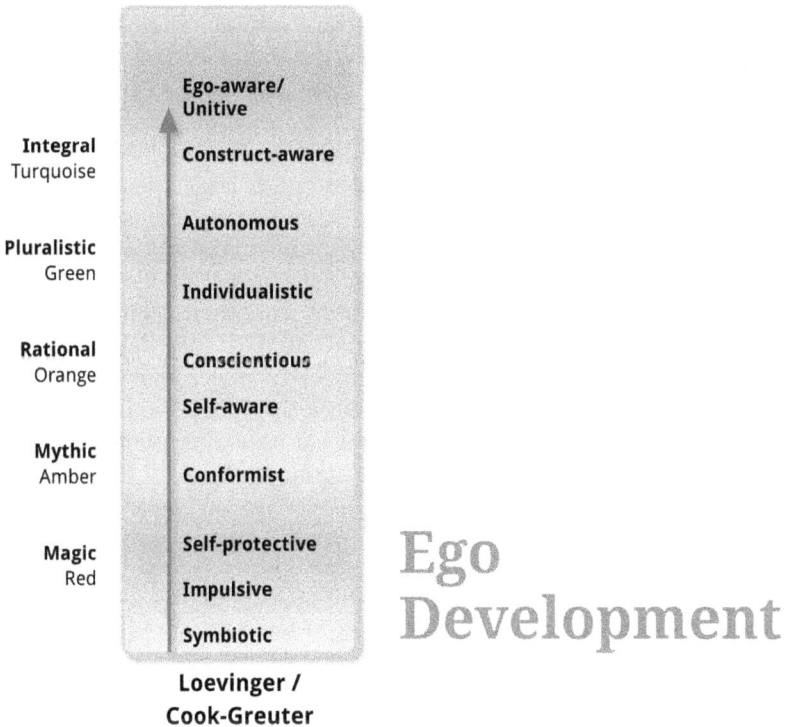

	Ego-aware/ Unitive
Integral Turquoise	**Construct-aware**
	Autonomous
Pluralistic Green	**Individualistic**
Rational Orange	**Conscientious**
	Self-aware
Mythic Amber	**Conformist**
Magic Red	**Self-protective**
	Impulsive
	Symbiotic

Loevinger / Cook-Greuter

Ego Development

Figure 7

Ego development is another important secondary indicator when determining one's levels of religious orientation. Often, ego development is used to describe a person's "self-sense." A self-sense is like a nebulous cloud comprising each individual's separate identity. Clearly, one's "self-identity" plays a major role in how he or she might relate, practice, or interpret his or her religious tradition. As a secondary indicator in religious orientation, ego-development signs help to orient an individual on the vertical spectrum of complexity. Let's take the ego-development stages one at a time to see how they unfold.

According to Cook-Greuter, humans begin their journey at birth, completely fused with the environment and initial caregiver (symbiotic).[105] They have no capacity to tell where their own identity ends and the world begins. Eventually, an individual's sense of self begins to solidify and they grow first to embrace a self-identity that is only concerned with instantaneous personal satisfaction (impulsive) to an identity that is constantly in a "test of wills" with other human beings (self-protective). Next, individuals move to a stage in which they tend to be easily influenced by their surroundings and tend to become whatever their particular social group determines appropriate (conformist). In the case of the conformist level of ego development, the individual has separated the self-sense from the environment but not from his or her group, class, or race (hence is ethnocentric). Today, this conformist stage is the resting place of a large majority of the world's population. The lucky few who continue ego development not only find a true sense of individuality (individualistic) but also move on to a stage in which they begin to integrate all previous levels of egoic identity (autonomous) into a healthy continuum. Finally, as ego development reaches its peak it transcends itself. At these highest stages, the "individual" begins to identify with an awareness not limited to a single "point of view" (unitive).

The unitive stage of development has several implications when it is understood from within a religious context, hence for the sake of this book's central analysis this stage of development is worth exploring in further detail. At Cook-Greuter's unitive stage, one's self-sense individuates when necessary but is not confined to a single personality or "point of view." The unitive individual begins to identify with what he or she perceives to be a single awareness that moves through all individuals.[106] Unlike the fusion with the environment that exists in the first symbiotic stage, here the individual has completely *transcended and included* the external environment within his/her own awareness. That is to say, unlike the symbiotic stage of ego development in which individuation has not yet occurred, the unitive individual has access to a properly differentiated individual consciousness that serves as a useful construct when needed. Ultimately, higher stages of ego development allow selfish desires to subside offering one the capacity to take on universal issues facing the whole of humanity.

Values Development

The work of Clare Graves is the best work to date that clearly articulates and explores the development of human values within a complete bio-psychosocial system. A comprehensive account of Graves' research was published in 2005 in a volume edited by Christopher Cowen and Natasha Todorovic called *The Never Ending Quest.* In their book, Graves agrees with the basic sequence of human development. He puts it this way: "The psychology of the adult human being is an unfolding, ever-emergent process marked by subordination of older behavior systems to newer, higher order systems."[107]

Graves was also quick to point out that an individual's level of psychological development influences the particular preferences that he or she has in life. He writes:

> The mature person tends to change his psychology continuously as the conditions of his existence change.... When a person is centralized in one of the [stages] of equilibrium, he has a psychology which is particular to that [stage]. His emotions, ethics and values, biochemistry, state of neurological activation, learning systems, preference for education, management and psychotherapy are all appropriate to that [stage].[108] [109]

It is clear to see how Graves' system might also easily account for changes in ones religious preference over the course of a single life. Graves' research offers one of the first comprehensive systems of human emergence. For the purpose of this book's presentation, this book uses only a small portion of Graves' research and focuses on the way in which values unfold in an individual's psychological development.[110]

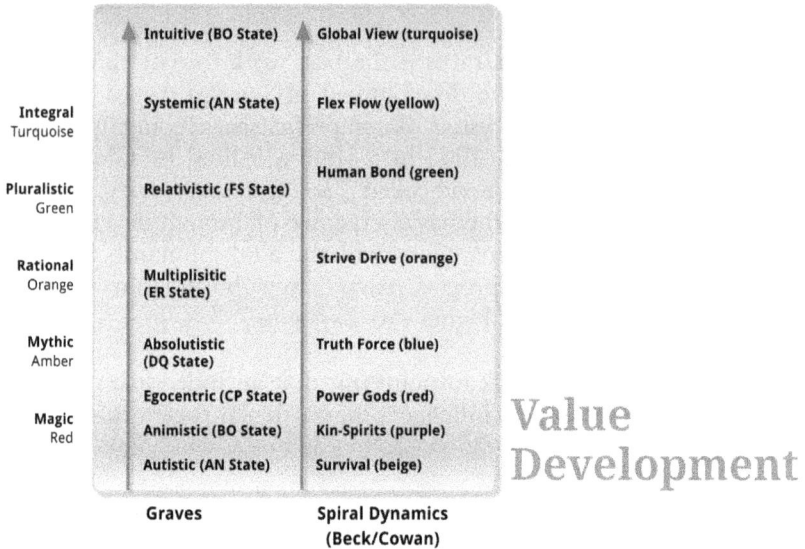

Graves		Spiral Dynamics (Beck/Cowan)
Integral Turquoise	Intuitive (BO State)	Global View (turquoise)
	Systemic (AN State)	Flex Flow (yellow)
Pluralistic Green	Relativistic (FS State)	Human Bond (green)
Rational Orange	Multiplisitic (ER State)	Strive Drive (orange)
Mythic Amber	Absolutistic (DQ State)	Truth Force (blue)
Magic Red	Egocentric (CP State)	Power Gods (red)
	Animistic (BO State)	Kin-Spirits (purple)
	Autistic (AN State)	Survival (beige)

Value Development

Figure 8

Graves' work was popularized by two of his students, Don Beck and Christopher Cowen, in a book titled *Spiral Dynamics*. Graves' research, as simplified by Beck and Cowen, uses its own color scale ranging from beige to turquoise. Although shown above in figure 8 for purpose of enabling correlation, the presentation in this book avoids using such colors in its description of values in order to prevent confusion with its own colorful spectrum of religious orientation.

As this book unfolds, the details of Grave's work will be highlighted in each of the situations in which such secondary evidence is helpful to determine religious orientation. For now, two relevant aspects of his research are worth noting before moving on.

1. Interestingly, as development of values increases over time, each stage alternates between placing an emphasis on the individual and then shifting at the next stage to emphasize the collective. Taking a closer look, we find that as the spiral begins at its most basic levels, those with values centering on survival place greater attention on the autonomous individual rather than the collective. Those who value survival are worried first and foremost about their own individual survival. It is not until one's own sense of self is secure that one can move to include others.

With the next stage of unfolding, called BO State (Graves) and Kin-Spirits (Beck), greater value is placed on the communal or collective instead of the individual. At this stage, one recognizes the vital importance of family and ancestors. As the CP State (Graves) and Power-Gods (Beck) structure emerges, emphasis returns to the individual and a focus on personal power. This oscillation between autonomy and communion occurs all the way up the spiral. Such distinctions become important when we reach an integral level of development wherein equal emphasis is given to both autonomy and communion.[111]

2. Graves is clear in his writing that development over time is not always all good news. At each stage of development there are often new problems that emerge alongside the positive changes. Graves writes:

As man starts his transition from the absolutistic form for existence, the ordered, authoritarian, submissive way of life, and as man moves through the stage of independence on into the sociocentric ways for being, five definable and describable states of existence emerge, one after another, in our ordered hierarchical way. These five states, each of which has a strong flavor of selfish independence in them, have brought more that is good to man and more that is bad for him than all states of existence which preceded them.[112]

It is precisely this sort of understanding that allows us to keep a sense of humility as development unfolds. If we can remember that each new stage of understanding is in itself limited and only a precursor to the next emergent stage, then we can remain in a place of discovery and learning, never settling at some artificially selected apex of human development. Graves reminds us that there is always further to go and more room to grow.

Moral Development

Lastly, our analysis of the stages of religious orientation takes into careful consideration a final secondary indicator called moral development. Moral development was most notably researched by Lawrence Kohlberg and has since been expanded upon by Carol Gilligan among many others.

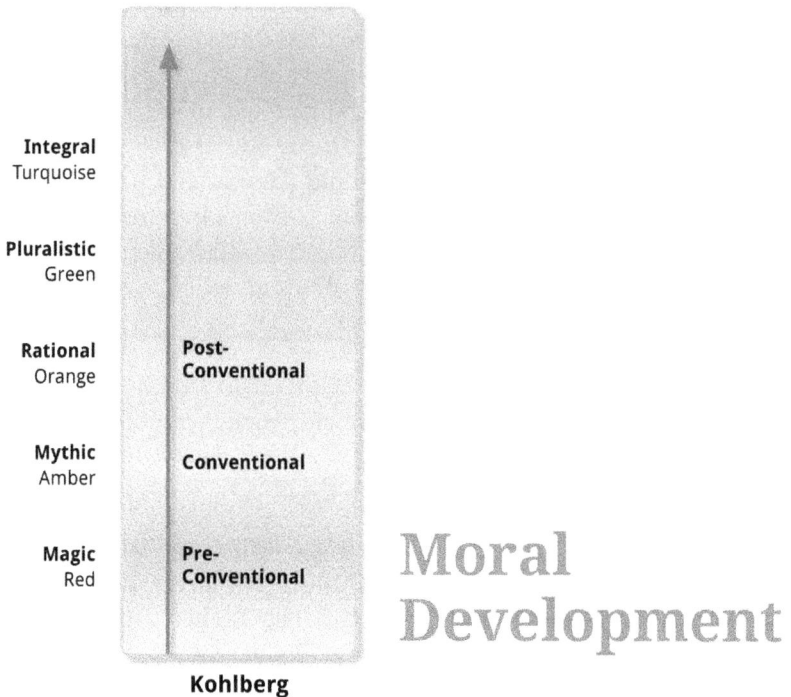

Figure 9

Understanding moral development is rather intuitive. Moral intelligence is the capacity or way in which one determines what is right and wrong. At its earliest stages, there is no real ethical distinction between different actions. Individuals simply act on impulse and do as they please without the consideration of others (pre-conventional)[113]. In the middle range (what are called conventional levels) of moral development, , individuals look to outside authority (laws and rules) to decide ethical dilemmas. Finally, in post-conventional moral development, individuals can make decisions of right and wrong based on their own internal moral compass. Individuals at the post-conventional stage take all others who might be affected by their choices into consideration before making ethical decisions. Analyzing behavior as a method to infer religious orientation often rests strongly on criteria that involve moral development. We discuss the critical role of moral development in more depth in chapter six where it helps us to determine the difference between an Islamic extremist and an average Muslim at a mythic level of development.

Conclusion

Three specific points and two broad points of conclusion are useful at the close of this chapter. First the specifics: (1) the above secondary lines of development (cognitive, ego, values, and moral) all help to determine an individual's religious orientation in a given context wherein either the faith line of development is uncertain or an individual's ultimate concerns are not activated directly, (2) In circumstances in which faith development is known, secondary lines of intelligence can serve to reinforce a faith assessment by averaging the secondary lines together to determine the general "center of gravity" of an individual, and (3) although conducting an analysis of one's religious orientation without specifically administering precise developmental tests may be somewhat speculative, when observational signs and expressions of primary and secondary lines are used, it helps to ensure an analysis is at least as close as possible to predict the behavior, action, or style of interpretation of a religious adherent.

More broadly, the academic research offered in this chapter is used to establish the fact that varying levels of developmental complexity are a very real phenomenon. If we are to use models of reality that are in sync with current research, we must include this vertical dimension of hierarchical analysis. Not only will including a developmental lens prove more accurate, but if based on sound research as shown in this book, the inclusion will allow us to create maps that help to guide religious adherents to more sophisticated levels of expression, ultimately allowing them to contribute to the well-being of the planet and its inhabitants. Finally, if we jettison a more sophisticated developmental approach to religious analysis and fail to move beyond the flatland of the postmodern paradigm, we run the risk of many religious traditions remaining trapped at lower levels of religious orientation. Religions that are restricted to traditional or mythic levels of development often instigate and propagate ethnocentric belief structures that create blockades, conflict, and violence in the name of religion—hindering further growth and development on a global scale.

Chapter 3
The Stages of Religious Orientation

Next, pushing the application of Integral Theory forward, we explore in detail the five most relevant stages of religious orientation. As a reminder, religious orientation represents the way in which an individual's level of psychological complexity and capacity for care influences his or her interpretation of a particular religion. If we are to move beyond the pluralistic approach, often limited to a single axis of extremist versus moderate, we must add and acknowledge a vertical dimension of depth and development to religious analysis.

Flavors of Religious Orientation

The core purpose of this chapter is to articulate the flavor of each vertical level of religious orientation. Building on the academic research articulated in chapter 2, the following pages describe some of the most significant developmental signs one might find when testing or observing each level of complexity. This chapter not only serves as a foundation for categorizing the religious action and interpretation of others, but it also offers personal relevance to any reader interested in using religion as a technology for happiness but unaware of which developmental level is most appropriate.

An Integral Psychograph

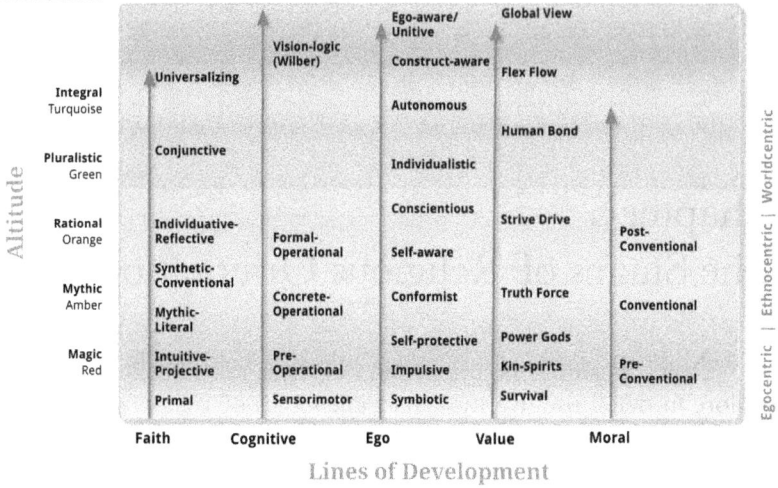

Stages of Religious Orientation

Altitude

Altitude	Faith	Cognitive	Ego	Value	Moral
			Ego-aware/Unitive	Global View	
	Universalizing	Vision-logic (Wilber)	Construct-aware	Flex Flow	
Integral Turquoise			Autonomous		
				Human Bond	
Pluralistic Green	Conjunctive		Individualistic		
			Conscientious		
Rational Orange	Individuative-Reflective	Formal-Operational	Self-aware	Strive Drive	Post-Conventional
	Synthetic-Conventional				
Mythic Amber		Concrete-Operational	Conformist	Truth Force	Conventional
	Mythic-Literal				
			Self-protective	Power Gods	
Magic Red	Intuitive-Projective	Pre-Operational	Impulsive	Kin-Spirits	Pre-Conventional
	Primal	Sensorimotor	Symbiotic	Survival	

Lines of Development

Egocentric | Ethnocentric | Worldcentric

Figure 10

Each altitude, across each line of intelligence, has somewhat of a similar "flavor": Red (magic/powerful) tends to be ritualistic, amber (mythic/membership) is absolutistic, orange (rational/reflective) is inquisitive, green (pluralistic/relativistic) is contextually sensitive, and turquoise (integral) is comprehensive. These flavors appear in each line of development and help to give a taste of how each stage of religious orientation might show up in the world.

Below, I describe five altitudes and the corresponding signs that accompany them. Each description includes indicators from both primary and secondary lines of intelligence. Descriptions are intended to train the reader to be more aware of the various elements of behavior, expression, and action that might suggest a particular level of development. Although the articulation of the various signs in each line appear horizontally across each level, they are not meant to imply that human beings develop evenly across all lines at all times.

Magical-Powerful
The ritualistic flavor of **red** altitude

The first altitude of religious orientation shows signs, expressions, and behaviors related to intuitive-projective and mythic-literal faith development. An individual here leans toward literal interpretation of sacred texts, often focusing on one or two verses of scripture in particular. The individual at this stage tends to be overly concerned with power and is often distracted with the supernatural elements of faith. Magic individuals value rites and rituals, and may be extremely superstitious. Other signs to look for at this level of religious expression are self-protective tendencies in ego development. One may see an individual here with a primary focus of avoiding existential punishment and seeking eternal reward. Some individuals at this level have a tendency to place responsibility and blame outside of themselves. The individual at this red altitude may show signs of pre-conventional morality or perhaps the beginning stages of conventional morality. At this level of religious orientation many individuals act without much consideration for others. If lower stages of moral development are present, right and wrong are constituted by impulse rather than authority or reason. Fear of wrathful deities (or a single God) often keep people at this stage in line.

Mythic-Membership
The absolutist flavor of **amber** altitude

An amber altitude of religious orientation corresponds to Fowler's synthetic-conventional stage of faith. At this stage an individual's ultimate concern begins to shift away from self-gratification and ego-centered drives toward an emphasis on role and identity. Often an individual at a mythic-religious orientation still maintains somewhat literal interpretations of scriptures. The individual at this stage often develops the desire for a personal relationship with God. In Islam, this period allows a deepening of one's submission to Allah. Christians, during this time, feel a drive for true companionship with Jesus. Hindus may be drawn more toward Bhakti Yoga, a practice involving love and devotion to God. At this stage, one's personal faith or set of beliefs provide deep meaning and courage for living. Other important signs to look for that may point to this level of development are values that focus on an absolute "truth" and a puritanical sense of right and wrong. The individual at this stage may show signs that indicate a preference for hierarchical structure and order even if such structure tends to be oppressive or abuse its power. Usually, an individual at this stage of development is willing to control impulses in exchange for deferred fulfillment. The individual with mythic religious orientation often shows indications that approval of his or her group is of the utmost importance. He or she is often kept in order through feelings of guilt. In many cases, the individual's own identity extends to that of his or her own group, family, or religious community, while seeing the views of those outside the group as either wrong, un-religious, or out of line with the one *straight* path.

Cognitive development at this stage most often demonstrates Piaget's concrete-operational thinking. The individual has the capacity to think in logical progressions, but in most cases does not "reflect about thinking" or consider whether their own belief systems are in themselves a coherent and logical system. Similarly, one might notice actions and demonstrations of Kegan's third-order "traditional" consciousness. The person expressing mythic stage tendencies in a given context lacks a definite capability to think entirely as an autonomous individual so morals and a sense of right and wrong often come from an external conventional authority (i.e., one's group, society, the Church, the Qur'an, the Vedas, dharma, or duty).

Rational-Reflective
The inquisitive flavor of **orange** altitude

Orange altitude correlates to Fowler's scale at the individuative-reflective level of faith development. Individuals at this level of development begin to question and examine all of their existing beliefs. They begin to scrutinize the myths they believed without hesitation at the previous stage, in order to find deeper meaning. For the first time individuals recognize the ability to have their own opinions outside the restrictions allowed by the group or scripture.

Due to the pragmatic and reflective nature of this stage, individuals may become agnostic or atheist; both of which represent healthy expressions of religious orientation at this stage of development.[114] Sometimes an extreme rational orientation, taking an atheistic stance, may try to rid the world of all lower levels of religious expression, declaring that they are immature and even childish.[115]

Looking at the secondary indicators of orange altitude, Graves' values meter may show signs of a strive-drive capacity. The individual at this stage is likely to place a strong emphasis on autonomy, independence, and success. He or she is usually emphatic about embracing the value of the scientific method, evidence, and *tried-and-true experience*.

Piaget's formal operational stage and Kegan's fourth order of consciousness propel individuals to reflect upon their own thoughts and beliefs.[116] This means that one will move beyond blind belief in particular religious ideologies, to now *operate* on them to improve them consciously and critically.

Although it is important to remember that an analysis usually gives the most weight to signs of faith development, a religious adherent with a center of gravity near an orange altitude may show secondary indicators of particular relevance. An individual at this stage may show signs that demonstrate Loevinger and Cook-Greuter's individualist and Kohlberg's post-conventional moral development. This stage on Kohlberg's scale is usually noticed when the moral compass begins to develop within. A post-conventional shift allows one to see the deeper principles that rest behind laws and written scriptures. The inward gaze also results in individuals resting on their own prowess for answers through personal experience and direct knowledge.

An orange level of religious orientation is usually marked by the fact that the person's sphere of care and compassion expands to embrace the entire world. This worldcentric awareness induces a deep notion of universal tolerance. As one scholar points out, "tolerance begins when we no longer see a group as other but as a concrete human community with real and ancient values. This cognitive leap is a difficult one, especially when the cultural other happens to be a religious other."[117] It is at this stage that rather than identifying with others because of race, religion, culture, or a belief system, the individual begins to see the underlying common connection that we all have as human beings. With this understanding comes the birth of and care for universal human rights.

Pluralistic-Relativistic
The sensitive flavor of **green** altitude

Signs or tests that demonstrate Fowler's conjunctive level of faith most often indicate a pluralistic level of religious orientation. The individual at this stage begins to realize that life's issues don't have to be black and white. The individual becomes comfortable with and may even enjoy the embrace of paradox. Pluralistic individuals recognize the deep truth that all traditions are simply different perspectives of the one Ultimate Reality.[118] The religious pluralism expressed from this stage goes beyond the tolerance expressed in the rational stage to now actually take on a full embrace of other religious traditions. Individuals at this pluralistic level begin to recognize the cultural embeddedness of their own religious beliefs. As a result, they begin to search out other spiritual systems. They search not with a desire to convert those of other faiths but in order to take other perspectives, to find out how another's view may be able to supplement their own. They begin to ask questions: What areas of knowledge are missing in my own religious system? Do I have any blind spots? Just as red-colored spectacles make the viewer unable to see red, the conjunctive individual begins to examine other traditions to see what his particular set of spectacles may be preventing him or her from seeing. For the first time in development, religious experience is cross-referenced with those experiences described in other world traditions in a serious fashion that actually gives value to the experience of the other. The pluralistic individual begins to see that the deep structures of these experiences are similar (e.g., esoteric nondual realizations), despite the fact that surface features might appear different (merging with Christian God vs. merging with the Buddhist Dharmakaya).[119]

The individual at green altitude will show actions and behaviors that demonstrate a deep value for connection with other people. They find great significance not only in community but in the unity and equality of all people. With sensitivity to the needs of others, this stage begins to recognize that majority rule and democracy alone (if left unchecked) can end up imposing a tyranny of the majority on the minority. As a result this level values that everyone has an opportunity to speak and be heard. No decisions are made until all come to some form of consensus. A feeling of interconnectedness often results in social activism in the world. Harvard professor Paul Hanson's "hermeneutic of engagement" or what he describes as the "interpretive method that ties study with worship and reflection with action in the world,"[120] although present at times in lower levels, becomes a necessity at a pluralistic level of development and beyond. All those concerned with social justice and global goodwill interpret their tradition in new ways so as to ensure positive social action in the world.

Individuals at this stage, with their nuanced sensitivity to culture, identity, time, and place, tend to despise the broad universals and hierarchy that they often embraced in earlier mythic and rational stages. They often stand against such notions noting how dominating and repressive they can be. From this viewpoint, stages of development are disenchanting. There is a sense that "it is not right to value one level more than any other."[121] It is in this stage that we see a clear confusion between dominating and healthy hierarchies. There is tendency at this stage to abandon hierarchies altogether.

Through testing or observation one might see signs of ego development that exhibit individualistic or autonomous features. As individuals begin to reach these higher stages of ego development, they develop the desire to go beyond the limits of their own individuated self.

Integral
The comprehensive flavor of **turquoise** altitude

At the integral stage[122] of religious orientation one will likely notice signs of Fowler's universalizing stage of faith. Having taken the perspectives of other religious traditions, supplemented one's beliefs, and uprooted one's own worldview from the limiting perspectives of his or her own culture (to whatever degree possible), the individual at turquoise altitude begins to find a vast and sophisticated mental resting place. With the universalizing level of the primary indicator (faith) lit up, integral religious adherents have found a center within themselves with regard to their own personal beliefs. The search to find individual truth that began with ferociousness in the inquiry of the rational/orange stage, now starts to settle as the individual actually learns how to rest in and as truth itself. God (or Ultimate Reality) is seen as both immanent and transcendent, as Self and other. God is recognized from first-, second-, and third-person points of view.[123] God/Godhead is seen, at least in part, as the causal ground from which all form and knowledge originally arise.

The integral stage recognizes the importance and value of all preceding levels. For example, an integral level sees that green altitude served as a filter to neutralize all dominating tendencies. Passing through the pluralistic level ensures oppressive tendencies do not resurface when healthy, natural hierarchy returns at the integral stage.

Beyond the primary indicator offered through faith development, secondary indicators may help to indirectly predict the orientation of an individual at this level of complexity. Through observation, one might look for actions or behaviors that demonstrate flex-flow and holistic/global values. With a clearer picture of the universe, the individual at this level of religious orientation will likely begin to demand more integrative open systems and forms of decision making by consent[124] rather than majority rule or the time-consuming process of consensus. Religious adherents at this stage will likely agree to employ decisions quickly upon suggestion, unless there are substantial objections. The flex-flow nature of this level allows decisions to be implemented at an astonishing speed, because individuals are aware that course corrections can be made along the way. Integral religious orientation recognizes the importance of both equality and value distinctions. One has a deep desire to make sense of the world, to order it, and to organize the fields of knowledge that previously seemed disconnected. The individual is thirsty for knowledge and the experience of other religions, not only to supplement their own understanding, as in the pluralistic stage, but now to organize and help draw clear maps for other travelers to follow. Spirituality is no longer something that can be valued as an object, it is entirely embedded into every moment, making it impossible to avoid.

Integral religious orientation is unique in that the individual now has a developmental perspective sensitive enough to implement hierarchy without domination or abuse. This perspective allows the individual to embrace all the levels of orientation that have come before it, from magic to mythic to rational to pluralistic. Integral religious orientation understands that the preceding levels serve as the vital foundational elements that support the higher stages. Without the lower levels of development, integral levels would not be possible. Trying to jettison lower levels of orientation would be like committing a slow but certain suicide. In fact, not only should lower levels not be destroyed, they should be embraced in agape, nurtured, and each stage made as healthy as possible. It is by way of these levels that the integral thinkers of tomorrow will blossom.

At turquoise altitude one may see signs of a moral development that has reached to the further limits of Kohlberg's post-conventional stages. One may notice that an individual at this level makes moral judgments in a more sophisticated way than those of the previous pluralistic stage wherein decisions are made considering the greatest good for the greatest number. At an integral level, decisions are made based on the greatest good for the greatest span and the *greatest depth*.[125] Here, depth represents the degree of and potential for the highest levels of complexity and care (e.g., human beings all have greater capacity for complexity and care than an ant or a fish). A religious adherent with an integral level of awareness takes both span and depth into consideration when making ethical decisions.

Because cognitive development is necessary but not sufficient for faith development to mature to the integral level, cognitive intelligence has expanded to Wilber's vision logic and Kegan's fifth order of consciousness. All perspectives are taken into consideration without privileging any single viewpoint. This allows a clearer picture of the whole to emerge, both within and outside of religious contexts.

Signs may be observed at this stage that point to a level of ego development that Cook-Greuter dubs "unitive" or "ego-aware." In this stage, the religious adherent might show behavior and or actions that demonstrate that the individual is no longer restricted to their own individual ego. There is a spaciousness that allows them to effortlessly glide between multiple perspectives and states of consciousness. To quote Cook-Greuter: "Though [individuals] at the Unitive stage are aware of themselves as separate and unique embodiments, they also identify with all other living beings. The separation of self from others is experienced as an illusion..."[126] The experience of an individual's "I-am-ness" is recognized and felt as the same I-am-ness that exists within every other living creature, an I am-ness that smiles softly back in bliss every time it is recognized and acknowledged.

Developmental Disclaimers

In conclusion, three disclaimers ensure that the method of developmental religious pluralism and the stages listed above are used appropriately:

1. As mentioned in the book's introduction, it is not my intention for the stages of religious orientation to be used to pigeon hole an individual to a particular altitude. The latest research out of Harvard on adult development (Fischer, Commons, Stein, Heikkinen) reminds us that individuals experience large developmental swings due to context dependent variables. This means that individuals express varying levels of psychological intelligence in different contexts. Some settings allow for greater levels of complexity. For instance, individuals may "scaffold" or build upon the thoughts and ideas of others allowing them to work at a higher capacity then they might on their own. Other circumstances (e.g., life conditions of great stress) may cause an individual to express actions and behaviors lower than his or her capacity. All this is reiterated here so that we (a) hold the classifications of specific individuals lightly, yet (b) simultaneously maintain the deep importance of adding the broader outline of developmental stages to religious analysis.

2. Outlining each rung on the ladder can help individuals become as healthy as possible at whatever stage they might currently rest. As passionate global citizens it is not always our responsibility to point out where other individuals fall short. Perhaps the best method to encourage healthy development is to help institutionalize an outline like the one above in each tradition, and hope that the insights provided encourage individuals, on their own accord, to work at consciously developing through the stages.

3. Religious traditions should feel empowered by this model of religious orientation rather than resistant. Given the fact that religions seek prosperity and goodwill, helping individuals follow the map provided in this chapter, so that they might develop to higher levels of compassion and embrace is perhaps the single most beneficial thing religious traditions can do for humanity. Rather than feeling disempowered by the advances of

modernity and postmodernity, religious traditions that embrace developmental pluralism can now have the opportunity and power to invigorate progress and social change in ways not previously possible. If such a developmental embrace occurs, we will be one step closer to implementing Wilber's notion of the conveyor belt.

4. If we can agree that empowerment and social engagement is desired, and that the actualization of the conveyor belt is optimal, then our religious traditions must immediately begin working on two key areas: (1) Within their own communities, religious leaders must make the path of development clear and each stage of religious orientation must be acknowledged as valid and authentic. When acknowledgement is reached by a critical mass, the stigma and resistance currently surrounding the transcendence of mythic/traditional religious orientation will be removed. Adherents will be able to move beyond what Wilber calls the "pressure cooker lid" preventing rational stages of development from emerging out of the dominant mythic forms of religion so popular today.[127] (2) Outside of their own communities, religious traditions must demonstrate to the external world that they acknowledge and embrace the entire developmental path. Stepping beyond blind faith of mythic orientations to stages that represent rational religious inquiry and beyond, will allow religious traditions to once again integrate into the academic, scientific, and political domains with a mutually respected and trusted voice.[128]

Chapter 3 - The Stages of Religious Orientation

Part 2: Evidence

Opening Comments

Now that the key features of each altitude have been delineated, part 2 of this book offers examples of each level of religious orientation from within four of our world's most populous traditions. Each chapter begins with a brief overview of several relevant features of the religious tradition itself, followed by examples of interpretation stemming from magic, mythic, rational, pluralistic, and integral stages of development. Part 2 has two objectives: (1) It provides evidence that the stages of religious orientation are in fact universal phenomena that emerge from within all religious traditions regardless of region, culture, or particular sets of religious teachings, and (2) it offers a clear developmental roadmap within each tradition that can be used to navigate the major roadblocks to human evolution. Ultimately, these two objectives serve to allow human growth to reach toward the higher levels of complexity and care necessary to confront and solve today's most pressing global problems.

The style in which I deliver the snapshots of religion offered at the beginning of each chapter requires at least a few preliminary comments: As the reader can find detailed in appendix 2, it was common, with the emergence of the modern study of religion in the West, for scholars to divide human systems of belief and practice into large monolithic blocks. These blocks of shared value, eventually became what we commonly call the major world religious traditions (Judaism, Islam, Taoism, Buddhism, Islam, Hinduism, Christianity, to name a few). We now know, however, that the early *essentialist* approach to religion, although adding heuristic value, is not necessarily an accurate map of reality. In fact, religious systems are far more nuanced and more sophisticated than the early scholars of religion first posited. As today's postmodern currents of thought clearly show us, religious belief is influenced by linguistic, regional, and cultural factors, as well as the historical time period in which they arise. In addition, religious belief is deeply influenced by the socially constructed identity of each individual adherent. It is only when we keep in mind the degree of carefulness offered by postmodern scholarship that anything at all can be said of a particular tradition.

The reader is likely aware by now, one of the core purposes of this book is to include the postmodern contributions yet still find a way to bring even more nuance and sophistication to religious analysis. To this end, although the brief snapshots of each tradition provided could be confused as general sweeping categorizations, each is made in light of the intention of this book to bring an entirely new level of granularity to the study of religion. My work here honors important postmodern guidelines and moves beyond into post-postmodern considerations.

Chapter 4
The Christian Conveyor Belt

Snapshot of Christianity

There are over two billion Christians in the world today.[129] No single universal version of Christianity exists under which all adherents around the world unify. Rather than one monolithic version of Christianity, there exists a diversity of versions of the faith with characteristics that depend upon and are influenced by multiple variables. The following snapshot offers a pragmatic attempt at painting a few broad strokes in order to orient the reader to the general contours of the tradition.

The history of Christianity is diverse and full of complexities. For nearly two thousand years the majority of Christian adherents around the globe learned that the general progression of Christian thought was somewhat linear. Beginning with the teachings of Jesus as articulated by his disciples in the New Testament, continuing through the early Council of Nicea in 325, to the Great Schism between Eastern (Greek) and Western (Latin) branches, until finally the major Protestant reformation was led by Martin Luther in 1517. However, with the recent discoveries of manuscripts like the Nag Hammadi Library and the Dead Sea Scrolls, it is clear that such a simplified progression needs to be reanalyzed by even mainstream adherents. With primary sources offering alternative views now directly available to us, we know for certain that there were multiple ways in which the Christian faith was interpreted from its very inception. According to Princeton professor Elaine Pagels, "the fifty-two writings discovered at Nag Hammadi offer only a glimpse of the complexity of the early Christian movement. We now [are beginning] to see that what we call Christianity—and what we identify as Christian tradition—actually represents only a small selection of specific sources, chosen from among dozens of others."[130]

Despite this early diversity, and any legitimacy that such scriptures might hold, the early Christian Church viewed all teachings outside of the approved orthodoxy as heretical. Within two hundred years after the death of Jesus, "Christianity had become an institution headed by a three-rank hierarchy of bishops, priests, and deacons, who understood themselves to be the guardians of the only 'true faith.' The majority of churches, among which the Church of Rome took a leading role, rejected all other viewpoints as heresy."[131] Even if some of the religious elite were in fact aware of dissenting perspectives, there was no room for the voices to be heard in any sort of wider constructive dialogue. An integral perspective attempts to be as historically and factually accurate as possible, so that our views of our world's traditions can break free of unwarranted biases.

According to some sources, beyond the broad categories of Catholic, Protestant, and Eastern Orthodox, the Christian faith of today is composed of "over 33,000 distinct denominations in 238 countries...."[132] Multiply this figure by the conditioning influence of the world's regional cultures and the multiple levels of psychological development that influence the interpretation of each individual and the scale of variation suddenly becomes immediately apparent. No matter how precise we might be with our studies of the Christian tradition, we will always only scratch the surface of the complexity of the Christian faith.

Despite the daunting diversity, there are a few basic principles that nearly all Christians agree upon. For one, the Christian faith commands at least some type of relationship to the religion's founder, Jesus of Nazareth. Among all of the claims that revolve around the person and teachings of Jesus, there is almost universal agreement that Jesus was an ethical activist who consistently and proactively encouraged his followers to take action against the injustice of the world. For his more orthodox followers, Jesus is nothing less than an incarnation of the one and only God. Hence, the Greek term Christ, or the anointed one, is closest to the Hebrew word messiah; giving him the commonly used title Jesus Christ.

In addition to a relationship with Jesus, adherents today are likely to also have a direct (or indirect for those who lack literacy or language skills to access it) relationship with the teachings of the Holy Bible, the collection of teachings composed of the Old and New Testament. However, beyond these basic claims, as we will see, interpretation of the Christian faith cannot be strictly categorized. Nonetheless, even with variation, the value, integrity, and depth of serious commitment to faith remains as strong as ever.

In this second decade of the third millennium we find ourselves living in unprecedented times, wherein religion in general and the Christian faith in particular, are undergoing significant transformation.[133] In order to better understand contemporary Christianity, it helps to take a closer look at how the Christian tradition evolved out of the Middle East and Europe to accommodate various cultural and regional contexts overtime:

> Over the past five centuries or so, the story of Christianity has been inextricably bound up with that of Europe and the European-derived civilization overseas, above all in North America. Until recently, the overwhelming majority of Christians have lived in white nations, allowing theorists to speak smugly, arrogantly, of "European Christian" civilization of the history of the world.... Over the past century, however, the center of gravity in the Christian world has shifted inexorably southward, to Africa, Asia, and Latin America. Already today, the largest Christian communities on the planet are to be found in Africa and Latin America. If we want to visualize a "typical" contemporary Christian, we should think of a woman living in a village in Nigeria or in a Brazilian *favela.*[134]

As accurate as it might be, Jenkins' description above of the "typical contemporary Christian" might be surprising to the majority of Western Christians. The face of Christianity is evolving and so are the ways that its adherents are interpreting its central message.

Examining the issue of religious accommodation with more granularity, we need to look no further than how Christianity dramatically transformed as it moved from Jewish and Hellenistic roots "into the Germanic lands of Western Europe during the early Middle Ages."[135] The changes resulted in vast repercussions in almost all spheres of human inquiry and action. For example, "in art and popular thought, Jesus became a blond Aryan, often with the appropriate warrior attributes." Simultaneously, "Christian theology was reshaped by West European notions of law and feudalism." Furthermore, notes Jenkins, "European Christians reinterpreted the faith through their own concepts of social and gender relations, and then imagined that their culturally specific synthesis was the only correct version of Christian truth."[136] This same sort of cultural accommodation is prevalent today. Each regional group, lacking external exposure, believes in some way that their particular iteration is correct.[137]

The two examples above help to set the context of Christian thought within a more careful framework that acknowledges cultural and historical accommodation. It is only with this type of postmodern awareness that we can begin adding a more integrally informed developmental perspective. A developmental lens begins to show us that even within the same culture, time period, region, and social class, there are still radically different versions of Christianity according to the stage of religious orientation of the individual. Both a postmodern approach that includes cultural and historical sensitivity, as well as a post-postmodern approach that includes psychological development are necessary if we are to use a lens that is truly integral.

To generalize using our developmental model, most mainstream Christians (in both the East and the West) tend to hold a mythic level of orientation towards their faith. Most of Christians who are at a mythic level believe in miracles, in divine resurrection, and in a virgin birth (all items that are reevaluated, but not necessarily discarded, at the rational stage of development and above). However, because not all individuals are fortunate enough to evolve to the levels of complexity required for the mythic stage of development, there are some cases in which Christianity needs to be *translated down* in order to make inroads that satisfy psychological needs at lower levels. Below we explore an example of Christianity as it is expressed from its most basic level of complexity: a magic orientation.

Magic Christianity

As a result of developmental expressions related to primary and secondary indicators, we learned in chapter 3 that a magic level of religious orientation may show some of the following signs: focus on power, literal interpretation of scripture, a reliance on superstitions, and an unrelenting emphasis on ritual. In the first piece of evidence offered below, we find all of these key features fully present in magic Christianity.

Magic-Extreme Christianity:
George Hensley and the Snake Handlers
Health: extreme   Stage: magic

Serpent handling began within the Pentecostal movement at the turn of the twentieth century.[138] The tale of the movement's inception is often told as follows: In 1908, a man by the name of George Hensley decided to climb a mountain in Appalachia to pray. Deep in prayer, Hensley had a profound religious experience. All of a sudden and without warning he "felt the power of God on him."[139] Upon looking down at the ground he saw a rattlesnake. Filled with both excitement and curiosity, he seized the snake in confidence. As the story goes, he successfully held the snake without being struck.[140] According to the particular Christian scripture he valued, the fact that he was not bitten was a sign that he was a true believer, engulfed in the Holy Spirit. This event marked the beginning of the holiness movement centered on snake handling.

Certain religious orientations, especially those stages that interpret the faith and scripture literally, tend to latch on to particular verses to help promote and reinforce their beliefs. Leaders and founders of sects often choose scriptures that give meaning and courage. The snake handler movement is a prime example. The following passages serve as the fundamental fulcrum around which most of the rituals and practices supported by George Hensley revolve:

Behold, I give unto you power to tread on serpents and scorpions, and over all the power of the enemy: and nothing shall by any means hurt you. (Luke 10:19)

And these signs shall follow them that believe: In my name shall they cast out devils; they shall speak with new tongues; they shall take up serpents; and if they drink any deadly thing, it shall not hurt them; they shall lay hands on the sick, and they shall recover. (Mark 16:17-18)

In addition to ritualized snake handling at services, these "believers" also engage, as the scriptures encourage, in the practice of drinking poison. It is not uncommon for "deadly things" such as battery acid and strychnine to be consumed as a ritual expression of their faith.[141] Despite the fact that most Pentecostals rejected both snake handling and drinking poison, the movement managed to spread across the United States to communities reaching as far south as Florida and as far north as Ohio.[142]

Overall, the actions such as handling snakes, drinking poison, and speaking in tongues are included to encourage a direct personal connection to the Holy Spirit. Dennis Covington, a journalist, decided to engage in the rituals and practices first hand in order to more profoundly understand the belief system and the accompanying religious states that they valued. He describes his first experience handling a rattlesnake as follows:

It was exactly as the handlers had told me. I felt no fear. The snake seemed to be an extension of myself. And suddenly there seemed to be nothing in the room but me and the snake. Everything else had disappeared.... The air was silent and still and filled with [a] strong, even light. And I realized that I, too, was fading into white.[143]

Before moving on to the analysis, it is important to note that not all snake handlers or Pentecostals hold a magic level of religious orientation. As Harvard professor Harvey Cox puts it, "some Pentecostals want to cooperate with Ecumenical groups. Others do not. Some feel at home in the evangelical or even fundamentalist household. Others want to dissociate themselves..."[144] However, after acknowledging the internal diversity of developmental levels within the movement, it becomes clear that there are certain qualities and a particular shape to the sect that tends to attract individuals of the magic altitude.

Let's look at a reconstructed psychograph of George Hensley to see how an understanding of the stages of religious orientation helps to shed light on the analysis. Due to the extreme nature of their rituals, the level of fatality and injury that result, and the strict opposition to more moderate practices, this book suggests that George Hensley expresses an extreme version of magic Christianity. In other words, Hensley represents an extreme classification at a magic stage of psychological development.

George Hensley's Potential Psychograph

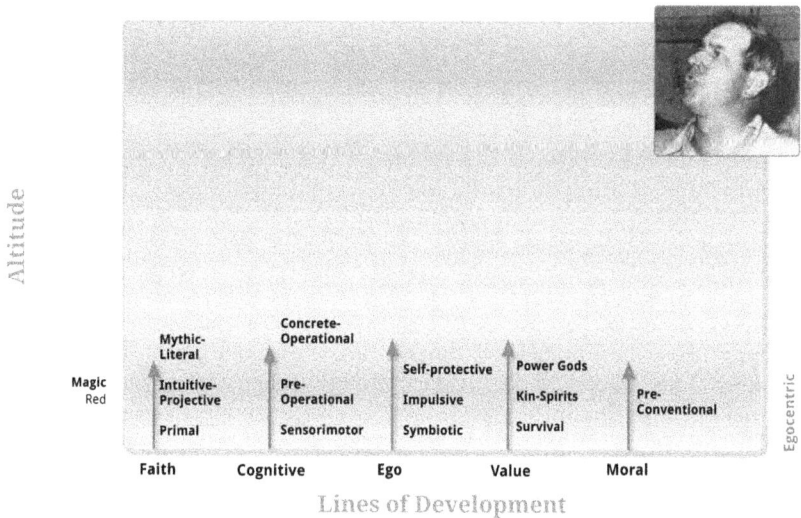

Photo Source: National Archives and Records Administration

Figure 11

This first explication examines signs and indicators from each line of the development one at a time. To reemphasize, the above psychograph in figure 11 and all of the potential psychographs in the following chapters represent reconstructed examples using the best biographical knowledge we have available. Because developmental psychometric tests were not employed on each individual considered, the psychographs are simply symbolic representations based on expression and action. It is my hope that this first detailed example will further clarify the general methodology employed over the next several chapters.

Faith

George Hensley shows signs that allow us to speculate that he borders somewhere between Fowler's intuitive-projective and mythic-literal level of faith development. Despite numerous deaths within the movement, he holds strongly to the belief that the Mark 16 scripture quoted above should be taken literally: "If they drink any deadly thing, it shall not hurt them." This type of expression is common for most adherents to a magic level of religious orientation. No amount of sickness, suffering, or death can convince magic adherents that perhaps the scriptures should not be taken literally. Other signs suggest there may still be remnants of intuitive-projective forms of faith development. At the intuitive-projective stage of faith, individuals often blur the line between fantasy and reality. Signs of this level of development are further suggested by way of the frequent type of spiritual experience encountered above wherein the qualities of strength and power are projected onto the snakes so that one may seek salvation from an external Holy Spirit.

Cognitive

George Hensley and the community that he inspired show clear signs of concrete operational thinking. Although individuals have the ability to think logically for most practical purposes, they lack the insight to reflect on their beliefs, and inquire into deeper meaning behind any of the scripture. No attempts are made to examine their faith as one whole coherent system. Instead small verses are stripped away and aggrandized, at times this is done even out of context. It is emotional impulse and not a deeper level reasoning that enters the snake handler's immediate awareness.

Ego

In figure 11 above, this book suggests George Hensley holds a self-protective level of ego development. It is common for those at a self-protective level of ego development to place blame and responsibility somewhere outside of themselves. Hensley gives credit to the Holy Spirit and blames evil spirits or even Satan for his woes. This redistribution of credit and blame is one key secondary indicator of a red level of ego development.

Values

When reading first-hand accounts, one repeatedly notices an emphasis on power.[145] Handling the snakes provides courage and strength in a world in which many of the individuals feel powerless. There is even some degree of discrimination that occurs between those who have been baptized by the Holy Spirit and those who have not. These signs, among others, suggest that Hensley holds a level of values development near what Beck and Cowen (via the work of Graves) calls *power gods*.

Morals

In this example, Hensley appears to show signs of pre-conventional moral development. For the most part Hensley's ability to take the perspectives and safety of all others into consideration is limited. He fails to take into consideration the ethical implications for the congregation itself if a poisonous snake were to escape and attack a member of the community. Others surrounding Hensley show pre-conventional morals through their adamant transgressions of local law (i.e., some practice snake handling in public where it has been forbidden). Choices to break the law, in this circumstance, are not made as result of taking multiple perspectives and reasoning beyond it (post-conventional), but because they simply don't want to follow the established rule and lack consideration for the reason as to why the laws were put into place (safety of both the practitioners and the surrounding community at large).

Worldview

Unlike those of mythic orientation who believe that membership in a belief system can itself be enough for salvation, George Hensley and many other snake handlers believe that faith and salvation is an individual affair. True salvation comes from the sacred gift of being engulfed by the Holy Spirit (also called being "Holy Spirit baptized"). This transformation is a personal affair and is not automatically the result of joining the group. This attitude shows signs of an egocentric worldview: "I handle the snake; I don't get bit; I have Faith…. You handle the snake; you get bit; you do not have faith." Secondary signs of an egocentric worldview are simply one more indication that we are likely dealing with a magic level of religious orientation.

Mythic Christianity

Mythic Christianity rises to a slightly more complex level of interpretation. At this stage in Christian development individuals tend to examine the Bible as a whole rather than the piecemeal fashion exhibited in the magic stage. At mythic levels of orientation, the Bible is seen as a collection of historical facts that are indeed divine revelation. The character of Jesus is blown up to mega-proportions and represents a super-figure in history. As Joseph Campbell explains, Jesus symbolizes the "hero" of the Christian legend. In our common parlance, when mythic levels of religious orientation show up in individuals alongside expressions of health that are closer to the extremist end of the spectrum, we tend to call them "fundamentalists." According to the research of Martin E. Marty and R. Scott Appleby (founders of the Fundamentalism Project) most individuals who are considered fundamentalists all possess a variety of "family resemblances" that show up in diverse cultures. Such common characteristics include, "a reliance on religion as a source for identity; boundary setting that determines who belongs and who does not; dramatic eschatologies; and the dramatization and mythologization of enemies."[146] We see many of these characteristics expressed by mythic level orientations in all four of the religious traditions explored throughout the next several chapters but focus on how such characteristics arise within the Christian context.

Below we look into two horizontal classifications of mythic Christianity. First, we examine an *extreme* version of the mythic level Christianity as expressed by Jerry Falwell. Then we take a more general approach to the *moderate* version of mythic Christianity expressed by the majority of practicing Christians today.

Mythic-Extreme Christianity ;Jerry Falwell
Health: extreme   Stage: mythic

Our first example of mythic Christianity examines the life,

behaviors, and interpretations of religion offered by the Christian leader and spokesman, Jerry Falwell. This book suggests that Jerry Falwell represents an extreme classification within a mythic stage of Christian interpretation.

Given the nature of the mythic level of interpretation and action and its common association with fundamentalists, the first question is, what is a Christian fundamentalist? The book *The Evangelicals* provides several answers:

> In 1910, a consensus emerged around the "five fundamentals" of faith.... These beliefs which were not to be compromised in any way were "the inerrancy of Scripture, the virgin birth of Christ, his vicarious atonement, his bodily resurrection, the historicity of Christ's biblically recorded miracles."[147]

Christian fundamentalism is a defining characteristic of mythic extremism and it is our hope that the following evidence offered from Falwell's life helps to paint a clarifying picture.

Interestingly, Falwell's life is documented rather well. So well, in fact, that through biographical accounts we can track a transformation in his psychological stage of development as his average level of awareness shifts from a red altitude (distracted by power) to its current and more traditional level of amber altitude (focuses on conventional conformity). Some accounts show that in his earlier days, Falwell was a troublemaker. "Before he converted," explains Harding, "Jerry was a 'prankster' and a neighborhood 'gang leader'."[148]

When using the Integral Psychograph one can imagine the altitude at which Falwell must have resided during his gang-leading days: egocentric, with power values and perhaps even a self-protective ego. The mythic system of Christianity that he was introduced to helped him to transform from red to amber altitude (magic to mythic), resulting in what Harding calls "a conversion." Because mythic orientations to faith offer only black and white options of right and wrong, religion can be very alluring for an individual who might lack his or her own moral compass.

At amber altitude (in both the extremist version expressed by Falwell and the moderate classification expressed below), the religious adherent likely has an ethnocentric mode of awareness. Mythic Christians observe the "absolute uniqueness of Christianity as the one faith by which all must be saved."[149] Falwell's famous comment "Mohammad is a terrorist" while in an interview on *60 Minutes* is just one example of how an individual at this level of development lacks the ability to take the truths of other traditions and cultures into consideration.

Mythic-Moderate Christianity
Health: Moderate   Stage: Mythic

Although the majority of adult Americans who regularly attend church and consider themselves Christians may not fall into the category of *extreme* mythic orientation, many nonetheless still hold mythic levels of orientation albeit of less intensity.

In general, the moderate mythic Christian likely shows signs of faith development teetering between mythical-literal and synthetic-conventional stages. Although Falwell, described above, clearly expresses a belief system that leans toward the literal side, a moderate mythic Christian may lean more toward a focus on the miracles of Jesus or have a deep commitment to the epic stories of the Bible (synthetic-conventional). Moderate classification at a mythic altitude is the common religious orientation of many evangelical Christians and is the level of awareness expressed at most megachurches.

At amber altitude a strong focus is placed on "the traditional biblical concepts of the person and character of Christ, the special divine creation of humanity, [and] providence."[150] According to some at this stage, "the Bible is entirely true in the ordinary sense of accurately depicting historical events. The rule of inerrancy extends, not explicitly and by no means irrevocably (as it does to the Bible), to preachers and other 'men of God.'"[151]

It is likely that mythic Christians (of both moderate and extreme classifications) express signs of conformist ego development. The mythic level of Christianity places an enormous emphasis on role-identity. To be a member of the church, a responsible citizen, and part of true believers, one must conform to a particular set of rules and ideals that meet the satisfaction of the Christian community at large.

At a mythic level of orientation one releases the emphasis on power that we saw in George Hensley at the magic stage. This level sees a shift in values that now focuses on the truth-force. There is an absolute right and wrong. Things are either black or white. "You are either with us or against us" is a favorite catch phrase of this level.

Falwell and the expressions seen in many evangelicals are just two examples of how an individual at this level expresses conventional morals by placing authority in the Bible. Others, like mythic-oriented Catholics, might express conventional morals by giving ethical authority to the Pope or other religious leaders. In either case, moral decisions are left up to some sort of external authority.

Rational Christianity

Individuals entering the stage of rational Christianity tend to take one of four paths. (Although this book describes these four paths in a Christian context, similar paths are present in nearly every tradition.) Each path represents one of the ways that an individual can navigate their tradition using the new set of rational skills and competencies that are now available to them.

Within the Christian context, the first of four rational paths occurs when an individual decides to maintain his/her Christian beliefs but re-contextualizes them to fit his or her rational worldview. This is often titled the "de-mythologizing" of Christianity. A second route Christians can take as they exit mythic orientation is to hold their beliefs in limbo and declare themselves agnostic. This choice often means that the individual allows all other aspects of their life to flourish but determines that there is no way to know about deeper matter of spirit. As a third path, some individuals throw out religion altogether. In common vernacular, we call this person an atheist. Often the atheist allows the scientific sphere of knowledge to cannibalize the other value-spheres (art and morals). Rational individuals who have abandoned religion often view Christianity in particular and religion as a whole as infantile, owning no avenue through which reconciliation with rationality is possible (i.e., Freud, Dawkins, Harris, and Marx). A fourth path available for those exiting mythic orientation has emerged more recently in our history (especially in the West). As information regarding other cultures and belief systems becomes available, some individuals reject the Christian tradition only to embrace the practices and beliefs of another tradition. Often these other traditions give emphasis to experience rather than mere belief and as such are deeply compatible with an orange altitude. Those who take this fourth path are desperate to keep spirituality alive but find no plausible salvation in the mythic versions of Christianity that they are familiar with. The rise in popularity of American Buddhism can be partially explained by this phenomenon.[152]

The Demythologizing of Christianity

Religious scholar Robert Krapohl describes the relationship between a rational form of Christianity and modernity:

> In a theological context...modernism generally meant:
> (1) the contentious, intended adaptation of religious ideas
> to modern culture, (2) the idea that God is immanent in

human cultural development and revealed through it, and (3) the belief that human society is moving toward realization of the Kingdom of God. To accommodate the prevailing empirical epistemology, modernists conceived hermeneutical techniques for interpreting biblical texts that shifted from the literalist to the allegorical, mythical, and symbolic.[153]

All these elements play prominently in a rational level of orientation. Individuals at the orange altitude no longer take the Bible literally, nor do they see it as absolute truth. Instead they search for the underlying principles contained in the myths of the Bible. They ask themselves, 'what are the moral implications of the story?'

The founding fathers of the United States subscribed to an orange level of religious orientation. One early and noble attempt at de-mythologizing Christianity from this rational level of religious orientation came from Thomas Jefferson in what is known as the "Jefferson Bible." In the Jefferson Bible, or what was properly titled *The Life and Morals of Jesus of Nazareth*, Thomas Jefferson made every attempt to strip the Bible of those concepts no longer legitimate in the modern world. By removing the supernatural content and any other commentary he thought may have been incorrectly added by the Four Evangelicals, he attempted to uncover the true teachings and philosophy of Jesus.

These very same currents that attempted to de-mythologize and translate mythic beliefs into rational philosophies in the past hold profound value for us today in our modern world. If religions are able to translate themselves into rational language they begin to hold a solid voice of value in the public sphere. To quote American president Barak Obama: "Democracy demands that the religiously motivated translate their concerns into universal, rather than religion-specific, values. It requires that their proposals be subject to argument, and amenable to reason."[154] Below we discuss a clear example of a prominent religious leader attempting to do just such a modern translation.

Rational-Moderate Christianity: Bishop John Shelby Spong
Health: moderate   Stage: rational

In a world with the majority of Christians maintaining a mythic level of religious orientation or lower, it is often difficult to avoid controversy when expounding rational interpretations of faith. Those residing at a mythic level of orientation are often the first to declare any ideas threatening to their worldview as heresy. The case of Bishop

John Shelby Spong is no different. Although Spong himself may reside at more of a pluralistic altitude, his writings are certainly directed at an amber-orange audience, and hence provide fitting evidence for a rational expression of faith. Ultimately, Spong focuses on those ready to exit a mythic level of orientation and enter into the world of rational Christianity.

Commenting on the five fundamentals (as outlined in the section on mythic Christianity), Spong states:

> Today I find each of these fundamentals, as traditionally understood, to be not just naive, but eminently rejectable. Nor would any of them be supported in our generation by reputable Christian scholars.

> Scripture is filled with cultural attitudes that we have long ago abandoned and with behavior that is today regarded as immoral. Concepts such as virgin birth, the physical resurrection, and the second coming are today more often regarded as symbols to be understood theologically than as events that occurred in literal history. The substitutionary view of atonement has become grotesque, both in its understanding of a God who requires the bloodshed of human sacrifice as a prerequisite for salvation and in its definition of humanity as fallen and depraved.

> If these things still constitute the faith of Christian people, then Christianity has become for me and countless others hopelessly unbelievable. Surely the essence of Christianity is not found in any or all of these propositions.[155]

Without a doubt Spong has moved beyond the confines of a mythic orientation. He, with both passion and bravery, hopes to lead "countless others" through what he describes as a "New Reformation." Needless to say, all of this is difficult to swallow for Christian adherents and Christian leaders who blindly cling to a mythic level of orientation. Some dissenters have even declared Spong's work to be *un-Christian*. In response to such critiques, Spong reassures his audience: "I define myself first and foremost as a Christian believer…. My problem has never been my faith. It has always been the literal way that human beings have chosen to articulate that faith." In the preceding quote, Spong attempts to separate himself from the mythic-literal versions of Christianity that dominate the world. In essence, Spong not only declares himself a Christian but a *rational* Christian.

On his website, Spong is quoted as follows: "Martin Luther ignited the Reformation of the 16th century by nailing to the door of the church in Wittenberg in 1517 the 95 Theses that he wished to debate.

I will publish this challenge to Christianity...." Quite extraordinarily, almost every point below that Spong proposes is a direct challenge to the classic mythic level of religious orientation.

Here is Spong's list, in his own words:

The issues to which I now call the Christians of the world to debate are these:

1. Theism, as a way of defining God, is dead. So most theological God-talk is meaningless. A new way to speak of God must be found.

2. Since God can no longer be conceived in theistic terms, it becomes nonsensical to seek to understand Jesus as the incarnation of the theistic deity. So the Christology of the ages is bankrupt.

3. The biblical story of the perfect and finished creation from which human beings fell into sin is pre-Darwinian mythology and post-Darwinian nonsense.

4. The virgin birth, understood as literal biology, makes Christ's divinity, as traditionally understood, impossible.

5. The miracle stories of the New Testament can no longer be interpreted in a post-Newtonian world as supernatural events performed by an incarnate deity.

6. The view of the cross as the sacrifice for the sins of the world is a barbarian idea based on primitive concepts of God and must be dismissed.

7. Resurrection is an action of God. Jesus was raised into the meaning of God. It therefore cannot be a physical resuscitation occurring inside human history.

8. The story of the Ascension assumed a three-tiered universe and is therefore not capable of being translated into the concepts of a post-Copernican space age.

9. There is no external, objective, revealed standard writ in

scripture or on tablets of stone that will govern our ethical behavior for all time.

10. Prayer cannot be a request made to a theistic deity to act in human history in a particular way.

11. The hope for life after death must be separated forever from the behavior control mentality of reward and punishment. The Church must abandon, therefore, its reliance on guilt as a motivator of behavior.

12. All human beings bear God's image and must be respected for what each person is. Therefore, no external description of one's being, whether based on race, ethnicity, gender, or sexual orientation, can properly be used as the basis for either rejection or discrimination.[156]

Spong's bravery to challenge mythic level of orientation is a direct attempt to rescue Western religion and spirituality from its premodern fusion. It is only through attempts like his that there is hope for an evolving Christian religion fit for every age.[157]

The integral lens helps to provide an even more specific analysis. Faith development of the atheist, the agnostic, and subscribers to Spong's New Reformation must necessarily rest somewhere at or beyond Fowler's individuative-reflective faith. Individuals have come to recognize that they must critically evaluate their belief in the Christian "fundamentals." At an orange altitude, nothing should be taken as blind faith. All beliefs must be examined using the careful scrutiny of the intellect. Hence, Fowler's use of the term "reflective."

In order to reach individuative-reflective levels of faith, cognitive development must reach to or beyond formal operational cognition. Individuals must learn to make their own ideologies objects in their awareness. Some of the greatest contributors to our world (theorist, scientists, and inventors) all of whom we can assume had cognitive development far beyond formal-operational thinking (orange) have nonetheless been agnostics and atheists with a faith development stunted at orange altitude.

Rational Christians likely run the whole spectrum of ego development. In most cases however, one might look for a sign that ego development rests beyond the conformist stage. Very few groups of people alive today are aware of rational versions of Christianity. If one is resting in a rational orientation rather soundly, then this usually means that one has broken away from the social pressures to conform to the norm. In the future, as more and more people embrace rational levels of faith, it is likely that individuals might remain at a conformist level of ego development while subscribing to a rational religious orientation, simply because there will be a larger rational group with which to conform.

Often, Christianity at an orange altitude will show signs of values expressing Graves' strive-drive. No longer is the individual caught up in truth-force values of right and wrong. In order to surpass mythic orientation the individual must have an intrinsic "drive" to discover truth for oneself, even if pursuing the truth means moving beyond conformity, black and white distinctions, or a rebellion against traditional structure.

Because the rational stage of orientation is composed of a self-reflective faith, a mature ego, and values beyond truth force, any religious analysis might also look for signs of moral development that rests at post-conventional levels. Now that one can think for oneself there is no longer the need to look to the Bible or the clergy for authority.

It is also very likely that the worldview of the rational Christian has for the first time reached a worldcentric understanding. People are seen as human beings first and foremost, regardless of race, color, class, creed, or sexual orientation. In the example above, Spong is clear that no external description of a person should be grounds for discrimination or rejection. All are beings of equal stature; all deserve the same basic human rights and dignities.

In the following passage, Spong, who normally writes and speaks to an audience of an orange altitude, hints to the reader that even deeper, higher altitudes exist beyond the rational Christianity:

> God cannot be bound by the limits of our religious systems.... That realization will enable us to walk into an ecumenical future that will be so dramatically different as to be breathtaking. We will be enabled to see the Ground of Being in Moses, Mohammed, Buddha, Krishna, as well as Jesus.... The God who is the Ground of Being cannot be bound, not even by our religious claims.... Once that is understood, then it becomes apparent that none of us should denigrate the doorways through which others journey in their quest to enter the holy God.[158]

On that note, we are ready to venture to the next stage of religious orientation.

Pluralistic Christianity

As a general rule: the higher the altitude, the fewer the proponents. This equation is a direct result of the fact that everyone is born into the lower altitudes of the developmental spectrum and few continue to higher stages. Wilber describes this same phenomenon in the concise statement, "more depth, less span."

Due to the fact that a high level of complexity and cognition is required to embrace pluralistic levels of religious orientation, one is more likely to find expressions of pluralistic Christianity in academia than in mainstream society. Although as a culture we often express pluralistic ideals, few and far between are those individuals who actually have the capacity to maintain such a stance in any authentic sort of way with regard to their own beliefs.

In the description of pluralistic Christianity this book rearticulates a framework proposed by theologian Paul Knitter. Knitter's intellectual attempt has done its very best to find a cohesive marriage between the best of postmodernity and the Christian faith.

Pluralistic-Moderate Christianity: Paul Knitter
Health: moderate   Stage: pluralistic

Before explaining his model, Knitter begins by outlining his own spiritual path and how it has unfolded in three distinct stages: exclusivism, inclusivism, and pluralism (categories first introduced in chapter 1 via the work of Eck and Ferrer). Delightfully, we can trace Knitter's path over time directly to his level of psychological development as it unfolded to include more comprehensive and compassionate levels of interacting with the world.

Exclusivism (mythic)

Knitter explains that his "dialogical odyssey began pretty much as a monologue…. Other religious persons interested me not so much because I wanted to converse with them, but because I wanted to convert them."[159] This compulsion to convert manifests because he believed "we had the word and Spirit; they had sin and heathenism…"[160] It is clear here that Knitter is deeply rooted in ethnocentric beliefs. Using our developmental lens we can classify Knitter as being deep within a mythic level of orientation. Upon more and more encounters with other religions, Knitter found teachings and practices of "beauty and mystery." His development progresses to realize, "there was much I couldn't fit into my Christian categories; there was much that I liked…I had an uneasy but distinct sense that the old exclusivist model of Christianity as light and other religions as darkness didn't fit the facts."[161] Knitter's questioning shows signs that he is ready to exit mythic levels and enter into more tolerant, rational expressions of his faith.

Inclusivism (rational)

Next, Knitter matures to what he calls his inclusivist stage. Knitter associates the inclusivist model with the likes of Vatican II and Karl Rahner.[162] This shift in Knitter's orientation allows him to begin touching on a more reflective way of thinking. Although Knitter is not entirely at an orange altitude, due to his relentless ethnocentrism, rational Christianity is beginning to emerge.

He emphasizes Rahner and the inclusivist position through the idea of "anonymous Christians." More specifically this refers to the theory that "non-Christians are 'saved' by the grace and presence of Christ working anonymously within their religions."[163] It is not the fact that religions themselves are doing anything unique or worthwhile; rather it is the fact that Christ is working through their religions. Knitter continues to give a personal account of this stage in his spiritual development, "I myself was not able to imagine that such wisdom and grace in other traditions could be anything else but 'reflections' of the fullness of truth and grace incarnated in Jesus the Christ."[164] At this point, Knitter can show tolerance but fails to acknowledge each faith as a legitimate expression of the Ultimate Reality.

Pluralism (pluralistic)

Finally, Knitter describes his evolution to his current stage. A stage he calls pluralism:

> There were particular experiences and insights that shook and then rearranged my theological perspectives: When I realized that perhaps the Hindu claim of non-dualism between Brahman and Atman was not just an analog, but perhaps a more coherent expression of what Rahner was trying to articulate with his notion of the supernatural existential; or when I realized that the Buddhist experience of Anita (no-self), as much as I had understood and felt it, enabled me to better understand and, I think live, Paul's claim "It is no longer I who lives but Christ who lives in me" (Gal 2:20).[165]

All of which are profound and accurate insights. Knitter continues as he describes his experience of religious pluralism:

> It is not at all abandoning the Christian witness contained in scripture and tradition, but rather understanding it more deeply and thus preserving it… [O]ne sublates…the given Christocentric approach to other believers with one that is theocentric. Though we Christians claim Jesus the Christ as our necessary and happy starting point and focus for understanding ourselves and other peoples, we must also remind ourselves that the Divine Mystery which we know in Jesus and which we call Theos or God, is ever greater than the reality and message of Jesus…[A]ll religions could be, perhaps need to be…related to each other as all of them continue their efforts to discover or be faithful to inexhaustible Mystery or Truth…I had, indeed, moved off the bridge, from inclusivism to some form of pluralism.[166]

This move from a rational to a pluralistic form of religious expression is a rare and cherished step on the ladder of religious orientation.

Once at a pluralistic altitude Knitter began to create models that helped to explain the world from his new point of view. Using a global perspective, he explains that not only should we encourage dialogue among religions but also a "common commitment to human and ecological well-being." According to Knitter's pluralistic altitude, global responsibility goes beyond social justice to include eco-human justice as well; "Such a project in order truly to attend to the needs of all the globe, must be an effort by the entire globe and all its nations and religions." Gone are the barriers that he thought existed from earlier perspectives in his development.

> Knowing quite well that there will be challenges from within the Christian community, Knitter turns to the tradition itself for support. Out of his list of incentives to support a more pluralistic orientation, perhaps the most persuasive is the incentive provided in the First Commandment:

> If God's love is unbounded, ours *ought* to be. We are called upon to love each other as God loves us. This is, for Christians, the first commandment—which means that this commandment takes priority over all other commandments in all aspects of life. It also means that, in situations where one has to choose, loving one's neighbor takes a prior place to proclaiming true doctrine or to formally worshiping

God. No matter how important, even essential, orthodoxy and liturgy are, they cannot be made more important than loving our neighbor. We know the biblical images and refrains: first work things out with your alienated brother and sister, then go to church (Mt 5:23-24). Don't let the Sabbath observance, with its professions on faith and sacrifices, get in the way of doing good to your neighbor; better "break" the Sabbath (offend God!) than fail in loving your neighbor (Mt 12:12).[167]

Faith development in Knitter, according to the signs expressed above, appears to have reached at least to Fowler's conjunctive stage. Knitter has clearly gained the ability to hold what appear to be opposing ideas. As he himself points out, "here again we are teased by the psychologically tantalizing paradox of religious experience: the more deeply we experience and are committed to a particular expression of the Divine, the more we sense and are opened to the universality of the Divine."[168]

Here, it appears Knitter's cognitive development has reached early vision-logic. Knitter seems able to both reflect on his own beliefs and take in the perspectives of others. His understanding that the divine mystery is even greater than the confines of the message of Jesus is a deep way of adding up all perspectives and privileging none.

Susanne Cook-Greuter and Jane Loevinger would probably agree that Knitter's statements and autobiographical reports express ego development at or perhaps even beyond the autonomous level. His use of broad "social ideals" (i.e., religious dialogue should include as its premise global responsibility) points to a recognition of the deep interconnectedness shared with all of humanity.

At this green altitude, human connection and dialogue become central to what one values. Knitter's model focuses on proper communication between religious traditions. It is at this level that we not only have tolerance for others but also value deep human connections with the religious "other." The pluralistic level values the bond that comes from authentically seeing the religious "other" without imposing one's own preference or perspective.

Finally, it is clear that Knitter has moved beyond worldcentric views to what Wilber calls a Kosmo-centric view. Kosmo-centric implies a level in which perspective-taking has shifted beyond humans to include all sentient beings. Knitter notes, "More recently I have come to understand, even feel, the suffering not only of humans but of all sentient beings, including mother earth."[169] Kosmo-centric worldviews can be an indicator of stages of religious orientation at green and higher.

Extreme versions of the pluralistic level might extend cultural sensitivity to its maximum yet paralyzing intellectual potential. Those who do might abandon the idea of a universal truth all together, emphasizing, as do some deconstructionists, that everything is dependent upon context and interpretation to such a degree that there is no such thing as universal meaning.

Integral Christianity

For this and every tradition, an integral religious scholar can locate each of the examples discussed above along both a horizontal spectrum of health as well as a vertical spectrum of stages. A graph like the following provides a visual representation of where each piece of evidence supporting a developmental view or religious orientation might fall.

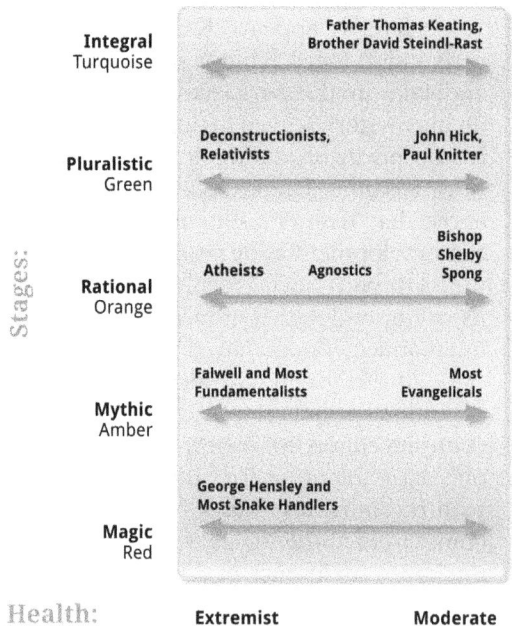

Evidence Along the Christian Spectrum

Stages:

Integral Turquoise		Father Thomas Keating, Brother David Steindl-Rast
Pluralistic Green	Deconstructionists, Relativists	John Hick, Paul Knitter
Rational Orange	Atheists Agnostics	Bishop Shelby Spong
Mythic Amber	Falwell and Most Fundamentalists	Most Evangelicals
Magic Red	George Hensley and Most Snake Handlers	

Health: Extremist   Moderate

Figure 12

An integral approach is clarified when it examines not the similarities but the differences between Knitter's approach at the pluralistic level and the approach one might take from an integral altitude. First, let's analyze the areas in which Knitter's system is partial. Knitter fails to recognize that human development is a central feature of religious studies. Although Knitter proposes a three-stage sequence for his own development, and in at least one case even mentions Fowler's stage model,[170] he does not make the stage outline explicit or try to demonstrate that the sequence might be a universal human truth within all religions.

Secondly, Knitter's mental framework forces him to commit the classic error of green altitude: he confuses dominating hierarchies with pathological hierarchies. Knitter's confusion between dominating hierarchies and natural hierarchies forces him to throw all hierarchies out the window. He explains:

> For a correlational dialogue to take place, the dialogical encounter will have to be carried out in egalitarian, not a hierarchical, community. Though all religious participants will speak their mind and make truth claims to each other, none of them will do so from a theological position that claims that theirs is the religion meant to dominate or absorb or stand in judgment over all others. A correlational dialogue cannot begin with one religion claiming to hold all the cards or to be superior in all respects over the others or to have the final norm that will exclude or absorb all other norms.[171]

Knitter's claim is true but partial.

What is true? Knitter is correct in that "one religion" should not attempt to demonstrate its superiority over all the others. This could indeed lead down a slippery slope to the dominating arrogance of exclusivism or inclusivism.

However, his argument is also partial? An integral approach to religious studies disagrees that hierarchies should be thrown out all together. Instead of claiming that *one religion is superior to another*, this book proposes that some perspectives and worldviews within the same tradition can indeed be more mature than others depending on their degree of compassion, embrace, and psychological maturity. This hierarchical judgment must be made from *the inside*. That means the developmental categorization can only be made from within the same tradition and culture.

With an understanding of developmental levels, we can see that dialogue can still occur with the presence and acceptance of natural hierarchies (as discussed in chapter 8). One at an integral level can clearly differentiate healthy from unhealthy hierarchies and has no reservations about using hierarchies when necessary. An integral religious scholar can make accurate observations that stages can and do unfold in a natural hierarchy of increasing compassion and embrace within individuals.

In addition to pointing out that Knitter confuses the two types of hierarchies, an individual with an integral awareness would note that Knitter's model focuses almost entirely on the spheres of culture and society. Seeing this as partial, the integral scholar would demand that the analysis be even more comprehensive. A truly integral model would include not only culture and society but also the sphere of the individual. Other than his own personal psychological analysis, Knitter leaves out an individual sphere of knowledge when applying his model to the world at large.

Knitter makes a valiant attempt at a new religious model, but until this point in his journey, he is still leaving out several features that an integral model would certainly want to include. Integral Christianity is currently being pursued in depth through the Integral Religious Studies Center at Meta-Integral. In practice, prominent Christian teachers like Father Thomas Keating and Brother David Steindl-Rast are leading the way.

EVIDENCE AND
EXAMPLES from
Christianity +

David Steindl-Rast
Paul Knitter
John Shelby Spong
Jerry Falwell
Hensley

Magic   Mythic   Rational   Pluralistic   Integral

Chapter 5
The Muslim Conveyor Belt

Next we explore how the model of developmental religious pluralism unfolds within the Muslim tradition. Once again, we find abundant evidence connecting various stages of development with real expressions of the Islamic faith.

Snapshot of Islam

As we attempt to describe the particular contours of the Islamic faith, it is crucial to remember dramatic effect that culture, region, and identity all have on the interpretation of faith. Rudolph Peters explains the internal diversity within the Islamic faith best when he writes: "Islam, like other religions, has a Janus face: it contains many different and even contradictory sacred texts and interpretation and, in addition, doctrines that are not uniform and monolithic, but can, in concrete contexts, be used to deliver widely divergent messages."[172] With this in mind, and careful to consider postmodern distinctions, the following pages explore some of the core characteristics of Islam in order to provide the reader with at least some orientation to the faith before we proceed.

Islam originated near Mecca, Saudi Arabia. Around the year 622 CE, a man named Mohammad (pbuh)[173] began having profound spiritual experiences. In these experiences Mohammad (pbuh) entered into a trance and received divine messages. The messages revealed through his prophetic experiences are preserved and transcribed in the holy book of the Muslims called the Qur'an.

Since the seventh century, Islam has spread to become the second most populous religious tradition on our planet. There are today over one billion Muslims and numbers are on the rise.[174] The Muslim community has spread far and wide beyond the Middle Eastern region of its founding. In addition to a strong and concentrated presence in Southeast Asia, India, China, Africa, and the Middle East, Muslims now make up the second largest religious tradition in the West with over 15 million adherents in Western Europe alone.[175]

Allah (God in Arabic) and his message for humanity, as articulated in the Qur'an, serve as the strict center of the Islamic faith. For those readers more familiar with the Christian or Jewish tradition, it is important to note that the status of the Qur'an should not be confused with that of the Bible or Torah. Instead, the Qur'an takes on a much more central role in the Islamic faith. Some scholars contend that the role of the Qur'an in Islam is closer in comparison, not to the Bible itself, but rather to that of the role that Christ himself plays for Christians. Islamic Scholar Frederick Denny, describes the relationship as follows:

> The place of the Qur'an in the life of the Muslims is only in limited ways like that of the Bible in the lives of Jews and Christians. Scholars have observed that in relation to Christianity, the Qur'an may be usefully compared with Christ, in that it is believed to be God's Word that has miraculously come down into the world in history and humankind. If in Christianity the "Word became flesh," in Islam it became a book.[176]

As a result, study, recitation, and memorization of the Qur'an play prominent roles in the religious practice of many Muslims. Within the Muslim context, it is understood that "reciting of sacred words is itself a participation in God's speech," explains Denny. As such, "it must be performed as perfectly as possible."[177] Furthermore, Denny continues, "the book is properly appropriated and applied only when it is recited live in a context of belief and obedience." In this way, orthoprax recitation serves as the fundamental way in which the Qur'an is both learned and offered as teachings.

Despite cultural, linguistic, and historical differences in overall beliefs, most Muslims see their faith as a natural evolution out of the two other monotheistic traditions that preceded it (i.e., Judaism and Christianity). As a result, Muslims recognize that Allah and the God worshiped by the Jews and Christians are one and the same. Not only do Muslims believe in the very same God as the other Abrahamic faiths but they too express reverence toward their prophets (i.e., Abraham, Moses, Jesus).

As Islam spread in the years after the death of the Prophet Mohammed (pbuh), two major sects arose: Sunnis and Shiites. The divide erupted around an argument over where proper authority rested in the continuation of the Prophet's (pbuh) lineage. Upon the death of the Prophet (pbuh), leadership shifted to one of his closest companions, Abu Bakr as-Siddiq. The decision was supported in full by the group that later became known as the Sunnis. The community of believers that eventually became known as the Shiites, however, believed that succession should follow in the family of the Prophet and be passed on to Mohammed's cousin Ali ibn Abi Talib. Today, the vast majority of Muslims in the Middle East, Africa, and Asia consider themselves Sunnis (nearly 75 percent), while only 15 percent, living mostly in Iran, Iraq, and Palestine, consider themselves Shiites.

With these basic preliminary comments in place, let us move on to address an area of particular relevance in our current global landscape: the relationship between the religion of Islam and those acts of violence perpetrated against humanity that claim Islam as a motivating force. Although we will look deeper into the phenomenon later in this chapter during our integral analysis of mythic Islam, a few preliminary comments here will help to set the proper tone.

Despite the assumptions that Islam and terrorism are always deeply connected, some scholars, like Rudolph Peters, question whether or not there is any sort of causal relationship between Islam and acts of violence whatsoever. Although terrorist attacks are indeed committed "in the name of Islam," according to Peters, such examples only prove that Islamic doctrines can be instrumentalized to political ends and "interpreted to justify such acts of violence, not that there is an intrinsic relationship between them." [178]

Like all traditions, the Islamic faith is full of internal diversity. "Among the Islamic texts and doctrines there are those that preach peace and tolerance, but also those that can justify violence and inculcate militants with a contempt for death and zeal for engaging in violent struggles." This book tries to drive home the central point that even more important than cultural context (a postmodern realization), interpretation is most greatly influenced by development (a post-postmodern realization). Peters explains that concepts like jihad, martyrdom, and "end of time," "are ambiguous and vague and need users to give them a specific meaning and content. What such users do is either select their ideas from a range of already existing interpretations and understanding, or create new meanings." As the chapter unfolds, we will learn that the relationship between terrorism and Islam is almost always linked to an individual with an extremist orientation who is interpreting the tradition through a mythic lens.

While exploring the first three stages of religious orientation within the Islamic tradition (magic, mythic, and rational) we uncover a telling situation. Like Christianity, Islam, in most of the world, can be linked to a moderate mythic level of religious orientation. The vast majority of Muslims take a traditional stance toward their tradition.

This stance is often composed of conventional orientations. This moderate expression of health, however, is by no means always the dominant voice. As the situation exists today in several countries in the Middle East, an extreme version of mythic orientation has grown to form an oppressive structure in both consciousness and culture.

Some forms of extreme mythic Islam represent the type of pathological hierarchy that any post-postmodern approach is careful to avoid. Rather than understanding religion through a developmental lens that acknowledges a depth of complexity and care while still validating all other belief structures, the extreme mythic level of interpretation places a stronghold on the tradition as a whole. Extreme mythic levels of interpretation claim to possess the one and only true expression of faith. As we shall see, when a pathological hierarchy like this has formed, it sets the conditions for one stage of development (in this case mythic) to both dominate lower stages (magic) and simultaneously prevent higher stages (rational, pluralistic, integral) from emerging. It is only with an integral lens that includes a developmental perspective that some of these nuances can begin to be explained.

Although we mention this type of pathological hierarchy here with regards to the Islamic faith, it is important to remember that similar currents of oppression/repression can be found in every religious tradition. With the proper mechanism in place to prevent pathological hierarchies, extreme versions of each tradition will continue to dominate lower centers of gravity (magic/red), forcing them to abandon their magic tendencies and conform to mythic levels.[179] Concurrently, extreme forms of mythic orientation will refuse to evolve to meet the rational needs of individuals who are intellectually more mature (rational/orange and higher).

Magic Islam

In almost all cases, because of the stronghold of those at mythic levels of development, magic orientation is almost entirely forbidden within Islam. Traditional expressions of Islam (mythic) dominate the main lines of communication through both mosque and media rejecting the use of charms, superstitions, and rituals that might jeopardize the singular authority of Allah.[180] As a result, very few cases of published material exist that offer fair expressions of magic levels of religious orientation.

In order to uncover the magic variations that do exist, one must dig deeper than published articles and books. For example, we find question-and-answer sessions on Islamic email threads and websites that specifically address the needs of these individuals at red altitude.

In the previous chapter, while discussing magic orientations of Christianity, we noted that snake handlers granted all authority to the Holy Spirit when handling snakes. They were steeped in both ritual and superstition to the exclusion of other relevant aspects of their faith. Islam, as expressed at this magic level of orientation, contains many similar "family resemblances." Recall, at a red altitude the primary indicator of faith development shows levels of Fowler's intuitive-projective stage. At this stage, individuals may think that their own individual thoughts can actually control the external environment. For example, one might believe that someone has fallen sick as a direct result of evil spirits or as a result of someone else's malicious spell. Consequently, an equally powerful spell of positive spirit may be needed to heal an ailing victim.

Even though mythic Islam stifles most magic orientations, those at this altitude turn to specific verses in the Qur'an for help and advice. As we explore below, some suggest the Qur'an contains passages that when recited can dismantle the powers of others.

To provide evidence of the deep superstition expressed at this level we look to an Islamic website where one Muslim seeks advice on how to ward off evil spells and spirits. The concerned Muslim asks: "I just want to say that I have read somewhere that to protect yourself from magic and jinns [ghosts], you should perform ruqayah. Please tell me what is *ruqayah* and what is procedure for performing it. I really urgently need to know so please if you can answer my question as soon as possible." [181]

In response to the individual's question, the person in charge of the *Islam Always* website administration answers: "The proper performance is to hold the hands in front of the face, blow into them (some say the blowing takes place after the reading), then recite Qur'an into the hands, and then wipe the hands over the entire body." [182] Adherents to this level of orientation take several of these ideas to heart and recite protective verses with their daily prayers.

In a second example, an Islamic website dedicated to educating the Islamic population devotes an entire section to black magic. [183] Due to the demand for answers, the site explains how each individual might actively find protection from the malicious spells of others. It is not to say that all forms of this type of practice always come from a magic orientation but rather that the expressions offer certain signs that, when interpreted by an integrally informed scholar, are understood to represent specific stages of development. It is always important that the analysis leaves room for exceptions and the possibility that some expressions and signs that appear to point to a lower level of development might actually be stemming from more mature structures.

As mentioned, mythic levels of Islam often deny or repress the concerns of those at this magic level of orientation. When asked the question regarding Islam's views on this type of magical information a scholar on the *Islamic Voice* website responds with the standard mythic level response: "Magic is mentioned on several occasions in the Qur'an, but always with disapproval and condemnation."[184] Despite the curiosity for answers, some individuals at a mythic level simply deny any reality to the needs of those at a magic orientation. An integral understanding, on the other hand, begins to both value and validate the needs of those at every level on the spiral of development. Simultaneously, the integral vision acknowledge that the ability to take more perspectives and hence the capacity for greater care increases with each new level of complexity. As development increases and a critical perspective emerges, it is likely the case that these types of magic beliefs are radically reevaluated and often abandoned.

Secondary indicators expressed by a magic stage of development within Islam may include signs that indicate values near Beck and Cowen's kin-spirits and power-gods. Loevinger and Cook-Greuter might argue that individuals at this stage are likely to possess a self-protective stage of ego development. Remembering that a self-protective ego shows signs of a primary focus that avoids punishment and seeks reward, Muslims oriented at this stage of complexity may focus relentlessly on the mercy of Allah in his willingness to bestow compassion. Others might focus on the power of Allah to punish and destroy the unrighteous. These secondary indicators of values and ego development are likely to result in an expression of Islam based on the "other-worldly" dichotomies that overly emphasize hell and paradise.

Mythic Islam

Expressions of mythic Islam are vast and diverse. First we explore the basics of this level of traditional Islam before focusing on one particular kind of mythic Islam called Wahhabism.

If mythic Islam were portrayed in two short and precise sentences, it might sound something like the following: "Find peace in this world through total submission to the will of the one and only God. Gain access to paradise by not wavering from the sacred teachings of the Holy Qur'an and the example set forth by God's prophet Mohammad, peace be upon him."

Analogous to the fundamentals of mythic-level Christians, adherents to traditional Islam subscribe resolutely to five main tenets, also called the "five pillars of faith."[185]

1. Most importantly, one must provide a confession of faith (*shahada*): to believe and profess there is no God but God (strict

monotheism) and that Mohammad (pbuh) is the messenger of God.

2. One must engage in prayer (*salat*): five daily prayers and a congregational prayer on Friday (*jum'ah*).

3. One must give an alms tax (*zakat*): this is a portion of income or wealth that is to be donated each year to the poor.

4. One must make a pilgrimage to Mecca (*hajj*): all those who are able and who can afford the trip are to travel to Mecca (the sacred center of the Islamic faith) once in a lifetime. This pilgrimage also has social and cultural implications: "Most importantly, pilgrimage is a symbol of Muslim unity and of the basic equality of all Muslims. All Muslims go on the pilgrimage wearing the same kind of clothing so that there is no distinction between rich and poor."[186] All are equal in the eyes of God.

5. The fifth pillar requires fasting during Ramadan (*sawm*): from sunrise to sundown Muslims "focus on all forms of self discipline." They "abstain from eating and drinking, if they are able to do so, as well as from sex, violence, and cursing." This is called "*jihad al-nafs* or struggle against oneself." This period also requires Muslims to "intensify their efforts at building their relationship with God."[187]

Mythic Islam: Wahhabism

With these few introductory notes about mythic Islam outlined above, we spend the rest of this section diving deeper into the mythic-level orientation with a look at a splinter ideology called Wahhabism. Wahhabism, or as some prefer it to be called, Salafism, is a strict fundamentalist movement within the Sunni sect of Islam.

In chapter 1 of this book, I introduced the concept of a horizontal spectrum of health that exists within each level of religious orientation. As a reminder, health represents the degree to which an adherent takes the defining characteristics of a particular altitude to their furthest implications. This is often determined by both the degree of intensity of engagement and a powerful influence of low levels of moral development. The spectrum of health used in this volume range from extremist to moderate.

In an exploration of this mythic altitude, degree of health is put to use as we contrast the following two versions of mythic Islam using the lens of Wahhabism:

- Ibn Abd al-Wahhab—a moderate version of mythic Isla
- Osama bin Laden—an extreme version of mythic Islam

Typologies of Mythic Islam

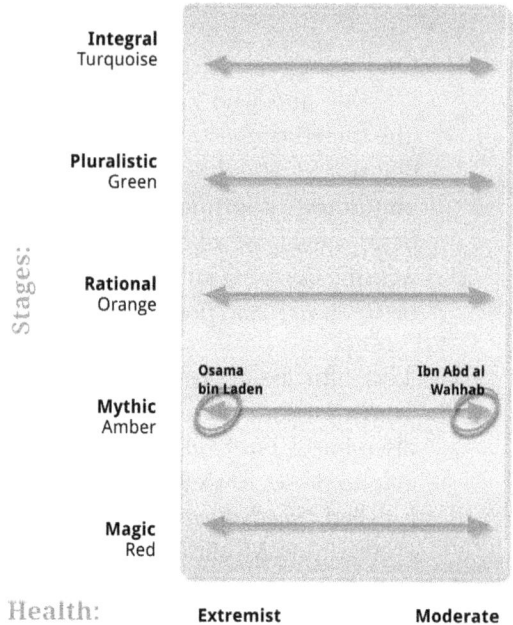

	Stages:	
Integral Turquoise		
Pluralistic Green		
Rational Orange		
Mythic Amber	Osama bin Laden	Ibn Abd al Wahhab
Magic Red		
Health:	Extremist	Moderate

Figure 13

Although both individuals listed above are considered Wahhabis, and both represent a mythic level of vertical development, it is important for us to make a distinction between the two horizontal classifications. As we see below, a variation in degree of health (moderate vs. extremist) can be the difference between a terrorist (Bin Laden) and a reformist (al-Wahhab).

Our new integral model suggests that the version of mythic Islam expressed by al- Wahhab and the version of mythic Islam expressed by Osama bin Laden were equal in altitude, but different in degree of health. Distinguishing between health classifications, even within the same altitude, provides a clear example of how precise and pragmatic the model of developmental religious pluralism can be.

Mythic-Moderate Islam: Ibn Abd al Wahhab
Health: Moderate   Stage: Mythic

Due to limited models of analysis, that use only a single-axis spectrum, some scholars are torn as to whether to call Ibn Abd al-Wahhab a moderate or an extremist. As a result of the extremist expressions of Islam that have now emerged in the name of Wahhabism, Ibn Abd al-Wahhab is often used as the whipping post. For instance, Islamic scholar Khaled Abou El Fadl contends that al-Wahhab was in fact just as radical as those extremists today. El Fadl reports that even al Wahhab's own family was disgusted by the radical lengths to which he took his teachings.[188]

Other scholars, contradict El Fadl, and claim that the Wahhabi founder, al Wahhab, has been entirely misunderstood.[189] They contend that extreme Wahhabism, as it is expressed today, by the likes of Bin Laden, has been distorted. Rather than linking current extremist views to al-Wahhab, these scholars argue that today's extremists are even more closely connected to the teachings of Ibn Taymiyya.

With the support of countless others in the Islamic community, Natana Delong-Bas dedicates an entire book to this intricate confusion between the teachings of al Wahhab and the extremist expression of Wahhabism today. Delong-Bas argues, "although it is often posited that bin Laden's ideology of global jihad has its origins in Ibn Abd al-Wahhab's writing because both are Wahhabis, the reality is that bin Laden's ideology owes far more to the writing of the medieval scholar Ibn Taymiyya and his contemporary interpreter, Sayyid Qutb, than it does to the writings of Ibn Abd al-Wahhab."[190] After compiling the various sources, and taking both sides of the argument into consideration, Delong-Bas' argument that al-Wahhab was not an extremist but more appropriately called a moderate at a mythic stage, holds more weight.

With a detailed exploration of both primary and secondary indicators of religious orientation, we see that in fact al-Wahhab expressed a version of Islam that was mythic in altitude and moderate in relative degree of health when contrasted to the interpretations, expressions, and behaviors of today's mythic extremists. Most of al-Wahhab's teachings moved beyond the mythic-literal stages of faith to the slightly more relaxed interpretations of Fowler's synthetic-conventional stages. When describing al-Wahhab, Islamic scholar Natana Delong-Bas writes, "looking back at original writings we see a reform movement encouraging more rights for women [and] a turning away from literal interpretation in exchange for conceptual understanding. He pursued the conversion of nonbelievers to Islam through education and debate rather than 'more militant methods, such as conversion by the sword.'"[191] Both clear examples of synthetic-conventional faith development and conventional morals.

In his time, al-Wahhab was surrounded by an Islam that was falling away from its traditional values and into what we describe as more magic interpretations. Not only were people examining the Qur'an with strict literal vengeance, but he also saw a dramatic increase in the use of superstitions.[192] His fight against magic versions of Islam was made in an attempt to restore the virtue of the Islamic faith at a mythic level of development. He believed things like "charms" were similar to worshiping false idols, any form of which was forbidden due to the fact that it took one's central focus off of Allah.

The potential reconstructed psychograph of al-Wahhab might look something like the figure below.

Mythic Moderate Psychograph

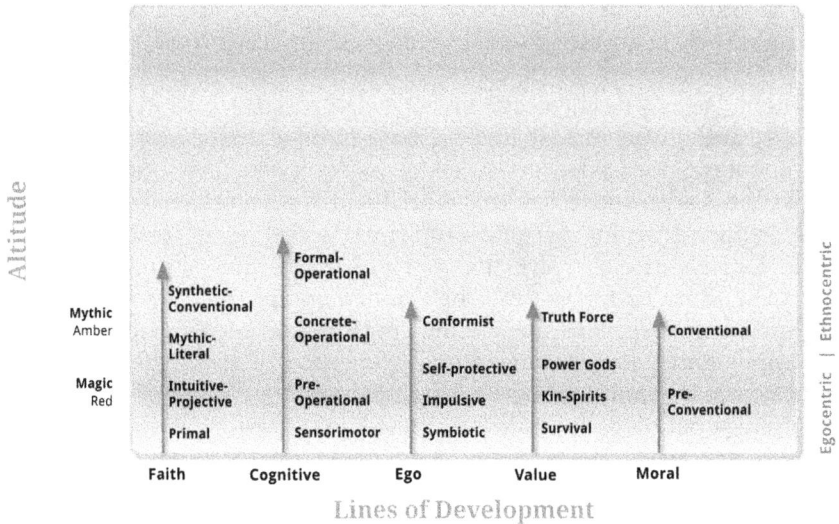

Figure 14

Ibn Abd al-Wahhab shared primary and secondary characteristics that we would attribute to today's moderate expressions of Islam. For instance:

> Ibn Abd al-Wahhab's vision of jihad was purely defensive in nature. He legitimated jihad only in cases in which Muslims had experienced an actual aggression. He did not glorify martyrdom because he believed that the only intent a

person should have in carrying out jihad was defense of God and God's community, not the desire for personal rewards or glory, whether on earth or in the Afterlife.[193]

133 It appears that despite the reputation that Wahhabism has today, al-Wahhab held many beliefs that directly contrast present day extremists. Delong-Bas makes a stark comparison:

> At the dawn of the 21st century it is clear that there is more than one type of Wahhabi Islam. The vision of Ibn Abd al-Wahhab was one in which Islam was to be revived and reformed in service of public order and welfare. It especially created public space and a balance of rights for women, as well as a legal methodology for indigenous reform based on Islamic teachings and law. A vision that offers hope for the future. The vision of Bin Laden is one in which global jihad is to define relations between Muslims and the rest of the world... Bin Laden's vision is one that seeks to cause fear and discord. [194]

We now turn directly to Bin Laden to uncover how in fact his particular extreme version of mythic religious orientation might differ from the moderate version of al-Wahhab, even while expressed from the same mythic altitude.

Mythic-Extreme Islam: Osama Bin Laden
Health: Extreme   Stage: Mythic

Obsessed with offensive jihad and strict interpretation of the Qur'an, Bin Laden and other extremists take Wahhabism, a once-reformist movement within Islam, and transform it into a breeding ground for terrorism.   Two of the most powerful notions expressed today by mythic extremist within Islam are martyrdom and jihad. Delong notes:

> Bin Laden, like Ibn Taymiyya and Sayyid Qutb before him, envisages the world divided into two absolute and mutually exclusive spheres—the land of Islam (dar al-Islam) and the land of unbelief (dar al-kufr)—a division that results in a necessarily hostile relationship... Because bin laden espouses a vision of a world in which good and evil are engaged in cosmic conflict, he believes that jihad must take on offensive as well as defensive capabilities and should

be a permanent state of being for Muslims. According to this vision, martyrdom should not be feared but actively pursued.... Anyone who resists the message of Islam or Muslim domination is to be fought and killed. [195]

Delong-Bas continues:

Ibn Abd al-Wahhab's quest was for broad social order in which Muslims could live peacefully and respectfully with both Muslims and non-Muslims. Bin Laden's vision leaves no space for non-Muslims or those who claim to be Muslims but do not act the part. Ibn Abd al-Wahhab's writings have inspired a variety of contemporary reforms, from context- and value-oriented reading of the Qur'an to legislation expanding women's rights and access to public space. Bin Laden's social vision is limited to jihad, suggesting a future of violence and destruction rather than peaceful construction.[196]

Islamic scholar Khalid Abou El Fadl uses the term puritan to describe those like Bin Laden that we would place in the category mythic/extremist. He explains, "the distinguishing characteristic of this group is the absolutist and uncompromising nature of [their] beliefs."[197] When these qualities combine with Grave's absolute truth-force values we are left with disastrous consequences. According to El Fadl, puritans are "intolerant of competing points of view and consider pluralist realities to be a form of contamination of the unadulterated truth."[198]

The most significant psychological difference between al-Wahhab (a moderate mythic Muslim) and Bin Laden (an extremist mythic Muslim) revolves around the secondary indicator of moral development. Al-Wahhab had an inherent respect for the sanctity of life. According to Delong-Bas, "he called for the maximum preservation of life—human, animal, and plant—during jihad, rather than their destruction."[199] Al-Wahhab's actions and writing tell us that he had, at the very least, what Kohlberg would call conventional moral development.

Despite the classification of a Wahhabist, Bin Laden's actions and statements tell a shockingly different story when contrasted with al-Wahhab himself. With little care for others and with little ability to take the perspective of the thousands who suffer as a direct result of violent attacks, Bin Laden resides at a low level of pre-conventional moral development. In this case, it is a secondary indicator (moral development) and the intensity of Bin Laden's ethnocentric nature that leads us to categorize him as an extremist.

Comparing al-Wahhab and Bin Laden shows why a more robust assessment of religious orientation does well to include both primary (faith) and secondary indicators (cognitive, ego, values, moral). Without it, using a more general postmodern or pluralistic approach that includes only cultural sensitivity and a spectrum of health (moderate and extremist), both al-Wahhab and Bin Laden are lumped together into the same category. In the classic pluralistic model, both are likely to be considered extremists due to their mythic tendencies. It is precisely these types of oversimplifications that this book tries to avoid by bringing a more nuanced and sophisticated integral classification.

In conclusion, it is vital to remember that although al-Wahhab's version of mythic Islam may be expressed through a more moderate typology than the extremist version of Bin Laden above, all those at mythic stages are likely to still possess an ethnocentric worldview. That is, mythic Muslims tend to be exclusivists. Even if they believe that individuals of different faiths can peacefully coexist (vis-a-vis al-Wahhab), Islam is understood to be the only true path to salvation.

Individuals at this stage with an ethnocentric orientation often quote the Qur'an directly: "Whoso desires another *din* [way of conduct] than *Islam*, it shall not be accepted of him; in the next world he shall be among the losers." (Qur'an 3:85) Authentic tolerance does not emerge until a rational orientation stabilizes. If we are to live in true mutual respect and tolerance rather than some form of bigoted coexistence, the ladder of religious orientation must be made clear and explicit across this and every tradition. From an integral perspective, it is an absolute necessity that adherents have the option to travel the vertical spectrum of complexity with freedom and confidence beyond magic and mythic forms to rational stages and higher.

Rational Islam

Just as we saw with the Christian ladder, most Muslims alive today tend to possess a moderate health classification and a mythic level of religious orientation. However, beyond the norm, there are some Muslims who move even further up the ladder in their psychological development to take a more individuative and reflective view of their tradition. These Muslims have acquired a rational level of religious interpretation.

Rational-Moderate Islam: Khaled Abou El Fadl
Health: Moderate   Stage: Rational

Challenges are inevitable any time one grows beyond the level of religious orientation that is most predominate in the given sociocultural context into which he or she is embedded. In both Christianity and Islam, mythic versions of interpretation are so copious that a rational stance is one of the most difficult places from which to orient. Despite the fact that it is indeed a more developed perspective, supportive structures have yet to be put in place that can allow the rational perspective to fully flourish.

Attacks from mythic adherents against those with a more rational approach are many. It is common for many Muslims who bring a rational and reflective lens to Islam to be accused of being contaminated by the West; as if rationalization equals Westernization. El Fadl tells us that "a considerable number of Muslims believe whole-heartedly that fellow Muslims who attempt to adopt a critical stance toward the Islamic tradition are nothing more than self-promoters seeking to placate the West at Islam's expense."[200] Because we now know through cross-cultural analysis that the rational (orange) level of orientation is not simply some form of yielding to Western ideology, we see more clearly that a reflective stance is simply the next appropriate rung on the developmental ladder.

Those with a traditional-mythic interpretation will likely continue to struggle endorsing anything other than their own belief system until a more clear understanding of developmental stages is taken to heart. Wilber uses an analogy to describe similar scenarios that exist across all traditions at this crucial developmental fulcrum. There is a steel ceiling (a pressure-cooker lid), between the mythic stages of development and the rational stages of religious orientation, Wilber explains. This ceiling prevents individuals from moving from amber (mythic) to orange (rational) levels of development.[201]

One of the intentions of this book is to help end the confusion between modernization and Westernization. Wilber's distinction between surface features and deep structures helps to shed more light on the issue and we will see how his ideas play out through the remainder of the book. In short, Wilber's distinction between surface features and deep structures allows us to more clearly see that rational levels of development will look different as they arise in different cultures and different features. The surface features of how each stage of development shows up will be conditioned by all of the factors that postmodern scholarship has strived to uncover. However, even with these surface differences, the deep structures of each developmental stage will stay fundamentally the same. In other words, even within a plurality of surface characteristics deep structures that represent an increased form of perspective taking and more critical distance from the tradition are sure to abound.

El Fadl sums up a solid description of a Muslim at an orange altitude in the following quote.[202] Below, I add the word rational after his term moderate to clarify that he is referring to what we would consider a moderate degree of health at an orange/rational altitude:

> Moderate [rational] Muslims are individuals who believe in Islam as the true faith, who practice and believe in the five pillars of Islam, and who modify certain aspects of that tradition in order to fulfill the ultimate moral objectives of the faith in the modern age...[Those at a rational stage of orientation] do not treat their religion as if it were a fossilized monument, but treat it as a dynamic and active faith... Moderate [rational] Muslims honor the past achievements of their fellow Muslims, but they live in the present. The reforms that they advocate are not intended to ignore or subvert the will of God, but are intended to realize the Divine Will more fully while respecting the integrity and coherence of the faith.[203]

One can sense how carefully El Fadl chooses his words in the quote above. His caution is a direct result of so many years of dominating forms of mythic Islam challenging his interpretation of faith the moment it appears to go astray from its fossilized and static mythic roots.

El Fadl uses the terms moderate and puritan to refer to what we would classify as moderate rational and extreme mythic respectively (I developed a full analysis of these two terms in the section "integral Islam" below). El Fadl explains the difficulty of this distinct split: "Although the schism between moderate [rational] and puritan [mythic] Muslims has become distinct, pronounced, and real, this division is not explicitly recognized in the Muslim world."[204] The distinction is not acknowledged precisely because all Muslims believe that there is a straight path to God. All Muslims are taught, as El Fadl explains to "unite in pursuit of the Lord's path and not divide."[205] This leaves adherents uncertain whether or not they should admit that such a divide exists. Once again, a developmental perspective would allow Muslims to embrace multiple interpretations without having to jeopardize their unity.

At the rational level of religious orientation, human rights and tolerance come to the foreground as elements of significant importance. When such qualities are acquired through authentic interest and genuine practice they usually inspire laws that protect the sanctity of all human beings regardless of race, color, class, or religion. Digging deeper into the heart of rational Islam, we can see these qualities blossom in El Fadl's thought.

Using the Qur'an for support, El Fadl attempts to provide several ideas as to some of the key realizations that might come as a rational expression of Islam works its way further into the currents of mainstream society. El Fadl suggests:

> The Qur'an and the Prophet Muhammad's traditions make clear that human beings have a right to certain entitlements and safeguards in life. In the Islamic jurisprudential tradition, the classical scholars…identified five protected interests: life, intellect, lineage, reputation, and property…. Therefore, the Islamic political and legal systems must protect and promote the lives of people (life); the ability of people to think and reflect (intellect); their right to marry, procreate, and raise their children (lineage); their right not to be slandered, defamed, or maligned (reputation); and their right to own property and not to have their property taken without fair and just compensation (property).[206]

In other words, although El Fadl sees many of the same rights that are protected in Western countries as valuable, he finds support for their roots within his own historical, cultural, and religious roots (a perfect example of modernization without Westernization). As he clearly articulates, human rights can and should be protected and supported by the teachings of Islam. Thus further proving that embracing rational values does not mean that one has to abandon the tradition of Islam, as some at mythic levels might fear.

As we have seen, mythic levels of orientation demonstrate several specific characteristics. They cherish structure, authority, and absolute notions of right and wrong. Because the very heart of Islam involves a complete surrender to the will of God, it is unlikely that one still resting at a mythic altitude could find it reasonable to declare any sovereignty as an individual. The individual, at mythic levels, would prefer external authority to personal sovereignty. Once at a rational capacity, however, adherents find a way to reconcile the apparent divide between human sovereignty and total submission to the will of Allah. El Fadl explains one such rational attempt: "Some moderates have argued that final authority rests with God, and so God is sovereign. However, God has delegated total authority to human beings to conduct their affairs according to their freewill."[207] Therefore, El Fadl believes that there is a divine responsibility imparted onto each human being.

A rational interpretation of Islam recognizes that God has no direct way of intervening in human lives while on earth except through the actions of others. Because God has delegated a certain amount of undeniable authority to human beings, it is our duty to uphold that obligation and to the best of our ability, create Godliness on earth. According to El Fadl, at the moment of creation God entrusted humanity with a deeply profound responsibility. Because God endowed humans with the capacity for self-reflection and rationality, God simultaneously gave each human the ability to reflect on right and wrong.[208] This rational interpretation strips away the mythic baggage dependent on external authority, while preserving the credibility of Islam with honor and integrity.

In the case of rational Islam this shift of authority allows many individuals to move into post-conventional levels of moral development. "The only way that Muslims can remain true to the moral message of their religion," says El Fadl, "and at the same time discharge their covenant with God is through introspective self-criticism and reform."[209] This ability for self-reflection and self-criticism is precisely what influences all Muslims who reach this level of development to express indicators of Fowler's individuative-reflective faith and Piaget's formal operational cognition.

Recall that development is often a process of transcendence and inclusion. Even if we transcend mythic notions of authority as described above, submission to the will of God still remains a central feature of the Islamic faith. How might this same central feature of submission look as we move up the spiral to orange levels of interpretation? In a beautiful passage El Fadl directly contrasts what we would call a rational interpretation of submission with an interpretation of submission from a lower altitude:

> Obeying God out of fear of punishment [magic] or out of desire for a reward [magic] keeps one vested in the paradigm of self-interest and the artificiality of the mundane physical world...To submit to the divine in a genuine and meaningful way is to elevate oneself to the transcendental and the sublime. To overcome the artificial physical world and to seek union with the Ultimate Beauty...Submission to God through fear and obedience is considered [by those at a rational level] a primitive and even vulgar stage of submission. Submitting to God through fear means that the worshiper has a tenuous relationship with God—a relationship that is driven by human self-interest or by primitive desire to avoid pain and seek pleasure. [From a higher altitude], submission to God means to have a relationship with God that is marked by

absolute trust and confidence in God…It is a surrender in which one is in complete tranquility and peace with that who is the object of surrender.[210]

In one final sweep, El Fadl expresses even higher levels of orientation as he explains the ultimate type of submission:

> The highest stage of submission is to love God more than any other, even more than oneself, and for those who achieve this lofty position of loving God absolutely and completely, they become God's beloved, endowed with true perception, wisdom and compassion. For human beings to love God necessarily means that they must love all that God has created and represents. It would make little sense to love God but hate God's creatures and creation. To truly love God, one must love all human beings, whether Muslims or not, and love all living beings as well as all of God's nature… In short, it is impossible to love God or be beloved by God and not exhibit the characteristics of Godliness.[211]

In short, it is by fully loving God and all creation that we, as individual human beings, are to share the most divine of all qualities.

Pluralistic Islam

Because lower levels of religious orientation (i.e., magic/mythic) rely heavily on strict literal interpretations of texts, those wanting to bring in higher ideals of rational or pluralistic stages of religious orientation must quote directly from canonical text if they are to grab the attention of magic and mythic adherents. When making the claim for a deeper understanding of religious plurality and diversity, the following two verses are often quoted from the Qur'an:

> O'humankind, God has created you from male and female and made you into diverse nations and tribes so that you may come to know each other. Verily, the most honored of you in the sight of God is he who is the most righteous. (Qur'an 49:13)

> Unto every one of you we have appointed a (different) law and way of life. And if Allah had so willed, He could surely have made you all one single community: but (He willed it otherwise) in order to test you by means of what He has

given you. Vie, then, with one another in doing good works! Unto Allah you all must return; and then He will make you truly understand all that on which you were wont to differ. (Qur'an 5:48)

We'll see how these phrases and others like them play into framing the pluralistic stage of development within the Muslim context.

Pluralistic-Moderate Islam: Abdulaziz Sachedina
Health: Moderate   Stage: Pluralistic

We explore pluralistic Islam from the perspective of Islamic scholar Abdulaziz Sachedina. All quotes are taken from his book *The Islamic Roots of Democratic Pluralism.*

To begin, Sachedina contends, "there is ample evidence to suggest substantial worldwide growth of a religious consciousness that points beyond particular religious traditions to embrace a pluralistic and tolerant attitude toward other faiths."[212] Sachedina's point supports this books idea of evolution and development.

Overall, the momentum of evolution means that with time, despite the fits and starts that are bound to arise, humanity is moving in a positive direction of more complexity and deeper embrace. Pluralistic and even integral interpretations will continue to grow and flourish as time unfolds.

According to Sachedina, the "lack of interest in religious pluralism and its intrinsic connection with democratic governance has helped to prevent a healthy restoration of interpersonal and intercommunal relations in the Muslim world."[213] Fortunately, as we have learned thus far in the book, a developmental perspective gives us the opportunity to transform all of these trends into opportunities for growth.

Building on his insight above, Sachedina still believes that many Muslims have the capacity for higher levels of expression. Unfortunately, as he sees it, dominating and repressive levels of interpretation (mythic) limit the current expressions of faith. In his own words on the subject, Sachedina explains, "I firmly believe that if Muslims were made aware of the centrality of Qur'anic teachings about religious and cultural pluralism as a divinely ordained principle of peaceful coexistence among human societies, then they would spurn violence in challenging their repressive and grossly inefficient governments."[214] If higher expressions were made available and then validated by the religious leaders in multiple communities, Muslims with a higher spiritual intelligence would be able to gain the momentum and strength needed to confront the repressive mythic levels that they currently face.

It would seem that Sachedina feels the values of religious pluralism deep within his being. Even if it is not explicitly stated, Sachedina has an intuitive understanding that improved relationships with the *religious other* are inevitable as higher levels of religious interpretation become more prominent. Moreover, he also sees that higher levels of religious interpretation will help to unfold socially engaged and democratic communities throughout the world.

Like most other pluralistic Muslims, Sachedina knows the strength and authority that the Qur'an holds for all Muslims at lower levels of religious orientation.[215] Without its backing, persuading others to embrace (or at least conform to) pluralistic expressions would be next to impossible. Using the following verse from the holy Qur'an, Sachedina explains the ideas he believes to be "fundamental to the [Qur'anic] conception of religious pluralism":[216]

> The People were one community (umma); then God sent forth the Prophets, good tidings to bear and warning, and He sent down with them the Book with the truth, that He might decide the people touching their differences. (Qur'an 2:213)

From Sachedina's viewpoint, the preceding verse contains three points crucial to Islamic pluralism: (1) the unity of humankind under One God, (2) the particularity of religions brought by the prophets, and (3) the role of revelation (the Book) in resolving the differences that touch communities of faith. He believes that any "Muslim government must acknowledge and protect the divinely ordained right of each person to determine his or her spiritual destiny without coercion. The recognition of freedom of conscience in matters of faith is the cornerstone of the Qur'anic notion of religious pluralism, both inter-religious and intra-religious."[217] So not only does the Qur'an support the notions of pluralism, according to Sachedina, but in fact, it requires that Muslims abide by such values as an intricate part of faith.

In our previous discussion regarding mythic Islam, we explored a quote from verse 3:85 of the Qur'an, "Whoso desires another din than Islam, it shall not be accepted of him; in the next world he shall be among the losers." From a mythic orientation this verse is used to support ethnocentric beliefs, assuming that all those who do not accept Islam will be punished "among the losers." However, from a pluralistic altitude a quite different understanding comes to fruition.

One important aspect of a pluralistic orientation is that it has gained the necessary skills to take into account both context and interpretation. Because the individual at a pluralistic stage has the ability to examine text more carefully from a higher level of developmental complexity, we find that the ethnocentric interpretation of this verse falls apart when studied alongside the preceding verses.

Sachedina begins his pluralistic analysis by reminding us that Islam is the name of the religion as well as the "act of surrendering." In this specific verse, according to Sachedina, "the word Islam refers to the act of surrender rather than to the name of a specific religion."[218] With this contextual understanding, the translation reads follows:

> Whoso desires to behave in any other way than surrendering [to God], it shall not be accepted of him [by God], who will punish the individual by making him among the losers in the world to come.

Sachedina, concludes that this new interpretation is more accurate, not only because it agrees with a more pluralistic understanding but more importantly because of the fact that both of the verses preceding it also use the term, he "submitted" or "surrendered" in the "literal sense rather than in the technical sense as derivatives of the name Islam."[219]

Perhaps one of the most significant developments of this pluralistic stage is the potential for the cognitive capacity to take all perspectives without privileging any one in particular. Wilber calls this stage of cognition "vision logic." In his own words, Wilber contrasts vision logic to the previous stage of cognitive development:

> Where [formal operational] privileges the exclusive perspective of the particular subject, vision-logic *adds up all the perspectives*, privileging none, and thus attempts to grasp the integral, the whole, the multiple contexts within contexts that endlessly disclose the Kosmos, not in a ridged or absolute fashion, but in a fluidly holonic and multidimensional tapestry.[220]

Without the ability to hold multiple perspectives simultaneously, one would have a difficult time inhabiting green altitudes with any stability. It is only with this capacity to hold a multiplicity of perspectives simultaneously that the ability to engage paradox (Fowler's conjunctive stage) is a realistic possibility.

Integral Islam

How might a more full application of an integral model help to clarify some of the above ideas?

An integral scholar would surely look at El Fadl's version of rational Islam with a closer lens, pointing out where it is partial and adding to it several new insights. Although acknowledging that his own division into two groups is an "inadequate oversimplification," El Fadl makes one crucial error that only an integral interpretation can mend. As is common in most modern and postmodern models, El Fadl speaks of two opposing groups of people, puritans and moderates. This clear and concise distinction can be taken a step further using the integral model.

Due to a lack of knowledge about developmental levels, El Fadl places his classifications on a horizontal spectrum similar to the one we described in chapter 1 (extremist vs. moderate). Pictorially El Fadl's spectrum is represented in the figure 15 below.

Puritan ⬅━━━━━━━━━━━━━━━━━━━━━➡ Moderate

El Fadl's Same Level Spectrum

Figure 15

El Fadl's horizontal understanding is reiterated when he claims, "few Muslims are going to be thoroughly moderate or thoroughly puritan. Most will fall somewhere between the two extremes, with a majority leaning toward moderation." This ability to "lean" one way or the other implies that everyone has the capacity for both of his versions of moderate and puritan alike and reinforces the horizontal, fluid nature of his approach.

Using a new understanding of psychological maturity we find that this is not necessarily the case. Not all humans have the capacity for higher levels of religious orientation. Not only are his two poles separated by a horizontal spectrum of health (extremist and moderate) as he assumes, but each is also separated by a vertical spectrum of levels (mythic and rational).

El Fadl's
Two Poles

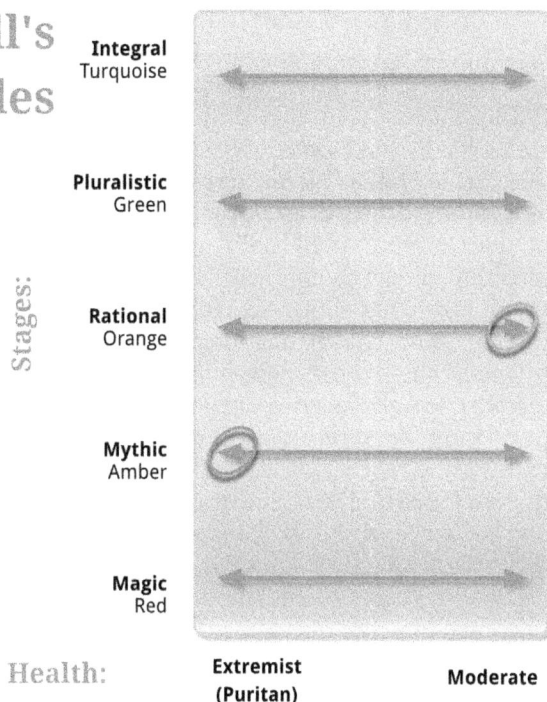

Integral
Turquoise

Pluralistic
Green

Stages:

Rational
Orange

Mythic
Amber

Magic
Red

Health: **Extremist**   **Moderate**
            (Puritan)

Figure 16

The classification El Fadl calls *puritans* we would place at mythic stage and extremist orientation. The classification he calls *moderate* we would place at rational stage and a moderate orientation.

We can find support directly in El Fadl's descriptions of each classification. For example, El Fadl contends that moderate Muslims must use reason to make choices for themselves. The capacity for interiorized reason and self-reflective cognition does not arise until rational altitudes, a concept with which El Fadl is clearly unfamiliar. Those with only mythic levels of development cannot lean toward the rational mode of moderation that El Fadl proposes.

We learned, conversely, that those at mythic levels of expression look to authority and do not have the capacity for internally directed decisions. Amber adherents simply do not have the capacity to authentically express such levels of orientation. In fortunate circumstances, we can hope for mythic adherents to become as healthy as possible at their level of development. For many this means a moderate expression of faith with conventional moral development. Unfortunately, this also means that the mythic individuals will likely still possess an ethnocentric worldview and conformist ego structure at best.

Adding the distinction between different altitudes may seem minor but it is absolutely crucial if we are to have a clear understanding of a world embedded in perpetual evolution and development. An example takes us deeper and provides evidence of how critical an inclusion of development actually is. Let's imagine we are conducting a case study on an Islamic terrorist. El Fadl would classify the terrorist as a puritan whereas an integral scholar would classify the terrorist as mythic extremist. In El Fadl's model the puritan has only one horizontal direction in which to move: from puritan to moderate. According to El Fadl's horizontal spectrum, every terrorist has the *capacity* to spontaneously change their degree of intensity and move from extreme to moderate. With a new integral distinction we now know that a terrorist actually has two directions for possible movement, horizontal translation or vertical transformation. Horizontal translation from extremist to moderate, although perhaps less violent, would still mean that an individual possesses ethnocentric, exclusive, conformist beliefs, and an external moral compass. It is only through positive vertical transformation, from a mythic to rational altitude that one gains the capacity to express authentic tolerance. It is only when authentic tolerance emerges that one will express true universal respect for the cultural and religious other.

Recognizing developmental levels allows us to insert healthy value judgments. It is better for a terrorist to vertically transform to rational levels of awareness than to simply translate horizontally to more healthy moderate expressions of mythic faith.[221] If we are to positively engage religion in the world, and the Islamic faith in particular, progress will only occur if scholars, practitioners, and religious leaders adopt a model that includes developmental variances in interpretation.

EVIDENCE AND
EXAMPLES from

Islam ☾

The
Conveyor
Belt

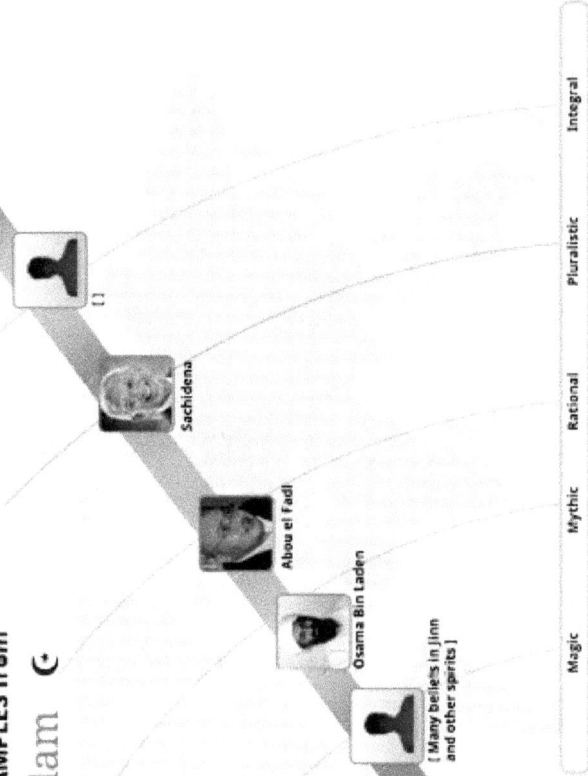

Integral

Pluralistic

Sachidena

Rational

Abou el Fadl

Mythic

Osama Bin Laden

[Many beliefs in Jinn
and other spirits]

Magic

Chapter 6
The Hindu Conveyor Belt

Snapshot of Hinduism

There are an estimated 900 million Hindus on our planet today, making it the third most populous religion in the world.[222] The diversity and complexity within the Hindu tradition is so profound that it can be argued that the term Hinduism in general is an inaccurate blanket term used by modern scholars to describe all of the indigenous traditions that were born on the Indian subcontinent. Consequently, there are times when I employ the plural term "Hindu traditions" to honor the diversity.

Difference in language, style of worship, and belief vary in India to such a degree that from one village to the next the practices may appear vastly different. Outside of India, the Hindu diaspora in America, Europe, and the United Kingdom takes on cultural traits of the West. Hindus in Southeast Asia are quite clearly molded and conditioned by the Muslim and Buddhist influences in countries like Malaysia, Indonesia (especially Bali), and Thailand into which they have integrated. All of this is to say that any attempt to characterize Hinduism as a broad category of "world religion" will fail to do justice to the true complexity on the ground. Theologian Hans Kung helps to confirm the argument:

> No Indian religion ever called itself "Hinduism," a word invented by Europeans. It was supposed to designate the religion of the Hindus, but unfortunately not enough was known about the Hindus when the term was coined. Westerners had not yet realized that Hindus had a number of different religions. Since then it has become customary to speak and write about Hinduism as one of the great world religions. And for some time people believed that there really was such a thing. Nowadays they know, without admitting

145

the fact, that Hinduism is nothing but an orchid cultivated by European scholarship. It is much too beautiful to uproot, but it's a test-tube plant and not found in nature.[223]

Even if the term Hinduism has itself been superimposed upon the Indian continent by scholars from the outside, Kung makes a sufficient counterpoint to endorse its use:

> Modern Indians characteristically do *not* utter indignant cries when we lump their religions together as "Hinduism". There are times when they might have, but not today. There are differences, to be sure; but, as Indians see it, stressing what separates them, insisting on the rightness of my religion and the wrongness of yours, is rather petty. This sort of attitude overlooks the fact that there has to be a variety of religions to offer approaches to the divine to a variety of people with different needs and at differing stages of development, to enable everyone to pursue his own access to divinity.[224]

It is true that broad statements about religious traditions are sure to stir-up disapproval in the minds of serious scholars. For instance, university professors, like Anne Monius and Francis X. Clooney, spend entire semesters at Harvard Divinity School looking at a single text or a single variation of Hinduism as articulated in a specific time in history, in a specific region of India. This degree of granularity is of course a necessity for specialists.

For the purposes of this book, however, a few broad orientating generalizations about the commonalities within the Hindu traditions are worth noting. The following descriptions are not true for all Hindus, in all cultures, in all times in history. Chances are however, that most individuals who identify themselves as a "Hindu" would be familiar with the basic foundations outlined below.

One place to start is by examining what it means to be a human being within the various Hindu traditions of India. As we shall see, the Hindu systems provide an entire philosophy of life and position the individual within a complex cosmology. According to most Hindu worldviews, at the most fundamental level a human being is a fusion of both mortal impulse and divine potential. The core of each human being is composed of pure consciousness, a self-awareness or I-AM-ness called Atman. As the sages of the Upanishads articulated, this Atman is none other than the very life force of all existence (Brahman). Knott quotes Sivaya Subramuniyaswami, as she explains, "we are the underlying consciousness and energy flowing through all things."[225]

The realization that I-AM-ness is none other than God gives

Hindus a unique outlook on the meaning and purpose of life. Understanding that Atman and Brahman are not separate (at least for Advaita traditions) becomes the central focus of the Hindu worldview. When the entire existence is seen as the Self, ethical and moral dilemmas become moot. One has no choice but to act for the benefit of all (apparently) separate selves, because in reality one understands all separation to be a result of ignorance (advidya/maya).

Ancient Hindu teachers realized that although esoteric contemplation and Self-realization might release one from the realm of endless rebirth and suffering (samsara), such practices do not disclose knowledge as to how one should live life on a daily basis. For the more mundane day-to-day activities, Hindus developed an elaborate system in which all human beings have a proper niche. In our discussion of the exoteric aspects of being human in the Hindu tradition we examine three interrelated categories: dharma, caste, and ashrama.

Using the insight provided by Harvard Scholar Anne Monius, one might loosely define the term dharma as one's particular responsibility and obligation to play one's part in "upholding" the cosmos.[226] The entire exoteric notion of being human rests on understanding the importance of dharma and the strict obligation that one has to fulfill it. On a practical level, dharma provides Hindus with both purpose and deep meaning in their lives. As we proceed it becomes clear how our other two terms, caste and ashrama, are intricately intertwined with determining one's dharma.

In the broad Hindu context, the word "caste" refers to a hereditary social class understood to be determined by past-life karma and implemented through the process of rebirth. In addition to the term caste, the term *varna* (literally *color* in Sanskrit) is also used to describe the class distinction among Hindus. Fair-skinned individuals tend to be members of one of the two higher castes: Brahmin (priests) and Kshatriya (warriors/rulers). Those of a darker complexion tend to be members of lower castes: Vaishya (merchants) and Shudra (servants). At the lowest level of the Hindu caste system individuals are given the title Dalit or Harijan, otherwise known as the untouchables.

A human being can also be examined from the context of the various ashramas, or four life stages: student, householder, forest dweller, renunciate. It is here that the Hindu philosophy of life comes clearly to the fore. At the early stages of life one is expected to acquire knowledge in the stage of the student. As one matures, the stage of householder takes hold and one is expected to raise a family and provide for them. Once family obligations are completed one is allowed to proceed to the stage of the forest dweller, a time period in which one can focus his or her attention on attaining moksha (liberation from the suffering inherent in cyclical existence). Those who have attained liberation (or have decided that they will spend the rest of their life pursuing nothing less) proceed to the stage of the renunciate. After performing a symbolic "mock cremation of themselves" (representing the death of their individual separate self), renunciates live out the remainder of their life void of name, obligation, or dharma, and spend their days teaching interested seekers.

Each caste has a particular dharma. In addition, each ashrama has a specific dharma. Therefore, defining a human being in the Hindu tradition greatly rests upon one's "duty to uphold the universe" as determined by both one's life stage (ashrama) and one's particular hereditary class (caste/varna). Knott uses the term varna-ashrama-dharma, to describe the "duties or obligations which fall to a person according to his particular social class and stage of life."[227]
Parish explains how being human is at least in part determined by the rites that each individual is obligated to perform according to their varna-ashrama-dharma: "The rites give salience to some ways of being a person, but mute other possibilities. They provide symbolic grounds for self-awareness, for knowing self in terms of particular cultural values, making it possible for persons to interpret themselves and their lives in certain defined ways...."[228] With four ashramas and five levels of caste (including dalits), we see that a human being in the Hindu context might fit into one of twenty particular niches, all with varying responsibilities and obligations.

To make matters even more dynamic, the learned few know the important difference between the exoteric and esoteric dimensions of their practice. All dharma discussed on an exoteric level is of a secondary importance when compared to the esoteric realization of the one Absolute Self. Sages teach that it is only through a deep experiential knowledge of this Absolute Self that the Hindu might truly discover true divinity.

Long before James Fowler's research into faith development, the Vedic traditions of India managed to derive an implicit understanding about the way in which individuals approach the idea of ultimate concern. For instance, the Mahabharata (an epic poem within the Hindu cannon) maintains that the human experience carries one through a predictable spectrum of ultimate concern. This path contains four progressive goals: (1) pleasure (kama), (2) wealth (artha), (3) duty (dharma), and (4) liberation (moksha). All four goals, like Fowler's faith development, are attempts to secure ultimate fulfillment.[229]

According to these early Hindu teachings, just as the child eventually outgrows the desire to play with toys, in time the individual outgrows his or her determination to find ultimate fulfillment in the pleasures of the senses (kama) or through worldly success (artha). However, understanding that not everyone will outgrow the first two stages of desire in his or her present life, Hinduism's doctrine of reincarnation explains that the pursuit of lower levels of desire may unfold over the course of several lives.

Religious scholar Huston Smith explains it in a slightly different way: "As long as people are content with the prospect of pleasure, success, or service, the Hindu sage will not be likely to disturb them beyond offering some suggestions as to how to proceed more efficiently."[230] For those who have realized the transitory nature of the first three Hindu stages of ultimate concern, Hinduism proclaims that it is only the desire for self-transcendence that might lead to everlasting fulfillment.

According to Smith, the final stage of life, called moksha, is experienced as a "release from the finitude that restricts us from the limitless being, consciousness, and bliss."[231] That is to say, ultimately, according to Hindus, the only thing that can satisfy the human condition is an experiential realization of infinite existence, knowledge, and joy. Anything less will leave the seeker unsatisfied and wanting more.

At their core, the Hindu traditions recognize that a metaphysical system void of the capacity to induce first-hand realizations would be useless. Therefore, Hinduism lays out specific scientific experiments, experiments that it claims, if followed as prescribed, will result in nothing less than a full realization of the absolute and with it, perpetual immersion in bliss.

In its own unique way, in addition to discovering several basic stages of faith, Hinduism also understood, as Howard Gardner came to research centuries later, that individuals all have distinct lines of development. Hindus acknowledge that individuals have different talents and temperaments. Accordingly, the great sages established scientific experiments for realization fit for all temperaments. Each type of experiment leading to realization they called a path of yoga. Hindus list at least five different types of yoga that individuals can follow in order to obtain ultimate fulfillment. A brief introduction to the various paths of yoga is useful now before we move on to examine the developmental evidence within the tradition itself:

Raja Yoga—This yoga is also called the royal path. Through Raja Yoga, one recognizes the Absolute through the use of meditation. Meditation thus culminates in a spiritual and religious experience called samadhi. Although types of samadhi vary, ultimately one recognizes the absolute and the relative are not separate. The lower self (jiva) and the higher self (atman-brahman) are experienced as one and the same.

Jnana Yoga—This path leads to recognition of the Absolute through knowledge and proper intellectual understanding. Jnana Yoga is fit for those individuals who excel at cognitive development.

Bhakti Yoga—The path resulting in recognition of the Absolute through devotion to the Divine. Bhakti Yoga is best fit for those individuals with well-developed emotional intelligence or a highly developed "affective" line. For bhakti yogis in one of the Hindu traditions, God is personal (Saguna Brahman, or God with attributes). As a bhakti, one often has a deep and profound loving relationship with God. Deep devotion to a personal God results in a complete dissolution of the lower self into the higher Self.

Hatha Yoga—This yoga leads to recognition of the Absolute through physical posture. Those not inclined to contemplation, worship, or meditation may choose this path. This path is well suited for those individuals whose bodily intelligence or kinesthetic line of development is strong. Hatha Yoga uses poetic movements of the body and intense posturing to sink the practitioner into a trance. Peak experiences in this trance results in samadhi. Just as with Raja Yoga, these experiences allow the practitioner to transcend the individual sense of self to rest solely in identification with higher Self.

Karma Yoga—This final path leads to the recognition of the Absolute through action. Karma Yoga does not presume that one is perfect in all actions, nor does it refer to a stance in which the individual refrain from all action. Rather it refers to maintaining awareness of the absolute *in all action*. Actions are performed for their own sake without attachment to or hopes that any benefit will come to the individual ego. One performs actions with neither selfish nor unselfish ideas in mind, for selfish ideas strengthen the ego and even unselfish action can reinforce the ego with thoughts like "I am such an unselfish person!" Karma Yoga is the path taught most explicitly in the Bhagavad Gita: renunciation *in* action rather than renunciation *of* action.

> Alexander Varghese explains the delineation succinctly:
>
> The eighteen yogas in the [Bhagavad] Gita are combined and reduced to four categories: Karma Yoga, Bhakti Yoga, Jnana Yoga and Raja Yoga. These four are compared to the bud, the tender fruit, the unripe fruit and the fully ripe fruit. These yogas need not be mutually exclusive. Some people practice all or combination of several ones.[232]

The paths of yoga described above are valued, and are explained as different but equal paths. Even more importantly, most individuals often practice more than one specific path. In a sense, an integral understanding ensures that individuals practice each type of yoga depending on their own Integral Psychograph and personal temperaments. Some are more inclined toward devotion, others toward contemplation. Varying lines of development may magnetize one individual to practice all five paths, others perhaps just one or two.

As Varghese points out, different yogas can even be combined and practiced together. For example, Karma Yoga can be combined with Jnana Yoga. All actions, though they appear to be separate in the relative world, are not, in their deeper reality, separate from God. Karma Yoga can be combined with Bhakti Yoga (prior to, in the midst of, and after all actions one dedicates the results to God). Finally, Bhakti Yoga and Hatha Yoga can be combined to form a type of full-bodied prayer or devotional dance.

Even with some of the complexities described above, an analysis cannot move beyond a critical postmodern perspective unless it also includes a greater sensitivity to nuances of development. Although the Hindu traditions may have had some intuitive understanding of the stages of ultimate concern might unfold, they certainly didn't posses the type of academic research uncovered by developmentalists over the past several decades.

As shown throughout the rest of this chapter, the stages of religious orientation flourish within the Hindu traditions. Because the Hindu systems developed in a fairly open environment of acceptance and embrace, we find that over time each stage on the ladder of spiritual development has been clearly expressed. As with all traditions, the particular characteristics of how each of the stages of religious orientation manifests according to the cultural, linguistic, and historical paradigm into which it is embedded. The examples below provide at least an initial word as to why a deeper engagement of developmental research is a necessity for religious scholarship of the future.

Magic Hinduism

Magic Hinduism refers to an expression of the tradition that focuses on power and is often steeped in rituals. (Often these rituals have lost any deeper meaning.) Early Hindu texts, called the Vedas, were originally composed by sages who likely possessed a magic level of religious orientation.[233] The teachings of the Rig Veda, for instance, consisted "mostly of prayers, invocations, and metaphysical speculations." The Artha Veda was composed of "magical spells and incantations."[234]

Today, as magic levels unfold, rituals are performed as ends in themselves without much awareness of transcendent meaning. Within the Hindu systems, adherents at a red altitude make offerings to deities from an egocentric perspective, often leaving them sweets, flowers, and milk in hope of *personal gain*. At this stage, religious practice, ritual and prayer focus solely on exterior elements (i.e., gods, goddesses, deities) rather than interior reflection and contemplation.[235]

Each developmental altitude finds its own peak at some point in history. Scholar Georg Feuerstein explains the important role ritual sacrifice (yajna) played in the peak of magic Hinduism during early Vedic times: "Every household had its own daily sacrificial ceremony to perform. In addition, the village or tribe came together on special occasions to participate in large-scale sacrifices, such as the famous fire sacrifice (*agni-shtoma*) and the horse sacrifice (*ashva-medha*), which was performed especially to ensure the reign of a successful king."[236] Daily sacrifices made by husband and wife included "invocations to Indra (the god of lightning and war), Agni (the fire god), and other deities of the Vedic pantheon. The purpose of the sacrifice was to win the favor of a particular deity."[237] At red altitude, sacrifice is performed in exchange for personal wish-fulfillment.

As the example above clearly shows, those performing rites and rituals at this level of development believe they might actually be able to influence the natural world around them. Using the model of developmental religious pluralism to determine religious orientation, signs of intuitive-projective faith would help to affirm a categorization at magic altitude. Similarly, this stage uses spells and sacrifices through devotion to the gods in hopes of gaining their "favor" for personal, often egocentric gains or protection. If inferring religious orientation through secondary indicators, ego development at this stage is likely to have not progressed beyond the self-protective stage.

A magic orientation in Hinduism is also likely to be marked by a preoccupation with special powers called *siddhis*. These powers include claims to things such as levitation or invisibility (feats analogous to Christian miracles).[238] Feuerstein explains, "the practitioners of Hatha Yoga have sometimes sacrificed their highest spiritual aspirations and settled for lesser, perhaps magical, goals in service of the ego-personality. Magic, like exo-technology, is a way of manipulating the forces of Nature, whereas spirituality is about the transcendence of the manipulative ego-personality."[239] Exhibiting a unique obsession with the potential power latent within the physical body, these adherents are likely to offer secondary indicators near Graves' level called "power-gods" on his values scale.

Mythic Hinduism

In our current era, mythically orientated Hindus are common in both India and the West. Mythic Hinduism is often closely linked with an emphasis on the great stories and tales from both the Mahabharata and the Ramayana (two of the world's longest epic poems).

Today, as a sign of the shifting currents of evolution, Hindu adherents are more likely to be familiar with the mythic tales of the Bhagavad-Gita (the most famous story within the Mahabharata) than with the many of the ritual and spiritual tenets of the Vedas that were composed using a magic level of orientation. Hindu scholar Arvind Sharma agrees: "The Gita is not part of sruti or revelation proper in Hinduism, and yet has come to enjoy at least a similar status and is certainly more widely known than the Vedas."[240] From a mythic level of orientation, some stories are believed to be not only unique tales of insight (as they might be seen at later levels of development), but as literal historical events whose stories should be taken to heart with great care.

This type of literal interpretation of the Ramayana, by mythic adherents, led to catastrophic events in 1992. Details of the events that came to pass help to demonstrate how a strict mythic interpretation of faith can lead to excessive ethnocentric conflict.

According to reports from 1992, Indian Muslims tore down a sacred Hindu temple in India and erected a mosque in its place. Hindus with a mythic level of orientation made the matters even worse. The very site on which the old temple rested and the new mosque was built was said to be the birthplace of the god Rama himself. In other words, mythic tales and stories passed down through generations and recorded in parts of the Hindu cannon described that the god Rama was actually born at a specific place on Indian soil. As a result, those with a mythic Hindu orientation concluded that the place of his birth should remain a sacred Hindu monument.

Members of the Hindu community were outraged and eventually managed to gather in protest. Fowler's mythic-literal stage of faith development reinforced the group dynamics. Later that year, the mosque was rampaged and demolished by Hindu activists, instigating riots and bloodshed on both sides which resulted in thousands of deaths.[241]

Mythic-Moderate Hinduism: M.S. Golwalker
Health: Moderate   Stage: Mythic

Other examples of mythic religious orientation are prominent among Hindu nationalists. Describing one example of Hindu nationalism the Rastirya Svayamsevak Sangh (R.S.S.), Klaus Klostermaier writes, "Hindu nationalists always had a sense of divine mission. They believed that the Hindus were a chosen people and that Hindu *dharma* was there to save the world." He continues as he quotes M.S. Golwalker, the second Sarsanghachalak (leader and philosophical guide) of the R.S.S.:

> The Mission of reorganizing the Hindu people on the lines of their unique national genius which the Sangh has taken up is not only a great process of true national regeneration of Bharat but also of the inevitable precondition to realize the dream of world unity and human welfare…. It is the grand world-unifying thought of *Hindus alone* [my italics] that can supply the abiding basis for human brotherhood…. This knowledge is in the safe custody of the Hindus alone.[242]

The phrase "Hindus alone" refers to a key indicator of an ethnocentric (mythic) level of development.

A mythically orientated individual often shows secondary indicators of values development centering around Graves' "truth force." Other secondary indicators like ego development cause the individual to express signs of Loevinger's "conformist stage." At the mythic level of religious orientation in the Hindu tradition there is a tendency to turn to structure and hierarchy to help organize the world. Often this impulse results in a stringent reliance or even promotion of the Hindu caste system.[243] The social reforms of India brought about, in part, by those who developed to authentic rational orientations within Hinduism, have made progress in improving some of the oppressive possibilities that emerge from mythic interpretations of the Hindu faiths.

Rational Hinduism

As is so often the case, more mature forms of religious orientation find ways to extract the deeper meaning behind the rituals and myths of the earlier stages. In Christianity, we saw this described as the "de-mythologizing" of religion. Here, in the Hindu context, Aurobindo describes how the Vedas did indeed contain similar knowledge to the Upanishads, however, they lacked the sufficient language and ability to communicate the message with the same clarity. Aurobindo explains:

> The Veda possesses the high spiritual substance of the

Upanishads, but lacks their phraseology; it is an inspired knowledge as yet insufficiently equipped with the intellectual and philosophical terms. We find a language of poets and illuminates to whom all experience is real, vivid, sensible, even concrete, not yet of thinkers and systemitizers to whom the realities of the mind and soul have become abstractions.[244]

Just as we saw in the other traditions, rational Hinduism is most often determined through primary signs of Fowler's individuative-reflective stage of faith development. At this level of Hindu expression, practitioners begin to reflect upon their practices and rituals. A critical lens is acquired at this stage through which one questions, scrutinizes, and dives deeply into the meaning behind their actions.

The Upanishads are perfect examples of how sages moved beyond the magic orientation offered in the Vedas to compose sutras using strict and pragmatic forms of logic.[245] A Hindu at the rational stage of development turns the lens of self-reflection inward and makes experience and experimentation the primary focus.

In many cases, the rational stage of Hinduism transcends an exclusive identification with the myths and stories so valued by previous altitudes. At the rational stage of Hinduism, cosmic myths and tales are either replaced by or complemented with contemplative philosophical treatises. If myths are held over from previous stages, the rational level of religious orientation reconfigures and reinterprets the once mythic ideas to accommodate a more modern worldview. An example helps to reiterate the point.

Rational-Moderate Hinduism: S. Radhakrishnan
Health: Moderate   Stage: Rational

As a Hindu progresses from mythic to rational stages of religious orientation, it's probable that a metaphysical concept like reincarnation will hold true. However, at the rational level of development, the adherent will abandon certain aspects of the magic and mythic interpretations. For instance, the notion that one might reincarnate as a lower life form such as an animal no longer holds very much weight. Radhakrishnan elaborates on a similar idea expressed through a rational lens: "When it is said that the human soul suffers the indignity of animal life, the suggestion is figurative not literal. It means that it is reborn in an irrational existence comparable to animal life and not that it is actually attached to the body of an animal."[246] This type of reconfiguration and reinterpretation is common as mythic beliefs are translated into a rational world space.

Radhakrishnan goes on to declare more of his rational religious orientation:

> The [rational] Hindu attitude to the Vedas is one of trust tempered by criticism, trust because the beliefs and forms which helped our fathers are likely to be of use to us also; criticism because, however valuable the testimony of passages may be, it cannot deprive the present age of its right to inquire and sift the evidence.[247]

Radhakrishnan continues as he explains that in his opinion Hinduism must be in line with modern science:

> Besides, our interpretation of religious experience must be in conformity with the findings of science. As knowledge grows, our theology develops. Only those parts of the tradition which are logically coherent are to be accepted as superior to the evidence of the senses, and not the whole tradition.[248]

In the above quote, Radhakrishnan delivers some of the core elements that stem from a rational lens. His view is based on both reason and evidence.

In the same line of thought as Radhakrishnan, the yogic practices established in India parallel the modern scientific progress of the West in three important ways: (1) Yogic practices begin with a hypothesis. In many schools of thought, this hypothesis claims that the ultimate nature of reality is nondual. (2) They offer a set of tests one can perform to test the hypothesis (often meditation, mantra, posture, etc.) (3) They require one to analyze the results. If one engages in specific yoga practices, he or she will be able to determine for his or her self whether or not the practices actually allow one to view reality as nondual. Yogas (various paths to liberation) and their exposition by Pantanjali were some of the first systems developed specifically to lead practitioners to Self-realization using a scientific method.

Using his own evolutionary model, based on the work of Jean Gebser, Feuerstein concurs, writing that "the psychospiritual technology of Yoga is the product of the early mental [rational] structure of consciousness." [249]

To conclude, one final example of rational Hinduism helps to ground the theory even further. Let us look into the case of Mahatma Gandhi. As a direct result of primary indicators pointing to individuative-reflective faith development, and secondary indicators expressing post-conventional moral development, Gandhi's decisions are made using his own internal compass of right and wrong. Rather than relying on the given and accepted social structure or scripture for answers, Sharma provides a narrative that explains the process by which Gandhi derived his moral reasoning.

Gandhi was once asked: "Where do you find the seat of authority?" Gandhi answered, "It lies here (pointing to his breast). I exercise my judgment about every scripture, including the Gita. I cannot let a scriptural text supersede my reason. Whilst I believe that the principal books are inspired, they suffer from a process of double distillation. Firstly, they come through human prophet, and then through the commentaries of interpreters. Nothing in them comes from God directly." [250]

Clearly, Gandhi shows signs of a post-conventional moral development. Rather than simply accept the accepted social norms as truth, each teaching must pass through his own moral reasoning to ensure it is as sound as possible. Any individual who has successfully passed through the filters of a rational stage of development will recognize Gandhi's approach.

Pluralistic Hinduism

Many are the names of God and infinite the forms through which He may be approached. In whatever name and form you worship Him, through that He will be realized by you.

Ramakrishna[251]

Religious pluralism is deeply embedded into the teachings and scripture of Hinduism. In fact, it can be said that because tolerance and pluralistic ideals are stated explicitly in scripture, Hinduism has an explicitly tolerant *shape*.[252]

Some pluralistic Hindus explain that spirituality and religion cannot be defined separately from everyday life. According to these adherents, making a distinction such as "I am a Hindu and you are a Christian" fails to acknowledge our fundamental interconnectedness and the underlying unity that we all share. Basing their argument on ancient Hindu teachings, like the one quoted above among others,[253] these individuals believe that Hinduism offers glimpses into a larger perspective called the Santana Dharma or eternal truth. In other words, all religious traditions are part of the same larger family comprising a single lineage in devotion to the one true ultimate reality.

These pluralistic beliefs are reinforced by Indian teachers who say, "Truth is one, but the people describe it in different ways. Those on journey to Eternity may differ, but once reached there, all differences sink into oneness."[254] Although acknowledging a diversity of perspectives, these individuals also value the deeper structures that each path can reveal.

Although the notion of Sanatana Dharma might sound like the inclusivist Christian strategy of Knitter, explained in chapter 4, the two should not be reduced to the other. The all-encompassing view of the Hindu pluralists who authentically express pluralistic values do not believe that all other religions are mere shadows of Hinduism. Rather a pluralistic Hindu acknowledges and values the significant differences in other traditions while simultaneously recognizing that all paths lead to God.

The pluralistic level of development, as we see below in our explication of the great sage Ramaskrishna, is first and foremost dependent on one's capacity to understand the relative nature of reality. The true pluralist understands that there is no such thing as an objective view void of obscuration and conditioning based on perspective. Hence, the Hindu pluralist understands that reality can only be determined within the matrix of inter-subjective experience with multiple paths and patterns to connect to shared reality.

Pluralistic-Moderate Hinduism: Ramakrishna
Health: Moderate   Stage: Pluralistic

Ramakrishna is an exemplary example of a modern-day saint expressing behavioral and interpretive signs of a pluralistic level of religious orientation. Ramakrishna's worldview allowed him to see a reality whose hallmark was harmony rather than disarray. Ramakrishna explains it in his own words:

> Men may partition their lands by measuring rods and boundary lines, but no one can so partition the all-embracing sky over head. The sky surrounds all and includes all. So the unenlightened man in his ignorance says that his religion is the only true religion and that it is the best. But when his heart is illumined by the light of true knowledge, he comes to know that above all these wars of sects and creeds is the one Existence-Knowledge-Bliss.[255]

Ramakrishna understood the powerful role religion might play as a unitive rather than divisive force in the world.

The life and work of Ramakrishna offers several signs pointing to a conjunctive level of faith development on Fowler's scale. For instance, after Ramakrishna gained full realization (moksha/liberation) from within the Hindu tradition, he began to reach out to other religious systems. His conjunctive level of faith allowed him the capacity to hold what appeared to be opposing ideas. Ramakrishna explains his immersion in the Islamic faith:

> I devoutly repeated the name of Allah, wore a cloth like the Arab Moslems, said their prayers five times daily and felt disinclined even to see images of the Hindu gods and goddesses, much less worship them—for the Hindu way of thinking had disappeared altogether from my mind. I spent three days in that mood, and I had the full realization of the sadhana [spiritual practice] of their faith.[256]

After dedicating his time to each tradition he claimed to have also realized the truths contained within both Christianity and Islam despite the external or exoteric discrepancies between religions.

Rather than jeopardizing his commitment to his tradition, as many religious adherents at lower levels often fear, Ramakrishna was able to deepen his devotion. Supplementing his own tradition with the ideas and practices of others allowed Ramakrishna to communicate his message to countless more individuals as an *insider* of their respective faiths.

Integral Hinduism

One of the greatest exponents of an integral version of Hinduism is the late, modern sage Sri Aurobindo Ghose. Aurobindo consistently pushed humanity to evolve to its fullest capacity. One secondary indicator that may point to an individual at integral levels of orientation is what Graves would call "global view" values. Beck and Cowen describe global-view values as a "focus on the good of all living entities as integrated systems."[257] Using a lens dedicated to integrating systems of thought and action, Aurobindo envisioned a revolutionary form of spirituality.

Upon reaching a turquoise altitude in religious orientation, one may also show clear signs of what Jane Loevinger and Susanne Cook-Greuter call the integral stages of ego-development. Cook-Greuter calls the higher of the two stages unitive/ego-aware, signifying a stable realization that has transcended the lower self (ego) and now rests in the higher Self. Aurobindo describes his own expression of a higher stage of ego development:

> In the last state of the soul's infinity and freedom all outward
> standards are replaced or laid aside and there is only a
> spontaneous and integral obedience to the Divine with
> whom we are in union and an action spontaneously fulfilling
> the integral spiritual truth of our being and nature.[258]

At these advanced levels of ego development acting in accordance with
and even as the Divine is a spontaneous overflow of being and action.[259]

Aurobindo has been perhaps the most apt modern sage to describe
the Hindu path from its higher altitudes. Testifying to and clearly
expressing Fowler's highest stage of faith (Universalizing), Aurobindo
explains that the path does not end with liberation (moksha). In fact
with the final liberation granted by moksha, one no longer has a desire
to escape the world or the realm of birth and rebirth (samsara). Rather,
union with the Divine is like being swept away by a warm current,
allowing one's own being to open up as a channel for the Divine to
interact in the evolving world. Aurobindo quotes from the Bhagavata
Purana: "I desire not the supreme state with all its eight siddhis nor
cessation of rebirth; may I assume the sorrow of all creatures who
suffer and enter into them so that they may be made free from grief."[260]
Although one might become ultimately freed through liberation, one
can overflow to new levels of fullness as new levels of complexity emerge
and the realization is shared with others. Aurobindo's outpouring of
compassion and care for others is a sure sign of the highest stages of
complexity and care. We can align his worldview here with Kosmo-
centric stages of unfolding.

Paralleling what James Fowler calls "universalizing faith,"
Aurobindo describes the culmination of the Hindu spiritual path:

> The truest reason why we must seek liberation is not to
> be delivered, individually, from the sorrow of the world,
> though that deliverance too will be given to us, but that we
> may be one with the Divine, the Supreme, the Eternal....
> This liberation and perfection are the divine Will in us, the
> highest truth of our self in Nature, the always intended goal
> of a progressive manifestation in the universe. The divine
> Nature, free and perfect and blissful, must be manifested in
> the individual in order that it may manifest in the world.[261]

And so it is, as evolution continues to march forward and new
developmental levels of intelligence emerge, even this integral level of
religious orientation will be transcended by higher levels of emergence.

EVIDENCE AND EXAMPLES from

Hinduism ॐ

Swami Durgananda
(Sally Kempton)

Ramakrishna

Radhakrishnan

Many Members of the
Bharatiya Janata Party

Many interpretations
of the Yajurveda

Magic   Mythic   Rational   Pluralistic   Integral

Chapter 7
The Buddhist Conveyor Belt

Snapshot of Buddhism

There are almost four million Buddhists alive today, making it the fourth largest of our world's religious traditions.[262] Like all of the traditions discussed in part 2, Buddhism is not a homogeneous block that is easily described without careful attention to detail. Taking the contributions of postmodern scholarship seriously, any description of Buddhism must begin with at least three essential questions that help to contextualize which version of Buddhism we seek to address.

First, we must make clear *where* the particular version of Buddhism to be discussed geographically resides. Next, we need to know *when* in history the form of Buddhism is arising. Third, we need to know something about the religious adherent interpreting the tradition and putting it into practice. If we can answer each of these questions and successfully -- identify a historical time period, a place with a particular cultural context and a general idea of the identity of the practitioner (social context, gender, etc.) -- then we have a better chance to avoid the oversimplified mistakes of modern scholars.

This chapter, as with all of our chapters, employs as much postmodern nuance as possible. Simultaneously, I ensure that the main points of the chapter are not lost in the particularities of scholarly carefulness. When a main point of interest risks being diluted, I take the liberty to make the details of the more nuanced postmodern approach implicit rather than explicit.

Looking at the Buddhist tradition using the broadest lens, one immediately notices that the Buddhist diaspora has spread throughout the entire globe. Since its birth on the border between what is now India and Nepal, Buddhism has successfully migrated to China, Tibet, Southeast Asia, Japan, Europe, Russia, Africa, the Americas, Australia, and the Pacific. In each new cultural setting, Buddhism recalibrates to meet the particular needs of its given host country.

Buddhist leaders like Ogyen Trinley Dorje, the 17th Karmapa[263] of the Kagyu lineage of Tibetan Buddhism, are quick to acknowledge Buddhism's capacity to adapt and evolve:

> As I see it religion must adapt to the changing needs of the people. The way things appear to people in the world is changing. And it is the responsibility of religion to adapt to these changes. We should try to preserve what is useful about our spiritual and religious perspective, and leave aside what is not useful. Human Psychology is evolving. As it evolves, we need to adapt spiritual customs to address the needs of individuals.[264]

Buddhism's ability to travel and integrate into diverse cultures and among diverse groups of people throughout many different historical epochs is one of its most admirable strengths. Buddhism continually finds a way to maintain its essence while simultaneously evolving to meet a plurality of needs.

Before going into too much detail about the tradition as a whole, it is useful to point to several misunderstandings that continue to surround Buddhism. For example, many Westerners continue to struggle with the notion that Buddhism lacks the one fundamental aspect that the three monotheistic Western traditions hold as central: a personal God. That is to say, unlike Judaism, Islam, and Christianity, Buddhism does not have a central teaching about a Divine Creator or Supreme Being.

Although adherents do respect and revere the historical figure of the Buddha, it would be an error to conflate this reverence to Judeo-Christian norms of theistic worship. According to Harvard professor Diana Eck, the Buddhist tradition goes to great lengths to explicitly state the fact that the Buddha was not divine: "When two wayfarers met the newly enlightened one, they asked, 'Are you a heavenly being? A God? An angel?' And he responded, 'No, I am awake.'"[265] The Buddhist delegates from Parliament of the World's Religions in 1993 make a similar argument:

> We would like to make it known to all that the Shakyamuni Buddha...was not God or a god. He was a human being who attained full enlightenment through meditation and showed us the path of spiritual awakening and freedom.[266]

They go on to say, "Buddhism is not a religion of God. Buddhism is a religion of wisdom, enlightenment, and compassion."[267]

Astonished by the degree of explanation that was required to deliver the point home, the Buddhist representatives were confronted with just how deep some cultural and religious biases can be. Even after 100 years of inter-religious dialogue, non-Buddhists still struggle with the concept.[268]

Historically, some Westerners with more clarity did make attempts to ease the confusion among their non-Buddhists compatriots. In an American culture where modern consciousness had not yet developed a postmodern sensitivity to cultural difference, there was a strong tendency to simply take the ideal of the Buddha and line it up with a more culturally familiar notion of a Supreme Being. Henry David Thoreau, for instance, acknowledged the difficulty that some fellow Westerners may have when he first articulated his deep reverence for the Buddha, "I know that some will have hard thoughts of me, when they hear their Christ named beside my Buddha."[269]

Other historical American figures like Colonel Henry Steele Olcott, tried to explain the concept of "no divinity" to an eager, although confused American constituent. In 1882, when Olcott conducted a question-and-answer exposition to help clarify the Buddhist tradition to those individuals more familiar with Western Protestantism, he was asked the same types of questions. In one occurrence a participant asked, "Was the Buddha God?" Upon his response, the group struggled to grasp the fact that within Buddha dharma there is no "divine" incarnation.[270] In both cases, Olcott and Thoreau did their best to sympathize with non-Buddhists still trapped in a modern monolithic cultural paradigm.

Common confusions and superficial essentializations about divinity aside, many Westerners are beginning to realize that Buddhism offers a vast variety of philosophical and psychological insight of significant relevance to our postmodern era. Although levels of understanding vary within all Buddhist traditions, as the evidence in this book demonstrates, it is useful to look at one particular cultural representation of Buddhism to provide the reader with at least some degree of generalized orientation about the tradition itself. Let us now turn to the cultural derivation of Buddhism that arose on the Tibetan plateau.

The Tibetan Buddhist system offers at least three specific orientations toward practice within the complexities of its sociocultural contours. These three broad orientations are often differentiated as the householder, the celibate monk, and the wandering Tantric yogi. When examined through a comparative lens one discovers that the three spiritual paths share both commonalities and differences.

At the most basic level any practicing Buddhist within the Tibetan cultural context, takes refuge in the three jewels: the Buddha, the Dharma, and the Sangha. Each of the three jewels can be expanded and explained one at a time.

Buddha: One takes refuge in the Buddha with the acknowledgement that the Buddha represents an experiment in consciousness that can be repeated by any human being. All humans have the innate capacity to awaken to a perspective that sees the world *nakedly* as it really is. This awakened perspective usually means a vantage point of unbroken non-duality.

Dharma: One takes refuge in the Dharma when he or she acknowledges the truth revealed in the Buddhist scripture and makes a commitment to follow the path to awakening.

Sangha: Finally, to take refuge in the Sangha, one must acknowledge and actively engage the trust and support of the community of fellow dharma practitioners.

In addition to taking refuge all Tibetan Buddhists also commit to the bodhisattva vow. The vow can be stated as follows: *I vow to cultivate the right view of reality as quickly as possible so that I may help release the countless other sentient beings into their own primordial awareness.* As one's commitment to the Bodhisattvic path increases, it is said that six particular perfections arise as a result. These six perfections or what can be called the Mahayana Virtues are generosity, morality, patience, courage, meditation, wisdom.[271]

Beyond this common foundation, differences in practice begin to arise depending on the specific characteristics of the individual practitioner.

Householder

The Tibetan cultural variation of Buddhism recognizes that not everyone is fit for monkhood. As a result, all adherents who decide to maintain a life engaged in the world pursue the path of the householder. Householders are free to earn a living (right livelihood), marry, and raise a family. The householder path has only minimal religious requirements but in exchange is often marked by the highest degree of social responsibility. Because of the householder's degree of social duty he or she is often categorized as treading the steepest and most difficult path to enlightenment.

In addition to the common Buddhist commitment of taking refuge in the three jewels (the Buddha, the Dharma, and the Sangha), the householder, at almost any level of structural development, commits to the *upasaka* vows, also called the five vows of a layman: not lying, not killing, not stealing, not engaging in sexual misconduct, and not indulging in personal adornments.[272] As we shall see, in each of the three orientations toward practice, vows play a vital role.

In addition to the social responsibilities of maintaining a family through "right livelihood," the householder engages in daily practices to cultivate merit and to train proper meditative awareness. Some more significant religious practices occur annually for extended periods of time. Roger Jackson describes one particular practice undertaken by the laity called *nyungne* (a fasting ritual lasting three days).[273] Filling the three days with "prayer, prostration, and ascetic practices focused on the great compassionate bodhisattva Avalokiteshvara," lay individuals temporarily release themselves from the social responsibility of being a householder, and find themselves completely absorbed in a life of exoteric spiritual practice.

Monk

Like the householder, the celibate monk also takes refuge in the three jewels and five vows. A monk, however, has a list of vows much longer and more demanding than the average practitioner. This list of commitments is expressed in the *pratimoksa* and *bodhisattva* vows[274] for all monks seeking full ordination.[275]

As part of the Tibetan Vajrayana tradition, the main goal of the Tibetan monk is twofold: (1) to focus relentlessly and continuously on the realization of enlightenment and (2) to share this realization with all other sentient beings. When all otherworldly obligations are removed to prevent obstacles to this realization, the monk is able to focus all of his or her single-pointed determination on the goal.

The diversity of praxis available to a celibate monk is voluminous. For instance, in addition to usual daily duties and responsibilities of upholding the monastery and studying scripture, a monk may partake in any number of meditations or visualization practices in order to perfect his own state of realization. One practice in particular as outlined by Janet Gyatso, in her article "An Avalokiteshvara Sadhana," is a practice called For All Beings Throughout Space. A brief look into the practice will provide the reader with a solid flavor of the Tibetan tradition.

In this particular practice, individuals visualize the bodhisattva of compassion Avalokiteshvara in order to "accomplish" identification with him.[276] As Gyatso explains, "It is believed that by visualizing themselves as having the prescribed features of the Buddha figure in these three dimensions—as looking like the Buddha figure, as chanting its mantra, and as assuming its mental state—the meditator will eventually become that Buddha in reality."[277] Tantric, or Vajrayana, Buddhism is rich with elaborate visualizations like the one described above.

Yogi

One final categorization helps to distinguish the multitude of paths within the Tibetan tradition. Beyond the householder and the celibate monk lies the category of the wandering Tantric yogi. Often Tantric yogins are called "great accomplished ones" or *mahasiddhis*.[278] Known for their lifestyle of complete and total freedom, mahasiddhas believed that the essence of enlightenment was present throughout reality, and thus any ordinary activity could be transformed into a Buddhist activity by directing it toward awakening the mind itself... Their special method of transforming daily activities into meditation practices involved seeing mundane things as mudra, as "seals" or "symbols" of deeper truths.[279]

As a common practice, the mahasiddhas transformed spiritual teachings into songs. Such songs were then passed down through oral teachings. Sages like Naropa, Milarepa, Tilopa, and Saraha represent the great lineage of mahasiddhas. As the Nalanda Translation Committee explains in Donald Lopez's *Religions of Tibet in Practice*, "each line [of their songs] implied or evoked a special symbolic 'code' meaning."[280] Embedded in each line of their songs, detailed meditation instructions are provided by the mahasiddhas on how to wake up the mind. For instance, one example of this type of pithy instruction is found in the book the *Songs of Naropa*. Here the great sage Tilopa instructs an exhausted Naropa:

> This self-knowing, while one is still defiled,
> Does not depend on other things,
> So self-existing wakefulness is just this.[281]

In these three simple lines, Tilopa points out that the true nature of Naropa's mind is always-present even when he appears to be caught in the throws of samsara.

Overall, mahasiddhas are known for their extraordinary powers acquired through the practice of yoga. Similar to the type of yoga described in chapter 6 on Hinduism, Tibetan Yoga is a sophisticated set of techniques for disciplining both body and mind.[282] Just as meditation itself fine-tunes the mind, yoga, as practiced by wandering Tantrics, purifies the various subtle energy channels of the body leading to extraordinary abilities and special powers called *siddhis*.[283]

Although useful for heuristic purposes, even the above description with its application of at least some degree of cultural sensitivity and appreciation of identity is still oversimplified. We still need a more sophisticated model that can bring more granularity to religious analysis beyond the postmodern paradigm.

Just as we explored in the previous three traditions, evidence exists within the Buddhist tradition to support the theory of stages of religious orientation. It is only when a more nuanced lens of developmental sensitivity is brought into the dialogue that our scholarship might enter an even deeper and more sophisticated conversation. We begin the analysis with examples of magic levels of Buddhist interpretation and practice and then proceed to provide examples from the rest of the developmental spectrum accordingly.

Magic Buddhism

Religious traditions that evolved out of the leadership of one particular charismatic individual demonstrate several unique characteristics, one of which is the fact that the system of belief is dramatically shaped by the specific religious orientation of the founder. Outside of the Jewish and Hindu traditions, most of the teachings that have become institutionalized were delivered through a particular psychograph of a specific person, with varying degrees of both structural development and different typologies.[284]

With this understanding in place, we notice that Buddhism entered our world through the psychograph of Siddhartha Gautama, the Buddha. It is likely that the Buddha was developmentally advanced for the time period in which he lived. With the luxurious conditions of his youth and all his basic needs met, life conditions afforded him plenty of time to grow and develop. In Abraham Maslow's Hierarchy of Needs stratum, The Buddha had all of his "deficiency needs" met, and could begin focusing on "being needs" like self-actualization and self-transcendence.[285]

Despite living over two millennia ago, developmental signs point to the fact that the Buddha may have reached a rational level of religious orientation. This triumph in development was especially rare due to the fact that most others alive during his time rested at a magic altitude. It is important to note that placing Buddha at a rational orientation takes nothing away from his degree of spiritual realization. During his time period, the Buddha could have simultaneously been at both the highest altitude available (orange rational) and had access to an awakened vantage point of nondual realization.[286]

With the exception of the rare cases in which the Buddha taught students who were able to see his orange world, Buddhism was most commonly translated down at least two stages in order to meet the psychological needs of its magic-oriented adherents. For some Buddhists, the rational Eightfold Path, or the contemplation and cognitive discipline required for the realization of the Four Noble Truths, so familiar to us today, were not the primary points of focus. Instead individuals resting at lower levels of religious orientation catalyzed other avenues of teaching and emphasis.

For example, we see that those at a magical stage of orientation developed a pantheon of gods and goddesses through which they could better understand the teachings of the Buddha.[287] "Of the 'countless' heavenly Buddhas and Bodhisattvas, some of the named ones became the focus of devotion as savior beings, with specific great beings also symbolizing and exemplifying specific spiritual qualities."[288] By focusing attention on exterior beings representing emotions and qualities, those at magical levels of orientation find legitimacy in teachings that might otherwise be beyond their capacity.

Magic-Moderate Buddhism: Many Adherents to Amitabha and Pure Land Buddhism
Health: Moderate   Stage: Magic

One prime example of Buddhism expressed through a magic lens revolves around Amitabha Buddha. This is not to say that all expressions of Pure Land Buddhism are at this level nor is it to say that somehow the religion itself is magic; of course, just as with all traditions, forms of Pure Land Buddhism have evolved as higher altitudes emerged. It is to say, however, that certain expressions that originate at this stage are easily interpreted through a magic lens.

Amitabha Buddha is of central importance in Pure Land schools of Eastern Buddhism.[289] It is believed that all of those who merely recite the name of Amitabha prior to death will be saved from further suffering. As a reward, these devout individuals will be reborn into the realm of the Pure Land. According to D.T. Suzuki:

> Pure Land devotional practices attracted monks and nuns who could not find spiritual solace in existing practices. It also opened gates of enlightenment to the general populace that had been excluded from the path. Although existing on the fringes of the major Buddhist schools, Pure Land became a powerful [way] of transcending this world of delusion, the realm of pain and suffering.[290]

Fowler's mythic-literal faith is most commonly exhibited at this level of religious orientation. Those at this stage interpret the Happy Land Sutra literally. Aspirants of Pure Land schools with a red orientation claim that in the Pure Land, "beings [will] be in their final life, of immeasurable length, except for bodhisattvas, wishing to be reborn elsewhere to aid beings. Its inhabitants [will] have the highest 'perfections.'"[291] This belief structure, similar to the Christian snake handlers, is egocentric in its orientation. For example, "If I repeat the name of Amitabha, I will be reborn in the Pure Land." This type of repetition is not concerned with immediate family or social group (although certainly may extend to such as it is translated up the spectrum of development).

1. Using secondary indicators, those subscribing to this system of belief often show signs of self-protective level of ego development. The ability to anticipate and seek reward is of great importance when one imagines the Pure Land. Recall as well that self-protective ego development propels individuals to avoid punishment. According to Paul Harvey, the Happy Land Sutra asserts that, "only someone who slanders or obstructs the Dharma cannot be reborn [in the Pure Land]."[292] Harvey's example, once again, demonstrates the tendency of a magic orientation, as it sets up systems for personal punishment and reward.

2. Magic interpretations of Pure Land Buddhism allow those who are leading selfish or even crime-ridden lives to find salvation. Harvey concludes the notion of gaining rebirth in the Happy Land has long provided a hope for people struggling with existence, living less than perfect lives. If currently unable to behave like true Bodhisattvas, the environment of the Happy Land will enable them to do so, and the immeasurably long life-span there will encompass the hugely long bodhisattva-path.[293]

3. Consequently, moral development indicators may very well show signs of pre-conventional stages. The Pure Land path offers forgiveness for all those who envision themselves as leading "less than perfect lives."

Mythic Buddhism

Mythic forms of Buddhism are widespread and tend to show up within multiple contexts and cultures. In extreme versions, mythic orientation may appear violent, as in the ethnocentric warfare of the Sinhala-Buddhists fighting with Tamil Tigers in Sri Lanka. In more moderate versions, mythic Buddhism might appear like the conventional religion we see play out in various communities of Nepal or Thailand.

Just as we saw with mythic levels of Christianity, Islam, and Hinduism, when Buddhism is expressed from the amber level of religious orientation it has several identifying characteristics. In chapter 4, we noted research conducted by Marty and Appleby describing the "family resemblances" of fundamentalists of different faiths. These characteristics include a strong sense of religious identity, strict social boundaries, and reliance on myth. Below we describe an extreme classification within mythic Buddhism as it is expressed in Sri Lanka by some Sinhala-Buddhists. These Buddhists share many if not all of the characteristics described by Marty and Appleby.

Mythic-Extreme Buddhists:
Sinhala Fundamentalism
Health: Extreme   Stage: Mythic

It is often surprising to see Buddhism expressed at ethnocentric levels. After all, we speculated that Buddhism itself entered the world through the Buddha's rational (worldcentric) psychograph. Because of this original orange altitude, the shape of Buddhism centers itself around tolerance and relaxed social barriers. However, despite its open and embracing contours, some Buddhists still proceed to explain away tolerance in the name of what they believe to be a higher good.

In the case of Sinhala-Buddhists, this higher good is Buddhism itself. The Sinhala-Buddhist fundamentalists see themselves as "protectors of the Buddhist teachings." According to Bartholomeusz:

> Sinhala-Buddhist fundamentalists identify Buddhist Sinhalas as the people who have been charged by the Buddha himself to maintain and protect Buddhism. In addition, they identify the island of Sri Lanka as dhammadipa, the island (dipa) of dhamma, the Buddhist teachings.[294]

These mythic oriented Sinhala-Buddhists show primary indicators between Fowler's mythic-literal and synthetic-conventional levels of faith development. For example, notions of ethnocentric superiority of the Sinhalese people are derived directly from the "mythohistory" called the Mahavamsa (a text composed by monks sometime around the fifth century). Taking the mythic stories as fact, adherents believe that the Buddha himself traveled to Sri Lanka and determined that it should be an island consisting of Buddhist teachings. As a result, "some modern readings of the Mahavamsa construe Tamils, the large majority of whom are Hindu, as the enemy."[295] Believing that the Buddhist path is the only true path, "the majority among fundamentalists argue that anyone can live in Sri Lanka as long as Sinhala Buddhists can enjoy cultural, religious, economic, and linguistic hegemony. Sinhala-Buddhist fundamentalism is thus inextricably linked to ethnic chauvinism, which privileges the Sinhala people above all others of the island."[296] Clearly, adherents to this orientation can be linked to our secondary indicator of an ethnocentric worldview.

Buddhist fundamentalists also express secondary signs of Graves' truth force. In protecting the island, adherents are righteous in their battle to maintain purity and goodness:

> Boundary setting (fueled by ethnic chauvinism) over who is the rightful heir to Dhammapida is tied to ideas about purity.... For Sinhala-Buddhist fundamentalists, their religion and hence their island, are vulnerable to corruption by impure forces deemed hostile to Buddhism....The protection of the dhamma thus means a focus upon purity, on only the righteous having sovereignty over dhammapida.[297]

Despite the fact that Tamils see themselves as just as adequately equipped to maintain purity of the land, these Buddhist fundamentalists refuse to abandon their ethnocentric views, infused with mythic-literal faith development and truth-force values.

Rational Buddhism

The most common interpretations of Buddhism imported to the West today arrive through a rational lens of development or higher. Unlike mythic versions of Buddhism, rational interpretations do not *exclusively* depend upon the external authority of scripture, the grace of deities, or even on the authority of the Buddha himself. Instead, the main focus of rational Buddhism becomes internal personal experience and subsequent validation by a community of the adequate (sangha). Just as we saw in Christianity, Islam, and Hinduism, a shift to a rational level of orientation occurs as a direct result of particular lines of development breaking through the orange altitudinal threshold.

Cognitive development around formal operational thinking allows the individual to critically reflect on his or her own ideology.

One can question the authority and the structure that was taken for granted at the mythic stage. As outlined above, the Buddha himself and his original teachings would be an adequate example of a rational religious orientation. Clearly the Buddha broke away from the Hindu traditions in which he was raised to uncover a new level of truth and understanding through reason and personal experience.

To take a more recent example of rational Buddhism we look at D.T. Suzuki, one of the greatest proponents of Zen Buddhism in the West.

Rational-Moderate Buddhism: D.T. Suzuki
Health: Moderate   Stage: Rational

A proper integral analysis shows that even if Suzuki did show signs of conventional or even ethnocentric altitude in some lines of development, his religious orientation was certainly rational. In fact we would say that Zen as a whole has a rational shape.[298] "According to Suzuki, religious experience is not merely a central feature of Zen, it is the whole of Zen....Zen eschews all doctrine, all ritual, all institutions..."[299]

Although any tradition, including Zen, can be hijacked by lower levels of orientation, Zen has a tendency to promote levels of interpretation that at least meet rational stages. In the Zen expressed by Suzuki, doctrine and scripture are placed as secondary to the personal experience directly observed in meditation. Along a similar line of logic, Graves' values show signs at strive-drive. Mirroring Suzuki's emphasis on testable experience, strive-drive values crown "tried and true experience" as king.

In his classic book *Introduction to Zen Buddhism*, Suzuki strictly contrasts his rational form of Zen with all forms of mythic religion as they are commonly known. When asked the question, is Zen a religion?, he responds as follows:

> It is not a religion in the sense that the term is popularly understood; for Zen has no God to worship, no ceremonial rites to observe, no future abode to which the dead are destined, and, last of all, Zen has no soul whose welfare is to be looked after by somebody else and whose immortality is a matter of intense concern with some people. Zen is free from all these dogmatic and "religious" encumbrances. When I say there is no God in Zen, the pious reader may be shocked, but this does not mean that Zen denies the existence of God;

neither denial nor affirmation concerns Zen. When a thing is denied, the very denial involves something not denied. The same can be said of affirmation. This is inevitable in logic. Zen wants to rise above logic, Zen wants to find a higher affirmation where there is no antitheses. Therefore, in Zen, God is neither denied nor insisted upon; only there is in Zen no such God as has been conceived by Jewish and Christian minds. For the same reason that Zen is not a philosophy, Zen is not a religion. [300]

Examining Suzuki's history, we see several indications that mythic levels of spiritual orientation have been abandoned and rational levels embraced. Suzuki was raised in a family practicing a type of Pure Land Buddhism known as Shin. Despite tendencies to interpret Shin Buddhism from magic and mythic levels of orientation (as described in the discussion regarding magic Buddhism), Suzuki became one of the main proponents to interpret Pure Land Buddhism using a rational lens. From an orange-level perspective, Amithaba is not understood as an external being that will save the practitioner from further suffering; instead Amithaba is seen as one's inner most self.[301]

D.T. Suzuki's Potential Psychograph

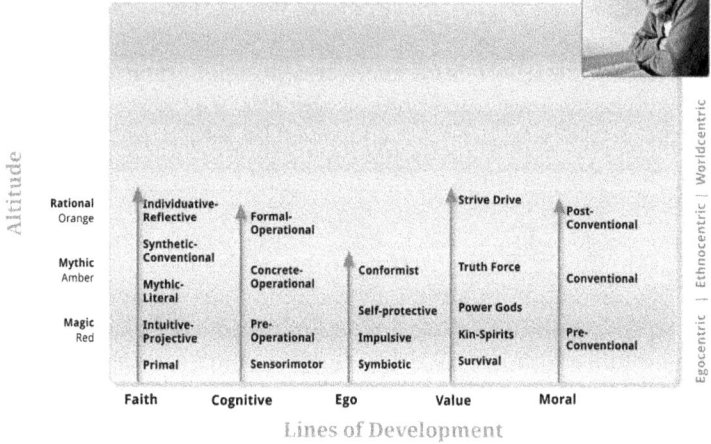

	Faith	Cognitive	Ego	Value	Moral	
Rational Orange	Individuative-Reflective	Formal-Operational		Strive Drive	Post-Conventional	
	Synthetic-Conventional					
Mythic Amber	Mythic-Literal	Concrete-Operational	Conformist	Truth Force	Conventional	
			Self-protective	Power Gods		
Magic Red	Intuitive-Projective	Pre-Operational	Impulsive	Kin-Spirits	Pre-Conventional	
	Primal	Sensorimotor	Symbiotic	Survival		

Altitude

Egocentric | Ethnocentric | Worldcentric

Lines of Development

Figure 17

Using the integral psychograph above, the trained scholar will notice that Suzuki has several areas of development that are lower in maturity levels than both his faith and cognition. Through the evidence provided in his writing, one can speculate that both his ego development and worldview rest near amber altitudes. Although this does not drastically effect his religious orientation, we do see examples of these underdeveloped lines in his comments and actions. Sharf points out that Suzuki places [his] understanding of Zen in the interests of a transparently nationalist discourse. Suzuki insisted that Zen is the wellspring of Japanese culture, and that the traditional arts of Japan— tea ceremony, monochrome painting, martial arts, landscape gardening, Noh theater, et cetera—are all ultimately expressions of Zen gnosis.... This is in marked contradistinction to the excessively materialistic and dualistic traditions of the West.[302]

Although Suzuki is indeed entitled to his opinion, one cannot help but notice the sense of privilege that he gives to his own Japanese culture over the West. This is a stark difference to the capacities that grow at the next stage of development wherein an individual in a similar circumstance would embrace both cultures to find the deepest value in each.

The case of Suzuki provides a perfect scenario as to why an integral approach using the model of developmental religious pluralism is so useful. Despite the fact that Suzuki has two lines of development stunted in growth, the Integral Psychograph allows us to contextualize these secondary indicators in reference to our primary indicator,

Suzuki's orange level of faith development.[303] This level of nuance is ideal for the type of post-postmodern scholarship necessary in the years to come.

Pluralistic Buddhism

One of the most common characteristics of green altitude is what the values scale labels "human bond." A human-bond level of values development expresses the need for deep connection, for sensitivity, for giving. Ninian Smart expresses a lens similar to that through which a pluralistic Buddhist might view the world: "The love which Christ self-emptyingly symbolizes, the compassionate non-violence which Buddhism expresses—these values are of even greater importance now than they were before..."[304] Due to a deep understanding of the interconnectedness of all beings and at least a broad understanding of the interdependency of life-systems, this stage demonstrates a drive to express care in the world stronger than any previous level of orientation.

In addition to values that show the need for human bonding, pluralistic Buddhists likely express cognitive complexity at a level wherein perspective taking is of primary importance. At this stage, paradox is no longer a problem because cognition can now hold multiple truths without contradiction. At green altitude, a type of simultaneous processing releases the mind from linear beliefs to one in which the individual understands that the more diversity of perspectives that are included in any given situation, the more accurate the snapshot of reality will be. Because Buddhism already includes a distinct focus on human psychological complexity and explicit emphasis on compassion, it easily comingles with the sensitivities and perspective taking of the pluralistic altitude.[305]

Pluralistic Moderate Buddhism: Many Involved with Socially Engaged Buddhism
Health: Moderate   Stage: Pluralistic

One prominent element of pluralistic spirituality is its preference for some form of social or global action. Proponents of Socially Engaged Buddhism tackle this issue head on. Although any given system of Buddhism can contain adherents of every level, Socially Engaged Buddhism is particularly magnetizing to those at pluralistic levels of development.

Each level of spiritual development has its own requirements for legitimacy. The pluralistic level re-labels Buddhism "Socially Engaged Buddhism" to meet its own level's prerequisites. Ken Jones in his book *The New Social Face of Buddhism* writes the following:

In its broadest definition socially engaged Buddhism extends across public engagement in caring and service, social and environmental protest and analysis, nonviolence as a creative way of overcoming conflict, and "right livelihood" and similar initiatives toward a socially just and ecologically sustainable society.[306]

To some describing Buddhism as "socially engaged" appears to be redundant. For instance, Thich Nhat Hanh makes the following argument:

Buddhism means to be awake—mindful of what is happening in ones body, feelings, mind, and in the world....If you are awake you cannot do otherwise than act compassionately to help relieve suffering you see around you. So Buddhism must be engaged in the world. If it is not engaged it is not Buddhism. [307]

Postmodern intellectual currents deeply influence those resting at a pluralistic altitude. To meet the requirements necessary to ascend to this level, cognitive development must push toward early stages of what Wilber calls "vision logic." At this stage there must be a natural competence to acknowledge all perspectives.[308]

From the pluralistic altitude one recognizes that ideas and concepts are, at least in part, molded by the culture in which they are embedded. More accurate pictures of reality only come according to the degree to which we can deconstruct our commonly accepted and culturally constructed ideas and beliefs. In the case of pluralistic Buddhism the desire to deconstruct shows up as a methodology capable of slicing through cultural baggage to reach the core of the teachings. Speaking of Socially Engaged Buddhism, Jones describes how important it is to deconstruct Buddhism to free it from its cultural baggage:

Buddhism itself—in particular as a Western import— also needs to be deconstructed as part of its own liberative agenda. With a light touch its mythic, cultural, institutional, dogmatic, and political packaging needs to be distinguished from its perennial diagnosis of and prescription for our human condition. And the subtle Western meanings imparted to Buddhism require similar treatment.[309]

In addition to serving the cultural sensitivities of the pluralistic stage, the process of deconstruction also reinforces the rational agenda that seeks to "de-mythologize."

As we have hinted in previous chapters, but not yet fully articulated, the pluralistic attitude creates emergent capacities for new levels of cooperation and collaboration. Understanding that global efforts for well-being are tasks not limited to Buddhists alone, Socially Engaged Buddhists look to other religions as complementary forces rather then opponents. Jones explains how some engaged Buddhists look to Christian ideals of external engagement to complement their own deep understanding of internal liberation:

> In their involvement in movements for peace and nonviolence, in their opposition to racism, poverty, and unemployment at home and abroad, and in the qualities that they have brought to this involvement, Christians have set an example that Buddhists are only slowly beginning to follow.[310]

At this stage the conjunctive level of faith development allows many Socially Engaged Buddhists to work together toward a common goal and look to each other to supplement their vision. Complementing an inward path of wisdom with an outward path of compassion helps to distinguish this stage.

Overall, the pluralistic stage of religious orientation has pushed beyond the mere tolerance expressed at rational levels and now fully embraces other perspectives with compassion, knowing that the diversity each perspective brings helps to make the evolutionary ecosystem even richer and more prone for success. When put to action, one sees this compassion expressed as a dedication to reducing the amount of unjust suffering in the world.

Integral Buddhism

If one examines the evolutionary progression of Buddhism from its inception around 560 BC to the present, three vertical shifts become apparent. In the Buddhist lexicon, these shifts are often referred to as the three turnings of the Wheel of Dharma. In essence, each turn represents a distinct evolution in the theory and practice of Buddhism. The three turnings of the wheel are relevant if we are to use an integral lens to see where Buddhism has been and in which direction it might be going.

The descriptions that follow are clearly oversimplifications. However they serve the purposes of creating broad brush strokes through which some patterns can be delineated. Generally speaking, the first turning of the Wheel of Dharma refers to the teachings explained in the Theravada Buddhist tradition. This turning is most notably recognized for bringing a new form of *wisdom* to the world. In the Theravada teachings, one gains a new way of perceiving the world beyond the confines of the limited self and free from the torments of everyday unhappiness.

The second turning, as explained in Mahayana Buddhism, consists of a move toward compassionate engagement; it is here that the ideal of the Bodhisattva enters the Buddhist teachings. Practice is no longer conducted primarily as a means to liberate oneself but as a means of service to all beings in the world.

Finally, the third turning of the Wheel of Dharma is called Vajrayana Buddhism. Vajrayana engages the fullest and most elaborated practices of nondual tantric teachings so that one might maintain full awakening and service at all times and in any given life circumstance. In Vajrayana, one learns to use every emotion, thought, and sensation, as a vehicle to moment-to-moment liberation.

It is commonplace for many to assume that the Wheel of Dharma has made its final turn in the Vajrayana cycle. Of course time will be the only true indicator of what is to come. However, those working within an integral paradigm suspect that a type of Buddhism is being set in motion that might be worthy of the term "a fourth turning."

Some have called this fourth turning Integral Buddhism. Using our integral lens, we can note several key characteristics that a fourth turning of the wheel of dharma would need to include. First and foremost, an integral form of Buddhism would take the rich phenomenological path of meditative states already so clearly explicated in the tradition and add to it a new post-postmodern understanding of psychological stages. An expression of Integral Buddhism would use this deep understanding of the complexity of structural development to validate and appreciate the fact that different expressions of Buddhism are appropriate depending on the level of the adherent. Along similar lines, a fourth turning would also include an understanding of how diverse cultures influence the way the tradition is interpreted. Consequently, Integral Buddhism would develop appropriate translations of its teachings for a diversity of cultural and developmental perspectives.

Integral Buddhism, as with integral versions of all traditions, would begin to acknowledge the possibility of new forms of intersubjective non-duality. Rather than isolating awakening to the confines of individual experience, Integral Buddhism builds upon the *socially engaged* attitude of Buddhist at the pluralistic altitude to explore what it is like to align with others who share both common vision and nondual awakening. The Integral Buddhist begins to realize that the power of collective enlightenment is exponentially greater than any single being working as an independent Bodhisattva. It is from an integral level of understanding that Thich Nhat Hanh's words, and others like them, start to make more sense: "The next Buddha may not take the form of an individual. In the twenty-first century the Sangha may be the body of the Buddha."[311]

A fourth turning of Buddhism would not only transcend but it would also include the very best from all previous levels. An integral form of Buddhism would include the allegorical interpretations of the myths and scripture so important at magic and mythic levels. Integral Buddhism would include the strict reason and experience required at orange altitude as well as the social responsibility and cultural sensitivity promoted by those at the pluralistic level. A fourth turning, similar to the one proposed above is being explored in various ways by spiritual teachers like Daniel P. Brown, Genpo Roshi, Diane Musho Hamilton, and Lama Surya Das.

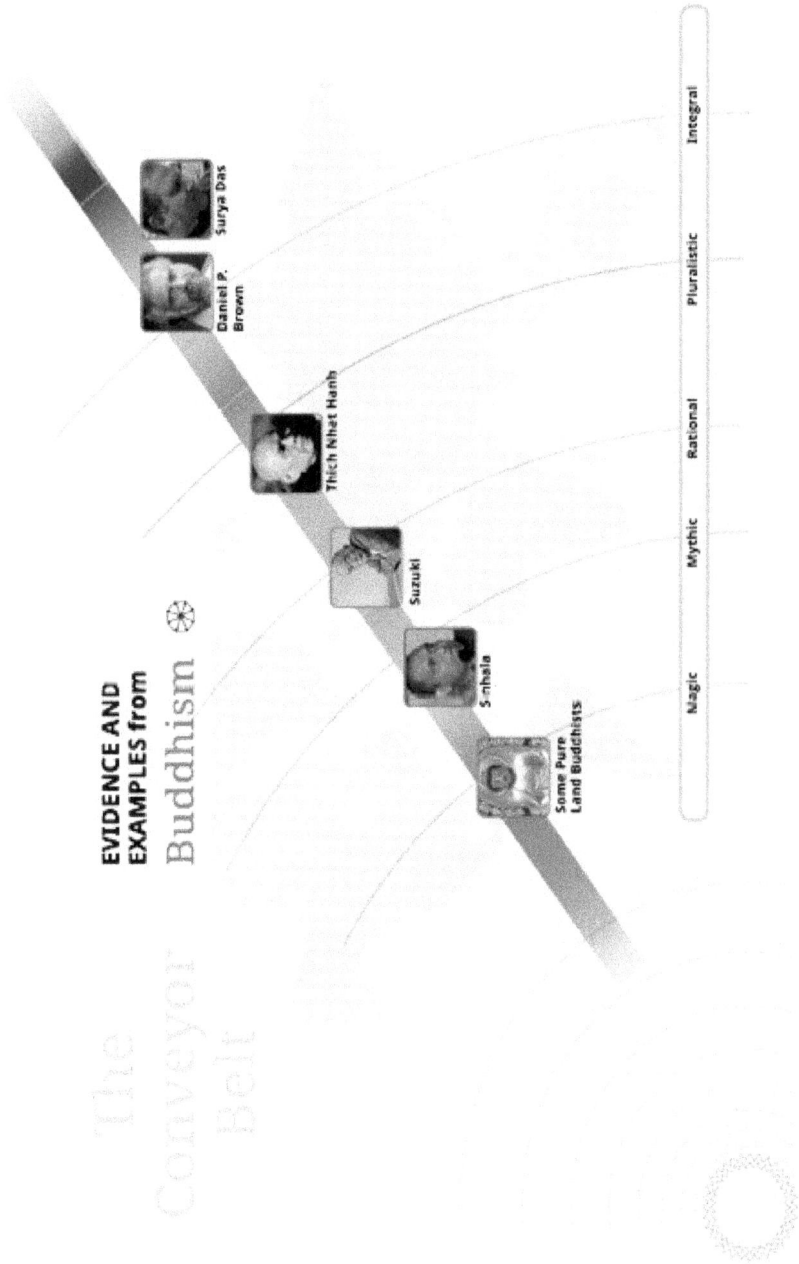

EVIDENCE AND
EXAMPLES from
Buddhism

The Conveyor Belt

Surya Das

Daniel P. Brown

Thich Nhat Hanh

Suzuki

Sinhala

Some Pure Land Buddhists

Magic   Mythic   Rational   Pluralistic   Integral

PART 3: ACTION

Chapter 8
The Future of Religious Dialogue

If we assume that the stages of religious orientation as outlined in the previous chapters are even vaguely correct, then an integral approach to religion has the power to revolutionize the way in which we engage religion and interact with religious adherents. Not only does a model that includes stages of religious orientation shift our understanding from two classifications of religious expression (extremist vs. moderate) to ten valid expressions of each religious tradition (2 degrees of health x 5 stages), but a developmental perspective also offers several astounding implications for immediate action.

One area directly influenced by a developmental approach, and the focus of this chapter, is religious dialogue.

Religious Dialogue

Because we live in an interconnected world where tolerance for the social, cultural, and religious "other" is a prerequisite for peaceful coexistence, it is a necessity that we ensure that the major world religious traditions engage in dialogue with each other. David Tracy writes, "dialogue among the religions is no longer a luxury but a theological necessity."[312] In agreement with Tracy, theologian Hans Kung's now famous statement says it succinctly:

No peace among the nations
without peace among the religions.
No peace among the religions
without dialogue between the religions.[313]

Let us first address the misperceptions about religious dialogue and the ways in which it often falls short. First and foremost, when conducted in its more sophisticated versions, religious dialogue is not just another form of pluralistic compromise. Religious scholar Gavin Flood explains that, "dialogue is not agreement or consensus, but can be the clarification of difference."[314] According to Flood, dialogue must also take into considerations the context of social discourse within which the conversation is occurring. All conversation and clarification "will necessarily entail reflexivity in delineating the boundaries of a discourse against another's," says Flood. As a starting point, Flood orients us to the fact that in its best expressions dialogue among traditions will not be composed of superficial agreements to some essentialized core, but will, on the contrary, consist of deep self-reflexivity and creative friction.

Along similar lines, Hans Kung aptly points out that dialogue must move beyond polite exchanges. "Dialogue will remain barren if it is limited to reciprocal gestures of friendship and courtesies and does not also lead to criticism of the other religion," says Kung. "However, if it is to be convincing, it must always include self-criticism."[315] Furthermore, if dialogue is to be understood and practiced correctly, it "can only take place between believing representatives of the traditions—that is, between men and women who have committed themselves wholly—in life and in death—to the integral message of their religious Way."[316] Kung correctly emphasizes that true dialogical exchange can only take place between those who have a strong commitment to a particular faith. With this commitment, however, participants must also bring openness and a willingness to be moved by the positions of others.

Using the work of the scholars listed above, we can list the characteristics that today's leading postmodern thinkers agree should be included in religious dialogue. As a foundation religious dialogue ought to include:

- Participants with a strong commitment to a particular tradition
- Participants seeking an honest understanding of the religious other
- Participants willing to be self-reflexive about the boundaries of the social discourse
- Participants willing to clarify differences
- Participants willing to criticize the religious other
- Participants willing to criticize one's own tradition
- Participants willing to be transformed by the experience

As we shall see as the chapter unfolds, these initial characteristics provide a solid platform upon which more sophisticated forms of integral religious dialogue can take place. For now, let us summarize the list above to define religious dialogue more succinctly. In the remainder of this chapter, I define religious dialogue thus: an exchange of ideas within a single tradition or between different traditions, so that both sides promote and are moved to deeper levels of understanding, respect, and mutual regard.

The Status of Dialogue Today

Both academics and world leaders show a consistent commitment to dialogue and continue to take steps in a positive direction.[317] In 2000, as the United Nations (UN) prepared to gather the heads of state for the Millennium Summit, an unprecedented gathering of preeminent religious and spiritual leaders from more than 120 countries arrived at the UN General Assembly Hall. This event, The Millennium World Peace Summit, was the beginning of an initiative for diverse faith traditions to support the United Nations and its agencies in their mission to foster peace, global understanding, and international cooperation. Joining forces in the spirit of reconciliation, progress, and dialogue more than 1200 pre-eminent men and women committed themselves to working together to solve the collective challenges of the twenty-first century.

In his opening address at the United Nations, Secretary General Kofi A. Annan emphasized the importance of the event: "This summit of religious and spiritual leaders is without doubt one of the most inspiring gatherings ever held here."[318] Sealing Secretary General Annan's conviction, the summit successfully delivered all that it promised, resulting in a common declaration signed by every religious leader in attendance to collaborate towards the dissolving of all animosity and disruption resulting from religious illiteracy, indifference, and intolerance. This proclamation of peace marked the largest written consensus among religious leaders that the world has yet to witness.

Influenced at least in part by the success of the Millennium Summit, the United Nations showed even further proof that there was serious international commitment to dialogue when it declared the following year, 2001, the Year of Dialogue Among Civilizations. More recently in 2008, the Custodian of the Two Mosques His Majesty King Abdullah Bin Abdul Al Aziz Al-Saud of the Kingdom of Saudi Arabia invited the Muslim World League to coordinate a dialogue between representatives of the world's religious traditions. Accordingly, the Muslim World League, under the leadership of its secretary general, His

Excellency Dr. Abdullah Mohsin Al-Turki, worked in conjunction with the government of Spain under the leadership of His Majesty Juan Carlos the 1st to host the first World Conference on Dialogue in Madrid. With a deep understanding of the importance of dialogue, the conference leaders declared that dialogue is one of the essentials of life. It is also one of the most important means for knowing each other, cooperation, exchange of interests and realizing the truth, which contributes to the happiness of humankind.[319]

The organizers of the conference developed clear intentions. Among some of the objectives set forth by the Muslim World League, the conference was proposed in order to "confirm the significance of religion as a basic rectifier for human communities"; it sought to "coordinate internationally world attitudes as well as confront positions contradicting sharply with mankind districts and social norms as well as values"; and finally, the conference was designed to "confront the conflict calls that promote the clash among nations and peoples."[320]

Although dialogue is an important ingredient to peaceful coexistence, it is simply an initial step in a much larger process. All individuals involved in the World Conference on Dialogue agreed that active engagement must follow mere religious exchange. Accordingly, in an effort to establish a comprehensive plan of action, the Madrid Declaration, signed by the participants, proposes the following steps (among others):

To disseminate the culture of tolerance and understanding through dialogue so as to be a framework for international relations through holding conferences and symposia, as well as developing relevant cultural, educational and media programs; to agree on international guidelines for dialogue among the followers of religions and cultures through which moral values and ethical principles, which are common denominators among such followers, so as to strengthen stability and achieve prosperity for all humans; [and to promote the] cooperation among religious, cultural, educational, and media establishments to deepen and consolidate ethical values, to encourage noble social practices.[321]

From dialogue to social action, many of today's efforts are heading in the right direction.

Adding a Developmental Paradigm to Dialogue

Heretofore, religious dialogue has only been conducted using the common postmodern sensitivity to culture and social context. Even today's most successful dialogues, like the ones described above, seldom look beyond cultural differences between religious traditions. The ideas in this book open new areas for even greater strides forward.

Significant breakthroughs occur if we add a developmental sensitivity to the equation. As we shall see, among other insights, a developmental lens informs us that the rational and pluralistic altitudes of religious orientation are the first stages to emerge in consciousness that demand a sincere understanding of the religious "other."[322] After addressing the more classical examples of religious dialogue, the following pages demonstrate how a developmental understanding of dialogue can prove both effective and pragmatic.

Taking a broad perspective, applying the model of developmental religious pluralism to religious dialogue allows us to differentiate at least five different types of communication: (1) inter-religious dialogue, (2) intra-religious dialogue, (3) inter-religious developmental dialogue, (4) intra-religious developmental dialogue, and (5) integral religious dialogue. Two of these styles of dialogue, inter-religious and intra-religious, already occur on a large scale throughout the world today. I fully support such efforts and encourage that these dialogues continue. The last three styles however, inter-religious developmental dialogue, intra-religious developmental dialogue, and integral religious dialogue are brand new ideas which, if successfully implemented, will help to create a global landscape that can successfully reduce religious turmoil, while simultaneously promoting our collective evolution.

Inter-Religious Dialogue

Inter-religious dialogue is best understood as a conversation between two or more different religious traditions in service of promoting mutual understanding. In agreement with this definition, the United States Institute of Peace (USIP) recently published a special report titled, "What Works? Evaluating Interfaith Dialogue Programs." "At its most basic level," explains the special report, "interfaith dialogue involves people of different religious faiths coming together to have a conversation."[323] Not just a verbal dialogue but a sharing of ideas, practices and beliefs that constitute true mutual exchange and mutual transformation.[324] [325]

A few case studies will help to make the significance of such dialogues more concrete.[326] In 2008, the most prominent Jewish and Hindu leaders came together to convene the second Hindu-Jewish Leadership Summit as part of an ongoing initiative of the World Council of Religious Leaders. The success of the first two events, and the agreements made between leadership of the Chief Rabbinate of Israel and the Hindu Dharma Acharya Sabha, have been powerful.

At the conclusion of the most recent summit, representatives of each party (Hindu and Jewish) signed an agreement acknowledging some of the fundamental commonalities between their two traditions. The agreements included the following, among others:

1. In keeping with the Delhi declaration [signed at the First Hindu-Jewish Leadership Summit], the participants reaffirmed their commitment to deepening this bilateral relationship predicated on the recognition of One Supreme Being...The parties are committed to learning about one another on the basis of respect for the particular identities of their respective communities and seeking, through their bilateral relationship, to be a blessing to all.

2. It is recognized that the One Supreme Being, both in its formless and manifest aspects, has been worshipped by Hindus over the millennia. This does not mean that Hindus worship "gods and idols." The Hindu relates to only the One Supreme Being when he/she prays to a particular manifestation.

3. As the two oldest religious traditions of the world, the Hindu Dharma Acharya Sabha and the Jewish religious leadership may consider jointly appealing to various religious organizations in the world to recognize that all religions are sacred and valid for their respective peoples.[327]

Not only did these declarations symbolize successful common ground between Jewish and Hindu representatives but also helped to establish a new mutual regard that jettisoned thousands of years of misunderstanding between the two faiths. At the conclusion of the gathering, the Secretary General, Bawa Jain, of the World Council of Religious Leaders declared: "The Hindu-Jewish Leadership Summits have been a source of tremendous inspiration. Barriers of a few millennia have been broken down. Intrinsic beliefs and knowledge of the world's two oldest religions, the Hindus and Jews, hitherto not shared, is now being transmitted across the world. This is historic!"[328]

A second powerful example of inter-religious dialogue was demonstrated when Abbot Thomas Keating convened a selection of leaders at his Monastery in Snowmass, Colorado (Keating is mentioned in chapter 4 as an example of a leader working from an integral level of religious orientation). Wayne Teasdale offers his direct endorsement of Keating's efforts: "In terms of the [inter]-religious dialogue and the future of this whole movement, Abbot Thomas Keating and his organization, the Snowmass Conference, which is composed of fifteen religions represented by one person, offers the most promising vision of how the religious traditions can and should relate to one another in a more universal way."[329] Teasdale's endorsement speaks directly to the caliber of the event.

In his book *Speaking of Silence*, Father Keating offers his "Guidelines for Interreligious Understanding." They are as follows:

1. The world religions bear witness to the experience of the Ultimate Reality to which they give various names: Brahman, the Absolute, God, Allah, (the) Great Spirit, the Transcendent

2. The Ultimate Reality surpasses any name or concept that can be given to It.

3. The Ultimate Reality is the source (ground of being) of all existence.

4. Faith is opening, surrendering, and responding to the Ultimate Reality. This relationship precedes every belief system.

5. The potential for human wholeness—or in other frames of reference, liberation, self-transcendence, enlightenment, salvation, transforming union, moksha, nirvana, fana—is present in every human person.

6. The Ultimate Reality may be experienced not only through religious practices but also through nature, art, human relationships and service to others.

7. The differences among belief systems should be presented as facts that distinguish them, not as points of superiority.

8. In the light of the globalization of life and culture now in process, the personal and social ethical principles proposed by the world religions in the past need to be re-thought and re-expressed.[330]

Most inter-religious dialogue, like that demonstrated in the summits and gatherings described above, are initiated by religious adherents who possess either a rational and or pluralistic level of religious orientation.

Although both of these levels engage in inter-religious dialogue with honest intentions, their motives come from different sources.

Most commonly, an individual with a rational level of awareness seeks to engage in inter-religious dialogue in hope of promoting tolerance and respect. The rational individual has very practical and pragmatic goals but is seldom open to large shifts in his or her own awareness (i.e., individuative-reflective faith).[331] In contrast, pluralistic individuals, although they too seek tolerance and respect, find deeper motivation in the insight that a clear and unbiased picture of reality will only emerge if a diversity of perspectives are engaged (i.e., conjunctive faith).

In other words, seeking to complement and perhaps even enhance their own perspective, pluralistic individuals engage in inter-religious dialogue as a positive way to supplement the shortcomings and blind spots of their own culture and tradition.[332] Although the above example is fairly benign, it starts to clarify how different motivations propel various levels of development.

At lower levels of development, however, motivations are less neutral and in some cases might even lead to problems.[333] As briefly mentioned above, some at lower levels of development engage in dialogue for personal gain. In other circumstances, when individuals involved are of a magic and mythic orientation, religious dialogue becomes a game of subtle persuasion. Dialogue from ethnocentric levels is often a matter of who can convert the other to the "only true religion." Such actions often lead to false gestures of respect and mutual regard.

The Islamic scholar Sachedina contends that the number of individuals moving into worldcentric altitudes is increasing: "There is a growing majority in every religious community that is in search of a tolerant creed to further inter-human understanding beyond exclusionary consequently intolerant institutional religiosity."[334] As more individuals move into worldcentric modes of awareness, they leave behind the ethnocentric beliefs that their own tradition is the "one and only truth." There is much reason to believe that interreligious dialogue among the world religious traditions, especially between those individuals with a worldcentric perspective and higher (rational, pluralistic, integral) will continue.

Integral
Religious
Dialogue

Integral altitude
across different
traditions

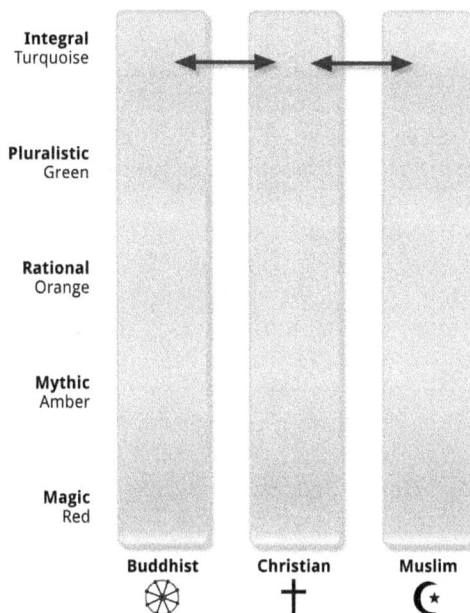

Integral Turquoise		
Pluralistic Green		
Rational Orange		
Mythic Amber		
Magic Red		

Buddhist   **Christian**   **Muslim**

Figure 18

Figure 18 above charts inter-religious dialogue as it might occur between a Buddhist and a Christian at the same level of religious orientation (rational). Although inter-religious dialogue can occur between any traditions and between any of the varying altitudes of religious orientation, our new understanding of development tells us that the most effective inter-religious dialogue will occur on the same level between different traditions. In the most ideal circumstances, inter-religious dialogue will maintain efficacy by matching level to level (i.e., orange to orange, green to green, etc.). As we shall see, it is best to encourage those of lower altitudes to only engage inter-religious dialogue tentatively until their altitude has been raised sufficiently through exposure to higher levels of development in their own tradition through intra-religious developmental dialogue (described below).

Intra-religious Dialogue

The classic term "intra-religious dialogue" describes a process of communication between various sects within the same tradition. This may involve Baptists speaking with Methodists in the Christian faith, Theravada Buddhists communicating with Mahayana Buddhists, or

Sunnis in dialogue with Shiites in the Muslim faith.

Intra-religious dialogue is not foreign to the world stage. In 2008, just before the Conference on Dialogue (mentioned above) was convened in Spain by the King of Saudi Arabia to promote dialogue among various faiths, the King also gathered more than five hundred Muslim leaders from around the world to meet in Mecca. The objective was to discuss Islam together as insiders of the faith, to clear up misconceptions between the various sects, and to speak with one voice before stepping into the larger arena of inter-religious dialogue with other faiths at the larger global conference. Ultimately, this pre-conference gathering was a monumental event for Muslims around the world and a perfect example of honest and engaged intra-religious dialogue at its best.

Those from outside the Muslim faith confirmed the significance of the dialogues. Reverend Dr. Shanta Premawardhana, director of the World Council Church's program on Interreligious Dialogue and Cooperation contends that this intra-Muslim conference unambiguously affirmed the Islamic legitimacy for dialogue, expressed the hope that their engagement in dialogue would be a means to counter allegations of extremism often leveled against Islam, and expected dialogue to contribute to confronting the difficult challenges of our day such as terrorism, violations of human rights and pollution. The Makkah Appeal is a strong encouragement for Muslims to engage in dialogue.[335]

Both inside and outside of the Muslim community this type of intra-religious dialogue is viewed as an important step forward.

It is not only the world's Muslims who engage in internal dialogue. Historically, the Christian tradition provides a strong precedent for similar action. Since the first meeting at the Council of Nicaea in 325 CE and the Council of Constantinople in 381 CE, the Catholic Church has held twenty-one major ecumenical meetings in the past two millennia. The most recent intra-religious dialogue among Catholics, called the Second Ecumenical Council of the Vatican, was held from October of 1962 until the final months of 1965. The gathering, which came to be known as Vatican II, was designed to, as Pope John Paul XXIII put it, "open the windows of the Church to let in some fresh air."[336]

Among the many monumental decisions concluded at Vatican II perhaps the most significant was the intra-religious agreement known as Nostra Aetate, the declaration on the Relation of the Church with Non-Christian Religions of the Second Vatican Council. The Catholic monk Wayne Teasedale speaks of the significance of Vatican II in general and the Nostra Aetate in particular:

In relation to the other religions, this openness and

sensitivity resulted in the establishment of the Secretariat for Non-Christian Religions on May 14, 1964, during the Council and prior to the promulgation of the counciliar decree Nostra Aetate on October 28, 1965. This secretariat (whose name was changed to the Council for Interreligious Dialogue in the reorganization of the Vatican government in 1989) has exerted enormous influence on the church's attitude towards the other world religions. Since its inception it has advanced the value of interreligious dialogue through publications, seminars, lectures, conferences and other dialogical situations all around the globe. It also facilitated and facilitates encounters between the Pope and various other spiritual leaders representing the great world religions, a practice begun and encouraged during the pontificate of Paul VI who was himself an ardent supporter of interreligious communication. During the pontificate of John Paul II, the Council for Interreligious Dialogue has expanded.[337]

Both of the examples provided above with regard to Muslim and Christian intra-religious dialogue offer sound examples of how powerful and productive it can be when individuals from within the same tradition come together to find a common voice. Other efforts around the globe like the World Buddhist Conference are encouraging signs that this trend is sure to continue.

Just as we saw in our discussion on inter-religious dialogue, intra-religious dialogue is primarily the domain of worldcentric leaders. However, like inter-religious dialogue, there may also be some leaders involved in intra-religious dialogue who possess levels of development at mythic stages and below. Consequently, these leaders believe that their own specific sect is literally the only true path. One needs to look no further than Protestant and Catholic confrontations in Ireland or Sunni/Shiite warfare in Iraq to see that collisions at lower levels of development (even within the same faith) can create major conflict in the world.

Figure 19 below shows an example of intra-religious dialogue among Baptists, Catholics, and Methodists within the Christian faith.

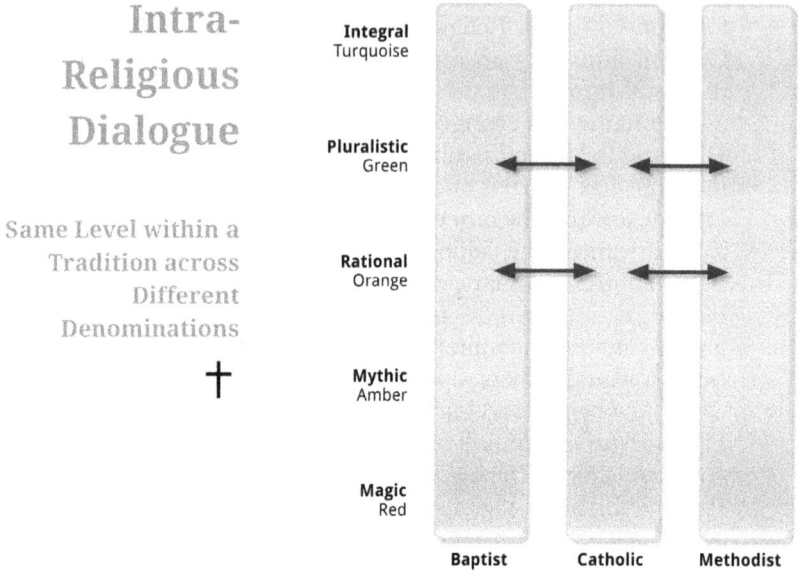

Figure 19

As we have explored, intra-religious dialogue is already in place today and it must continue. Like inter-religious dialogue, the most effective conversations will result from same level communication across diverse denominations.

The exchanges that result from intra-religious dialogue will serve as a harmonizing voice among diverse sects and denominations. If intra-religious and inter-religious dialogue improve through the use of a developmental approach, we can continue to build upon Teasedale's vision for an "international council of religions...[whose members] consult on a regular basis and [] speak with one voice in world affairs."[338]

Intra-religious Developmental Dialogue

Using a developmental model more explicitly liberates new potential for religious dialogue heretofore yet unrealized. We begin by introducing a type of exchange I call "intra-religious developmental dialogue." Intra-religious developmental dialogue consists of communication between different levels of religious orientation within a single tradition.[339]

Internal dialogue among adherents of the same faith (intra-religious dialogue) does not always unfold as smoothly as cited in the examples above. Charles Jones, associate professor in the school of theology and religious studies at the Catholic University of America, states the following:

> Problems emerge, not when Christians actually encounter people of other faith traditions, but when Christians gather and talk among themselves about these issues, and find that their fellow church goers do not necessarily share their deep convictions about other faiths. Things quickly break down when accusations of "betrayal of the gospel" or "intolerance and triumphalism" begin to fly, and when the discussants lack the concepts and the language to talk about the historical, sociological, psychological, and theological underpinnings of their positions.[340]

A developmental approach to intra-religious dialogue adds a new level of clarity to discontinuities and discrepancies within a single tradition. Not only will a developmental lens help to mitigate conflict but it will also help to harmonize the internal dynamics of each tradition.

The new understanding of the stages of religious orientation, presented in this book, helps to explain one of the reasons why adherents of the same faith or even same sect might indeed disagree. Using a developmental model, one quickly notices that it is not simply a difference in health (extremist vs. moderate) that creates ideological divide as many today might argue, but rather division comes as a result of a fundamental difference in the psychological capacity of each adherent. A Sunni Muslim expressing his or her tradition from a rational perspective and a Sunni Muslim expressing his or her tradition from a mythic perspective may very well have monumental theological disagreements, even if their culture, social identity, and degree of health are roughly the same.

Clash in Developmental Dialogue ☾*

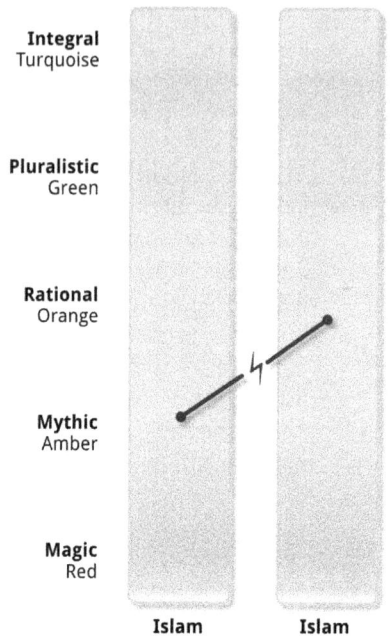

Figure 20

The graphic above shows how a rational expression of Islam might meet a mythic interpretation of Islam. The developmental canyon between the two perspectives results in what this book calls a "clash in developmental dialogue." Because each altitude has its own unique and valid perspective of the world, it is often difficult for two expressions of different altitude to find common ground.

In order for intra-religious developmental dialogue to be both successful and effective, at least one of the participating parties needs to have an integral level of religious orientation. The aperspectival nature of the integral level provides its representatives with the skills to travel up and down the entire spectrum of development, translating their viewpoints into a language appropriate to each altitude. The integral religious mediator has the capacity to meet the other parties wherever they are in order to establish clear channels of communication.

Intra-Developmental Dialogue

Different Levels within a Single Tradition

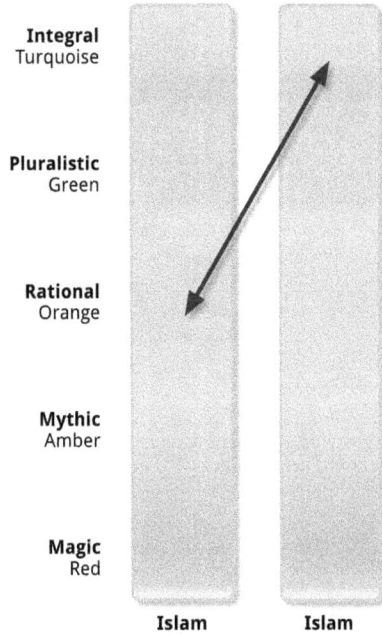

Integral
Turquoise

Pluralistic
Green

Rational
Orange

Mythic
Amber

Magic
Red

Islam   Islam

Figure 21

At first glance, the graphic above is helpful to understand how intra-religious developmental dialogue might take place. However, the graphic in its current form is also misleading to the untrained eye. For those less familiar with healthy forms of hierarchy, it may appear that the individual at an integral altitude is imposing a higher view upon those at lower altitudes. Although this arrogant approach may unfold when orange speaks to amber or even when green speaks to orange, this is not the case when the participant is at an integral level of awareness. More accurately, intra-religious developmental dialogue involving an integral participant can be represented as follows.

Intra-Religious Developmental Dialogue

Different Levels within a Single Tradition

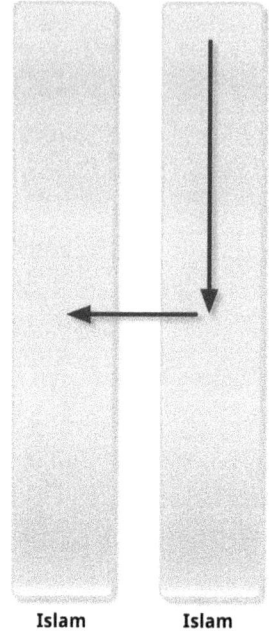

Figure 22

At an integral religious orientation, individuals have the capacity to glide effortlessly between various perspectives while maintaining an anchor at an integral level of development. This leads to a brand new type of interaction.

An integral practitioner takes several steps to ensure effective action. First, the individual at an integral level uses the primary and secondary indicators of behavior, expression, and action to assess the person with whom they are in dialogue. Then, like a tuning fork, the integral individual navigates the entire vertical spectrum adjusting his/ her perspective so that it resonates at the other participant's particular frequency. Once the integral individual has attuned his or her own perspective to match the perspectives of the religious other, he or she can then translate complex ideas from a turquoise altitude into a language that can be received and understood by an individual at any lower level of development.

Two immediate benefits come from this type of engagement: (1) Intra-religious developmental dialogue offers a significant opportunity for religious traditions to find greater internal agreement, allowing them to contribute even more to the modern and postmodern world, and (2) through this new type of developmental communication, those individuals at lower levels of religious orientation (more likely to cause violence, conflict, and harm) are exposed to the higher levels of interpretation and action. Although it is true that an integral adherent of any tradition cannot force those of lower levels of development to evolve, he or she can set the conditions so that evolution and further psychological development is a likely possibility.

Over time, as more internal religious dialogue occurs with at least one party at an integral level, we will see greater swaths of adherents within each tradition hopping onto the "conveyor belt" for an unprecedented developmental ride.

Inter-Religious Developmental Dialogue

Inter-religious developmental dialogue occurs between different levels of religious orientation across different traditions.[341] In figure 23 below, the graph provides an example of an integral Hindu in dialogue with a rational Muslim.

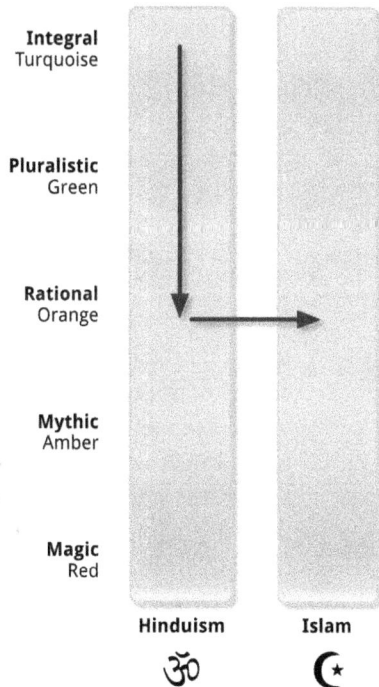

Inter-Religious Developmental Dialogue

Different Levels across Different Traditions

Integral
Turquoise

Pluralistic
Green

Rational
Orange

Mythic
Amber

Magic
Red

Hinduism
ॐ

Islam
☪

Figure 23

One can imagine how much more effective inter-religious dialogue would be if, like in the example above, the participants could all agree to reason as the foundation for shared agreement. Agreements made at this rational stage might allow religious values and opinions a more legitimate space in the public sphere. Such opinions are sure to be even more powerful if they are agreed upon across a plurality of traditions.

Like intra-religious developmental dialogue, inter-religious developmental dialogue is most effective when one of the parties involved maintains a religious orientation at an integral altitude. In inter-religious developmental dialogue the integral participant acts as a universal donor, moving with ease between varying levels of orientation and ensuring clear, concise dialogue throughout the entire spiral. Ultimately, inter-developmental dialogue will help to promote mutual respect, tolerance, and at times a deep embrace of the religious "other." Concurrently, like the benefits gained in intra-religious developmental dialogue, there is a chance that through exposure to higher levels of intelligence, participants may make positive strides up the spectrum of religious orientation.

Integral Religious Dialogue

The fifth type of dialogue introduced here is called integral religious dialogue. This form of communication involves several participants engaging in conversation, between different traditions or within a single tradition, who all rest at an integral altitude. When discussing religion among fellow integral thinkers we must take three steps to verify clear communication:

1. First, we must verify that the participants are all at an integral level of religious orientation and that they all share some sort of foundation or model on which to base dialogue (if this initial step is not ensured, participants may find it difficult to establish a common language). Right now, the best model to serve as foundation is Wilber's All Quadrant, All Level (AQAL) framework. A quick assessment of each other's level of awareness can be done using a snapshot of primary and secondary indicators as described in chapters 3 and 4.

2. Second, after having established the shared perspective and altitude that will serve as foundation, it is crucial to identify which level of religion the group is talking *about*. That is, each member of the dialogue must answer the question: "Are we referring to a magic, a mythic, a rational, or a pluralistic expression of

this tradition?" Establishing which level of religious orientation is in focus allows all parties involved to make sure they are all speaking in the same relative context.

3. Third, if the approach is to be truly integral, it is crucial that all parties involved in the dialogue identify not only which altitude they are talking about but also the particular *perspective* about which they are engaging.[342] In other words, the group must decide if they are speaking about a specific individual (I), the community and its shared values (WE), or the religious system itself (IT).[343]

One example helps to clarify the methodology to be used in a proper integral religious dialogue. Let's look at a situation in which a Buddhist, a Christian, and a Muslim are all engaged in integral religious dialogue. The graphic representation would look something like the following:

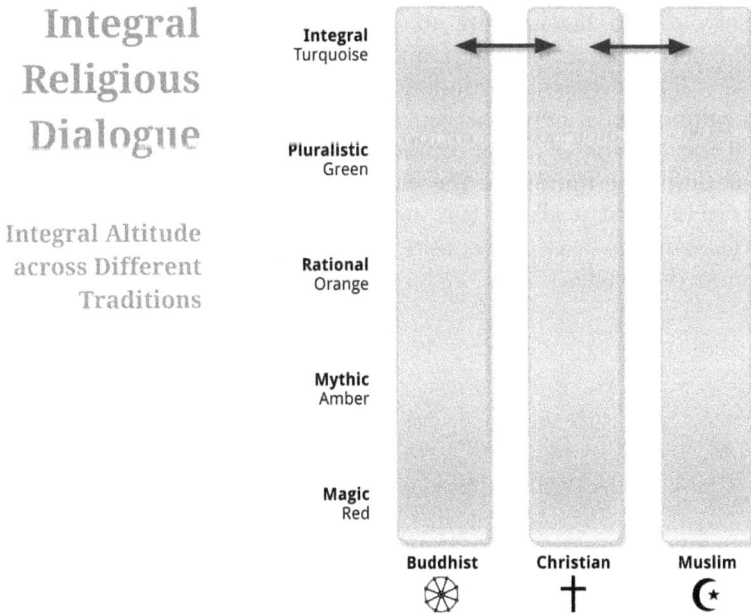

Figure 24

Following the three steps outlined above, all participants would first establish their understanding, desire, and capacity to engage in integral dialogue, and the common platform of engagement (AQAL). Second, all parties involved establish which level of religion they would like to discuss. In this case, let's say that all agree to discuss the mythic versions of their own particular traditions. Finally, let's say that all agree to discuss scripture or the religious system itself.

Having established the preceding three steps, the participants have successfully established what Wilber calls a Kosmic Address, also written as KA = (altitude + perspective of the subject) x (altitude + perspective of the object).[344] A Kosmic Address can be described as the altitude and perspective of the speaker in relation to the altitude and perspective of that which is being spoken about.

Integral religious dialogue is already underway. In 2005, forty spiritual and religious leaders gathered in Denver, Colorado, for the inaugural event of Integral Spiritual Center, "a collaboration between some of the most highly respected spiritual teachers in the world today, who, in addition to fully embracing their own particular paths, have come together to explore a trans-path path to the future."[345] As the subsequent meetings of Integral Spiritual Center have unfolded over the past several years, each spiritual and religious leader has made a commitment to sharing the deep insights of his or her tradition. To such an end, teachers are now in the process of taking turns teaching the other members of the center in the spirit of transformation.

The events surrounding Integral Spiritual Center signify the beginning of a new emergence in religious dialogue. "Out of the fire of this crucible of lineage minds melting into each other as the face of an unfolding tomorrow, the shape of future religion will be born, if it is to be born at all."[346] It is my hope that these five forms of religious dialogue will be deeply considered as a result of this book and put into immediate action.

Chapter 9
Removing the Barriers to Security, Connectivity, and Cooperation

This chapter explores three of the most significant ways a developmental perspective can help position religion as an ally to global progress and human evolution. When expressed through higher levels of developmental complexity (i.e., rational, pluralistic, and integral variations), religion can help to foster international security, human connectivity, and cross-sector collaboration.

Despite the fact that many theories place religion as either the largest barrier to areas of security, connectivity, and cooperation, or at the very least unrelated, it will be clear by the end of the chapter that religion also holds the potential to be one of evolution's most potent allies. Rather than treating religion as part of the problem and ostracizing it to the private sphere, the approach offered in this chapter uses the model of developmental pluralism to confront the negative aspects of religion head-on, transforming religion itself into part of the solution. Although it is true that religion expressed through only lower levels of development can be problematic, religion expressed through higher levels of religious orientation offers a vast resource for peace, prosperity, and progress. This chapter ends with a broad blueprint for action and a description of how the model of developmental pluralism might be most easily integrated into a national and international agenda.

Let's look at security, connectivity, and cooperation in brief before fully explicating them in the remainder of this chapter.

1. *International security*—Religion interpreted through higher levels of development naturally serves as an antidote to combat transnational terrorism. In other cases, religion expressed through rational, pluralistic, and integral lenses can serve as

a potent force in both conflict resolution and international diplomacy.

2. *Human connectivity*—Religion expressed through a more sophisticated lens has the capacity to generate positive social norms that emphasize interdependency and connectivity on the basis of our shared humanity. Connectivity that is established using rational, pluralistic, or integral lenses ensures that compassion extends to include all human beings, including those beyond the boundaries of one's own religious group.

3. *Cross-sector cooperation*—At its more complex levels of interpretation, religion has the power to cultivate transnational cooperation in service of social well-being and progress. Because religion at higher levels of interpretation is open to rational inquiry, it can successfully integrate and coordinate with various sectors of society that are also based on rational thought (including business, politics, civil society, media).

The idea of including our world's religions more prominently in the world through understanding various modes of interpretation is counterintuitive to those raised in the educational and social systems of the modern West. For years, social scholars have assumed that the pubic role of religion, positive or negative, was on the decline. Without a developmental understanding of religion, such a stance is logical. For centuries, scholars and practitioners have confused the whole of religion with its mythic interpretations (what Wilber calls the "level-line fallacy").[347] Now, however, an integral vision is liberating religion from its mythic chains.

Religion and the Global Stage

If we are to come up with an appropriate role for religion and discuss the ways it might lead to greater security, connectivity, and cooperation using a developmentally sensitive perspective, then it is vital that we more deeply understand where we are historically with regard to religion and its role on the global stage. A fitting place to begin is with the term "secularism."

One of the most widely accepted definitions of secularism comes from sociologist of religion Peter Berger.[348] In one of his early books, the *Social Reality of Religion*, Berger defines secularism as "the process by which sections of society and culture are removed from the domination of religious institutions and symbols."[349] Complementing Berger's definition, Scott Thomas, professor of economics and international development, helps to expand our understanding with the following:

> [Secularization theory explains that] the number of people who declare themselves to be believers and who regularly attend religious services will steadily decline as a country modernizes since the kind of cultural pluralism modernity creates undermines the stability of belief. There will also be a steady retreat of religion from the Public square, as social, economic, and political institutions are transformed toward religious and ideological neutrality and lose their religious identity.[350]

The type of secular ideology explained by both Berger and Thomas has been taught in our universities and classrooms, without critical reflection, for nearly fifty years. In short, secularism was assumed to represent the evolutionary step from premodernity to modernity in total. We now know however that there are multiple modernities, some of which may not include secularization.

Under the gaze of a self-reflexive eye, we begin to see that secularization theory itself is a type of ideology that lends to its own type of close-minded fundamentalism (demonstrated in part by the way that modern secular theory assumes itself to be the only correct view). Having served as the dominating, and often dogmatically imposed meaning making system of the international relations in the West, modern scholars point out that secular theory offers a very narrow view not unlike that of religious extremists, if only in a different context. Thomas elucidates a similar idea:

> Social theorists, who in the past tried to ignore or marginalize religion by explaining it away in terms of some other natural, social, or material reality, or by privileging an account of social theory based on secular reason, are themselves insufficiently self-critical or aware of their own philosophical (if not also quasi-religious or theological) assumptions, which no appeal to such secular rationality can justify any longer.[351]

Unfortunately, almost all current theories of international security blindly follow secular logic. First stemming from the Western Enlightenment, culminating in the Treaty of Westphalia, and continuing soundly into today's classrooms and diplomatic interactions, an unquestioning acceptance of the separation of religion and politics prevents our leaders from taking a more holistic approach to International Relations. Edward Luttwack explains:

> Astonishingly persistent, enlightenment prejudice [toward religion] has remained amply manifest in the contemporary professional analysis of foreign affairs. Policymakers, diplomats, journalists, and scholars who are ready to over interpret economic causality, who are apt to dissect social differentiations most finely, and who will minutely categorize political affiliations are still in the habit of disregarding the role of religion, religious institutions, and religious motivations in explaining politics and conflict.[352]

Luttwack's explanation provides just one example of how the "secular fundamentalist" stance, taken by most modern theorists, cripples their ability to accurately assess international conflict and violence, even in circumstances in which religion is an obvious factor. If it is true that our Western view on modernization has in fact been biased for decades and that secular theory can no longer be justified, what does this mean for the future of religion? Might an integral perspective include a vision that is not only post-postmodern but perhaps *post-secular* as well?

This book is being written at an opportune time when leading social theorists are beginning to recognize that perhaps their ideas about secularism and religion were in fact inaccurate. Almost forty years after his authoritative definition of secularism, Peter Berger clearly admits that his theories on secularism and modernization were incorrect. In his own words: "The idea is simple: Modernization necessarily leads to a decline in religion, both in society and in the minds of individuals. And it is precisely this key idea that has turned out to be wrong."[353] The implications of this realization are only now beginning to trickle down into the minds of theorists and diplomatic leaders. Until full assimilation of such truths has occurred, modern approaches still attached to the idea that secularism is a universal phenomenon will continue to find themselves in crisis.

David Brooks helps to explain the type of calamity that results from world leaders who fail to let go of flawed modern assumptions: "Our foreign policy elites…go for months ignoring the force of religion. Then, when confronted with something inescapably religious such as the Iranian revolution or the Taliban, they begin talking of religious zealotry and fanaticism, which suddenly explains everything. After a few days of shaking their heads over the fanatics, they revert to their usual secular analyses. We do not yet have, and sorely need, a mode of analysis that attempts to merge the spiritual with the material."[354] Scott

Thomas describes a similar type of cognitive dissonance:

> The global resurgence of religion taking place in the developed world— charismatic Catholics and Catholic conservatives, evangelicals and Pentecostal Protestants, New Age Spiritualists, Western Buddhists, and Japanese traditionalists—is part of a larger crisis of modernity in the West. It reflects a deeper and more widespread disillusionment with modernity that reduces the world to what can be perceived and controlled through reason, science and technology, and leaves out the sacred, religion, or spirituality.[355]

This inability to account for the interior dimensions of human experience is precisely what Robert Wuthnow is referring to when he explains that our current social theories, "expect rationality and produce cynical interpretations based on assumptions about self-interest. They stress cause and effect but leave no room for meaning and significance."[356] Theorists must see beyond Machiavelli's realist opinion that although religion is mere superstition, it is sometimes useful "as a type of ideology the state can use to gain legitimacy, promote social cohesion, and so maintain its power." Instead, theorist of an integral age will be better served if they follow Wuthnow's call to bring "meaning" and "significance" into our international relations theory.[357]

So where do these intellectual unfoldings leave us today? Elizabeth Shakman Hurd explains:

> If Westphalia signaled both a dramatic break from the past and "a consolidation and codification of a new conception of political authority" that was secular and also deeply Christian, then perhaps contemporary international relations is witnessing the gradual emergence of a series of post-Westphalian, post-secular conceptions of religiopolitical authority.[358]

An integral, post-secular worldview clearly recognizes that there is not one single, monolithic path to modernity but rather, as Eisenstadt puts it, there exist "multiple modernities."[359] Second, a post-secular world order must maintain all of the important contributions of modern and postmodern social theory and preserve the classical theories that have come before, while simultaneously jettisoning all those parts of the theory that no longer hold any weight (e.g., secularization theory). Finally, at the very least, a post-secular or post-postmodern shift in the way we relate to religion in the global sphere must take seriously those influencing factors that stem from interiority (e.g., culture, spirituality, meaning, significance). As Thomas puts it bluntly, "there is a distinction between studying an unconscious world of atoms or a range of mountains, and the conscious world of human beings with emotions, thoughts and intentions that are capable of representing the world to each other in meaningful ways."[360] In a post-secular world how do we know which version of religion to include? A developmental lens unlocks the potential to include only those versions of each tradition that prove to be most mature.

International Security

There is no doubt that religion is the source of much turmoil in the world. According to a recent book published on the relationship between religion and international relations, in 2001, "over half of the 34 serious conflicts around the world had a religious dimension to them."[361] A second author explains that a drastic "rise in religiously related conflict or terrorism by new religious non-state actors has taken place over the last 20 years."[362]

To show just how much of a driving force religion plays in conflict around the globe, Sam Harris lists several global hotspots: Palestine (Jews v. Muslims); the Balkans (Orthodox Serbians v. Catholic Croatians, Orthodox Serbians v. Bosnian, and Albanian Muslims); Northern Ireland (Protestants v. Catholics); Kashmir (Muslims v. Hindus); Sudan (Muslims v. Christians and animists); Nigeria (Muslims v. Christians); Ethiopia and Eritrea (Muslims v. Christians); Sri Lanka (Sinhalese Buddhists v. Tamil Hindus); Indonesia (Muslims v. Timorese Christians); and the Caucasus (Orthodox Russians v. Chechen Muslims).[363]

Given these facts, it serves us well to ask: Is it religion itself that causes all of these problems? Or is the trouble caused by the interpretation and consequent action carried out in religion's name? It is the main intention of this book in general and this chapter in particular to confirm that religion itself is a neutral force in the world. Religion can be used as a positive or negative tool depending on the religious actors who are involved in its interpretation. Religious conflict is most often caused by magic and mythic interpretations of each tradition wherein the group believes that they have the one and only truth. Conversely, a positive role for religion will only find its fullest expressions when each tradition is translated and expressed through a rational lens and higher.

Agreeing that the coming integral age might in fact be post-secular as well, we can look deeper at how religion might be more fully included into the discourse at the global level. One of the first things about which we need to gain clarity is which version of each religion to include. Taking a more careful look at the psychological infrastructure of those individuals who are acting out using religion as a foundation we see that religion has the capacity to build international security if it stems from higher levels of psychological complexity. The Constitution of United Nations Educational, Scientific, and Cultural Organization (UNESCO) argues along a similar vein: "Since wars begin in the minds of men, it is in the minds of men that the defenses of peace must be constructed."[364] Although focusing on the psychological dynamics of conflict is not a new idea, understanding the psychological and developmental dynamics of religious interpretation and conflict is, in fact, something only now emerging.

Commonly, religious violence is committed not simply because of irresolvable differences between religious traditions but rather as a result of varying levels of development between and among traditions. As described in part 2 of this book, magic and mythic levels of religious orientation often produce intolerant mental frameworks, represented by literal belief structures, and lacking critical distance and reasoning. When individuals at these lower levels of religious interpretation are challenged by those with opposing worldviews, they have the potential to act out violently against all those they consider to be outside of their particular group (i.e., Al-Qaeda). Often these violent actions are reinforced by a deep-seated belief that they are acting upon the will of God.

The following cannot be understated: If we are to reduce the amount of international conflict (including acts of terrorism) that transpire as a result of religion, we must find ways to ensure religious adherents are free to move away from egocentric and ethnocentric interpretations of religion (magic and mythic) to worldcentric interpretations of faith (rational pluralistic, and integral).

A post-secular society that takes religion seriously naturally creates a new role for religious and spiritual leaders to mitigate conflict and ensure international security. Due to the fact that secularization was always assumed to be an inherent part of the modernization process, the "public role for religious personal and religious institutions in society was still considered to be part of a traditional not modern society."[365] However, now that we have seen that there are in fact multiple paths to modernity, many of which do not necessarily include secularization, we need to start considering a positive role for religious leaders in the public sphere. Seeing this phenomenon clearly, Thomas points out the following:

> The study of International relations has recognized for some time that new types of non-state actors or nongovernmental

organizations (NGOs) can influence international relations. However, religious non-state actors, apart from some early studies of the Catholic Church, have not been investigated with any consistency.[366]

Furthermore, "the global resurgence of religion and globalization have contributed to new wars and internal conflicts in ways that call into question the adequacy of inter-state or conventional diplomacy to resolve them."[367] Thomas sees the need for multi-track diplomacy wherein the world stage utilizes "a variety of non-state actors in diplomacy, peace building, and conflict resolution."[368] The World Council of Religious Leaders has already begun to implement this post-secular strategy using what they term "religious diplomacy."

Religious diplomacy, or what Douglas Johnston of the International Center for Religion and Diplomacy calls "Faith Based Diplomacy,"[369] is gaining momentum around the globe. In his own work, Edward Luttwack notices that the conflict-resolution efforts of religiously motivated third parties can do more than merely offer a negotiating mechanism, a method of communication, or any other such purely procedural assistance. By introducing the authority of religion into the negotiating equation, they enable the parties, if they so desire, to concede assets or claims to that authority itself, so to speak, rather than to their antagonists.[370]

That is to say, if individuals feel as if they are making concessions in a peace treaty, yielding to God or a deeper reality rather than the opponent, the resistance to make such choices is greatly diminished. The implications for such a concept and the potential for religious and spiritual leaders to use religion as a unitive, rather than divisive, force in the world seems extraordinary.

Examples of religious and spiritual diplomats on both the world and national political stage are not an entirely new phenomenon. After all, Martin Luther King Jr., Mahatma Gandhi, and Desmond Tutu, among many others, have used a transcendent or spiritual basis to inspire major global change. What is novel in this proposal is the recommendation that such players be sought out in a conscious fashion in hopes that each might use his or her talents and skills to bring the reservoirs of wisdom contained in our world's spiritual traditions to the public arena.[371]

Thus far, the classic pluralistic model of religious analysis that encourages religious adherents to abandon extremist views to embrace moderate ones has failed to make any deep impact. Although the promotion of more liberal views of religion is useful, rhetoric alone without nuanced research to support the legitimacy of alternative views will continue to fall on deaf ears. The model of developmental religious pluralism, proposed in this book, is one of the first attempts to demonstrate, through supportive academic research, which levels of religious interpretation are most useful for global well-being and how we can successfully set the conditions for each higher stage of development to emerge.

Luckily, both evolution and education are on the side of all those who hope for a better future. As described in part 1 of this book, longitudinal studies of development show that, over time, development moves in a positive direction towards more complexity. That is to say, given the right circumstances and exposure to more mature religious views, individuals will gradually progress from lower levels of religious orientation to those of higher levels. In practical terms, the vertical spectrum offered by the model of developmental pluralism provides a roadmap that guides individuals away from views that may lead to terrorism, toward those views that are more inclusive and capable of greater care. The model of developmental religious pluralism is a goldmine for all those interested in directly combating religious extremism and global terrorism in the long term.

Human Connectivity

Religion is simultaneously the most potent catalyst and greatest barrier to realizing our shared human connectivity both individually and collectively. Because levels of religious interpretation vary to such large degrees, the role religion plays in the world is a dichotomous one. At one end of the developmental spectrum represented most often by magic and mythic interpretations of religion, individuals use religious teachings to promote the self-interest of their own specific identity group, dividing the world into believers and non-believers. At the opposite end of the spectrum, religion can be used for tremendous social good that extends beyond any single religious group to benefit all of humanity.

Because so few have used a developmental perspective to analyze religion, cultures have taken strides to curb the divisive tendency of religion but have had little success. In the West, many still think that ostracizing religion to the private sphere is the most appropriate form of action. Maintaining religion as a private affair, it is often said, will ensure that we keep our religious differences separate from our shared public interests. Such notions are now out of date as we move into a post-secular era of "multiple modernities."

Although a theory that tries to privatize religion has good intentions that try to remove those barriers that prevent human connectedness, it bases its argument on a secularization theory that theorists now see as inaccurate.[372] A solution that forces religion to the private sphere fails to take into account two important factors: (1) Even if the Western world keeps religion on the sidelines, many other countries around the globe with whom the West interacts engage religion publicly and explicitly. Therefore, failing to include religion in the international dialogue leaves a key piece out of the puzzle.[373] (2) The thought that individuals can successfully remove their private beliefs from public decisions is unrealistic. All religious individuals bring their beliefs with them from the private sphere into the public sphere (even if they do translate them into secular language). These two facts make the direct and indirect influence of religion unavoidable.

When we combine the ubiquitous and unavoidable nature of religion with the fact that the role of religion is on the rise in the world (outside of Western Europe), we are faced with a major dilemma. How do we deal with the inevitability and resurgence of religion around the globe? Can we engage religion in a positive way, despite its negative tendencies to be divisive at lower levels?

The model of developmental pluralism helps to show us how religion can add to human connectivity rather than divide. Although it was once thought to be the right solution to tuck religion away into the private sphere, we know now that such a task is not possible. If we are to engage religion in the open we must understand that higher levels of sophistication represented by rational, pluralistic, and integral interpretations of faith allow adherents to include a diverse array of perspectives. As perspective-taking increases so too does the ability to have empathy and compassion for those who might be of a different religious or ethnic group. If we are to increase levels of human connectedness we must ensure that religious adherents of higher levels of development (in all traditions) have a clear and legitimate place on the global landscape.

Coordination and Cooperation

Religion (as with any grand ideology like capitalism or Marxism) naturally creates the foundation for global cooperation and coordination that transcends national boundaries. As it currently stands, however, religious groups cannot successfully integrate or coordinate (to any large degree) with other sectors of society. Other silos of society that tend to seamlessly integrate and coordinate with each other (e.g., business, politics, science) refuse to allow religion into the fold.

It becomes obvious, when looking deeper at the phenomenon, that traditional forms of religion (magic and mythic) are denied a seat at the collaborative table for good reason. Unlike both business and politics which have evolved into modern expressions (rational, pluralistic, and integral) using reason as foundation, traditional forms of religion still trapped in an older paradigm do not base their truth-claims on logic or evidence. In addition, magic and mythic forms of religion are not open to rational inquiry or criticism. As a result these premodern forms of religion lack a common foundation on which they might build a working relationship with other sectors. A refusal to engage the demand for evidence results in a deep distrust between those sectors of society based on experientially based proof (rational, pluralistic, integral) and those based on faith (magic/mythic religion). Not only is a failure to integrate religion a disservice to the great teachings that do exist within our religious traditions but such a divide creates a systemic dysfunction preventing successful dialogue between the most fundamental pillars of society (politics, economics, spirituality).

Sam Harris, along this same line of thought, offers a relevant point in his book *The End of Faith* to which all religious adherents who care about the well-being of humanity should pay careful attention. Harris aptly points out that traditionally, religion is the only area of our modern life that we fail to demand the use of reason. He continues:

It is time we recognize that the only thing that permits human beings to collaborate with one another in a truly open-ended way is their willingness to *have their beliefs modified by new facts*. Only openness to evidence and argument will secure a common world for us. Nothing guarantees that reasonable people will agree about everything, of course, but the unreasonable are certain to be divided by their dogmas. The spirit of *mutual inquiry* is the very *antithesis* of religious faith.[374]

Harris' insightful quote needs one major qualification. Although his statement is true for religious interpretation as it is expressed through magic and mythic lenses, it does not apply to those expressions at rational levels and higher who are indeed willing to "have their beliefs modified by new facts." So although "mutual inquiry" might be the antithesis of magic and mythic stages, it is in perfect alignment with rational, pluralistic, and integral interpretations of every faith.

Despite being dubbed a new atheist, Harris' point is significant to all of those deeply engaged with religion and who care about its potential contributions to the world. Once religion can meet other sectors of society on the equal footing provided by a foundation of reason (rational levels of expression and higher), religion will become a trustable source of influence. At higher levels, a common language of self-reflexivity and critical analysis come to the fore that will allow religion to "return from exile," expressing a voice of ultimate concern on the world stage.

Ultimately, including religion more steadily into what are now assumed to be public spheres is still, and will always be, a dangerous affair that must be handled delicately and with careful ethical intention. To this end, we must be aware of the potential for exploitation on two fronts. First, there remains a strong possibility that if religion is included into the public sphere, it runs the risk of religious leaders and their institutions being exploited for political ends. As Kubalkova explains, religions are "broadly compatible with directive rules of any political organization and thus eminently suitable for political exploitation."[375] Second, if we are to give religious leaders a more direct role in global affairs, we must be cautious about the risk of religious leaders becoming corrupted by economic lobbyists and special interests. In other words, we must be careful that the power and influence that our religious leaders have on the masses is not exploited to meet the demands of specific financial or economic agendas.

Keeping the above cautionary notes in mind, this book agrees with the secretary general of the World Council of Religious Leaders when he suggests that the three pillars of society (religion, economics, and politics) should all be honored but clearly differentiated.[376] Simultaneously, it will be the role of any truly integral practitioner or theorist to make sure that such a differentiation of value-spheres is flexible enough that direct communication and coordination links can be established which allow the three pillars of society to work conjunctively with a common global direction and intention.[377]

Blueprint for Action

Although this chapter has taken a strong stance for why higher levels of religious interpretation are more likely than others to catalyze the well-being of humanity, it also emphasizes that all levels of religious interpretation deserve protection and honoring. The theory of developmental religious pluralism should not be used to dominate lower levels in pathological hierarchy or to force upward development. Rather the integral model should be used as a map that articulates and coordinates all levels of interpretation into a comprehensive spectrum of consciousness.

Nearly thirty years after first publishing his theory of faith development, James Fowler makes a similar point, totally aligned with an integral approach:

It should never be the primary goal of religious education

simply to precipitate and encourage stage advancement. Rather, paying attention to stage and stage advancement is important in helping us shape our teaching and involvement with members of religious traditions. Movement in stage development, properly understood, is a byproduct of teaching the substance and the practices of faith.[378]

Noting well that stage advancement will come as a *byproduct* of proper exposure, perhaps the single greatest thing we can do to promote developmental religious pluralism in the world is to expand the current definition of "religious freedom."[379]

Former director of the United States Office of International Religious Freedom, Thomas Farr, states that religious freedom is the right to pursue the religious quest, to embrace or reject the interior and public obligations that ensue, and to enter or exit religious communities that reflect, or do not reflect, one's understanding of truth of religious truth.[380]

Similarly, Article 18 of the Universal Declaration of Human Rights states the following:

Everyone has the right to freedom of thought, conscience and religion; this right includes freedom to change his religion or belief, and freedom, either alone or in community with others and in public or private, to manifest his religion or belief in teaching, practice, worship and observance.

If we are to ensure that the higher stages of development are to flourish, the definition of religious freedom must not only protect the various traditions of our world faiths (Hinduism, Judaism, Islam, Christianity, Buddhism), it must also clearly and confidently protect each varying level of development *within* any single tradition (mythic Muslims, rational Muslims, pluralistic Muslims, integral Muslims).[381]

A definition of religious freedom in line with the model of developmental religious pluralism needs to be successfully cultivated and propagated at least three different scales:

1. *Governments and International Organizations:* Both individual governments and international bodies like the United Nations must clearly define religious freedom using an integral definition that includes both a developmental and postmodern approach.

2. *Religious Leaders:* The world's most preeminent religious leaders must begin mapping all relevant developmental levels within

their tradition in service of greater religious freedom. Of equal importance, these leaders must signify to the masses that all stages of religious orientation are legitimate expressions of faith.

3. *Individuals:* Individual religious adherents must fearlessly embrace the level of religious orientation appropriate for their respective level of complexity and care. Rational adherents and higher must not fear that they are abandoning their faith. To the contrary, expressing higher levels of spiritual intelligence is one of the most significant ways to ensure that one's tradition survives in its most healthy forms in the years to come.

True enforcement of religious freedom, that allows religion to be expressed through each level of psychological development, will be an important key to offering real and sustainable global change. As long as each stage of religious interpretation is legitimized, direct exposure to higher stages of religious interpretation will ensure that shifts to more mature levels of development emerge as the evolutionary process continues.

Chapter 10
Developmental Religious Pluralism in Your Personal Practice

As our world's great religious traditions expanded and spread throughout the globe they represented one of the very first attempts to develop inner technologies to produce greater degrees of human happiness. Given the role that religion played historically, citing its potential as a positive force in human happiness, and noting the fact that billions of individuals in the world today still subscribe to one particular faith or another, why is it that so many others abandon religion entirely?

Several key assumptions continue to lead a large portion of humanity on an antagonistic path with religion. For starters, many individuals presume that living in a state of insecurity and existential angst is simply an unavoidable part of life. As a result, many consider religion to be a *crutch* leaned upon by the weak. From this perspective, religion is seen as offering a type of false security by proposing un-testable answers to life's most challenging questions.

Other opponents of religion assume that religion is a relic of the past, forever tied to a traditional level of consciousness. These individuals conclude that those who have evolved to higher levels of psychological development (positions that base their truth claims on evidence) can no longer make use of an *irrational* system that depends on dogma and blind faith rather than reason.

Both of these critiques have been powerful enough to persuade masses of people away from institutionalized religion. A recently published Swedish survey inquired into the religious habits of individuals in fourteen different democratic countries around the globe. The results were staggering. On average, 36 percent of those surveyed either never or mostly never attended a formal religious service.[382] Even more telling, church attendance in at least one prominent country in

Western Europe dropped by nearly 25 percent since 1974.[383]

The new model offered in this book provides a more sophisticated form of religious analysis that directly challenges the classic assumptions about religion that cause so many to reject it. With a deeper understanding of the developmental spectrum and the various legitimate interpretations of religion, it is clear that religion consistently adapts and evolves to meet the needs of each individual according to his or her stage of psychological complexity.

Using a developmental approach to religion, we can stop making the common error that all religion is pre-rational. To assume that religion as a whole is pre-rational conflates the entire category of religion into only those forms expressed through lower levels of psychological development. As demonstrated in this book, pre-rational levels that base their beliefs on blind faith alone (magic and mythic) are merely two stages of religious orientation out of at least five legitimate levels of interpretation. This means that three stages (rational, pluralistic, and integral) meet the modern demand for reason, refusing to simply accept beliefs without some form of evidence or injunction.

So, what does all of this mean for you, the reader? Have you abandoned religion in your own life? Are you curious to see if there is a particular religious perspective that still resonates with your own journey toward increasing levels of happiness? If you are interested in finding a more fulfilling purpose in life, but unwilling to sacrifice your desire for evidence and rationality, then applying the model of developmental religious pluralism to your own life may make way for even deeper levels of satisfaction.

This chapter helps to reinforce the fact that religion is still a relevant technology for happiness for all individuals, no matter how high one might have matured along the spectrum of psychological complexity. By the end of this chapter, you the reader will come to understand and digest three main points:

1. You will learn the tools needed to assess your own level of religious orientation. after which you can successfully integrate teachings from the appropriate stage of a particular tradition into your everyday life. Integrating a proper level of religious interpretation resurrects religion's capacity to serve as a technology for happiness.

2. Perhaps even more importantly, you will get a better sense of the fundamental teachings about happiness that exist at the heart of the contemplative teachings of our world's traditions. Discovering that religion might still have relevance today (via

an embrace of a proper level of religious interpretation) can open you to the storehouse of knowledge and practices that you may have otherwise ignored. Contemplative teachings, if properly understood and thoroughly practiced, point out the fundamental nature of the human mind. A realization, as we shall see, that results in nothing less than the individual living each moment in and *as* the creative evolutionary impulse.

3. You will be walked through a series of plausible scenarios wherein developmental pluralism is explicitly engaged and you can see firsthand how the contemplative truths of each of our religious traditions can be embraced.

Determining Your Level of Religious Orientation

To begin, let's try a personal practice together to demonstrate one of the ways that you, the reader, can apply the model of developmental religious pluralism to your own life. As made clear in chapter 2, the most ideal way to identify a level of religious orientation is to take an assessment test specifically tailored to measure faith development and other secondary indicators. Unless you have access, psychometric tests and the scoring required to deliver proper results are not plausible options. In lieu of a proper test, this book provides a methodology that can serve as a basic guide for self-assessment.

Before we begin, let's ensure that your mind is in the proper state for such contemplation. Ask yourself the following questions: Have I abandoned religion? Do I have meaning in my life? Am I connected to my purpose? Do I feel drawn to any particular tradition? What is the dominant tradition I am surrounded by in my everyday life?

If you need a visual reference as you work your way through the following exercise, please see figure 25.

1. To begin, at the top of a sheet of paper write, "My Religious Orientation."

2. Write your first name at the center and bottom of your paper.

3. Take a moment to consider the tradition you most closely identify with. If you have rejected religion all together, select the most popular tradition you are surrounded by in your community, country, or culture. Just above your name, write

down the tradition and circle it.

4. Draw an arrow leading from your name to the tradition. To the left of the tradition write the label "religious filter."

5. It is time to consider where you are developmentally. (You may have already begun this process as you've read through earlier chapters of the book.) Do you resonate more with the magic, mythic, rational, pluralistic, or integral approach to religion? Refer back to chapter 3 if you need a refresher on the various flavors of development.

6. Above the tradition you listed in your "religious filter," write down the developmental level (magic, mythic, rational, pluralistic, integral) with which you most closely resonate.

7. On the left side of the page label your response "developmental filter." Then draw an arrow connecting your tradition (according to your "religious filter") with your level of development according to the "developmental filter." (For example, if you've selected the Christian tradition, draw a line connecting it to your level of development. See figure 25.)

8. Finally, think about your everyday life circumstances. Do you tend to be intense, passionate, perhaps even "extreme" in how you relate to the world? Are there underlying elements of your psychograph that might cause you to lean more towards an unhealthy expression of your tradition? Or conversely, do you take a more even-minded, "moderate" approach to life circumstances? Do others look up to you for your balanced psychological health?

9. Write down either "extreme" or "moderate" above your "developmental filter." Please circle your response and write "health filter" directly to the left. Draw a line connecting the response you gave for the developmental filter to the response you just provided for the health filter.

Congratulations! You've just mapped your own religious orientation. Review your map to see which perspective you resonate with most. Let's say, for example, you labeled yourself as a Christian, at a rational level of development, who possesses a moderate classification of health (see figure 25 below).

My Religious Orientation

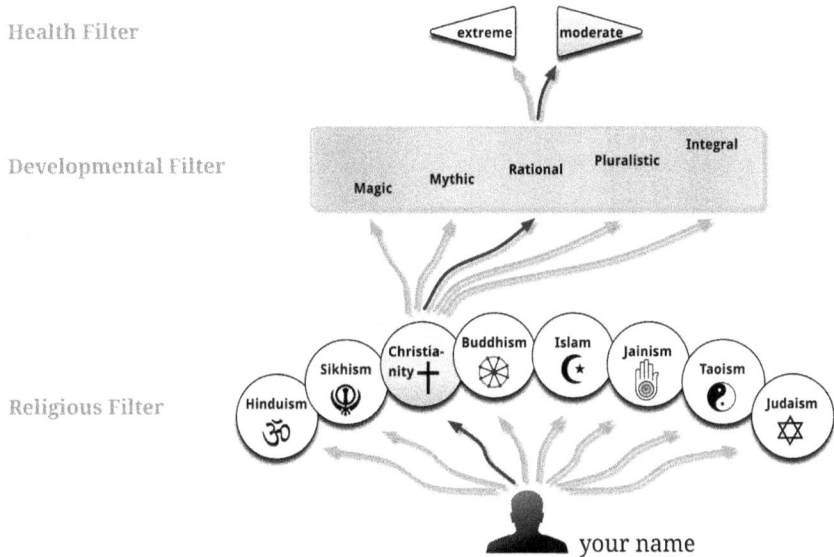

Figure 25

Within an otherwise confusing sea of religious perspectives, you now know that a *moderate Christian* perspective from a *rational* stage of developmental complexity will serve as the most effective technology for happiness in your life. As a result, you may resonate most with the teachings of Bishop Shelby Spong as found in his book *Rescuing the Bible from Fundamentalism.*[384] With over thirteen major world religions (Hinduism, Buddhism, Christianity, Islam, Judaism, Sikhism, Jainism, Taoism, Shintoism, Confucianism, Zoroastrianism, Baha'i, and various Indigenous traditions), five developmental levels (magic, mythic, rational, pluralistic, integral), and two degrees of health (moderate and extreme), you have now narrowed down your preference to a single orientation out of a potential of at least 130 perspectives (13 x 5 x 2 = 130).

Just imagine the degree of simplification you have just created in your life. Prior to doing this exercise there were at least 129 other perspectives that you may have come across in search of meaning. In all likelihood, you would have rejected almost all of them simply because you had not appropriately matched your own level of development with a corresponding religious expression that met your needs. With this new model in place, the classic assumptions that force so many to abandon religion lose their significant draw.

Religion will struggle to perform as a sufficient technology for happiness for the millions of modern and postmodern individuals in the world, unless we begin to understand that religion itself can be expressed not only through multiple degrees of health (extreme vs. moderate) but also through various levels of complexity (magic, mythic, rational, pluralistic, integral).

Let's explore some of the key take-a-ways offered thus far in this chapter before moving on.

First and foremost, examining religions through a developmental lens begins to release religion from a conflated identification with a traditional level of consciousness. Far too often religion is reduced to extremist orientations or traditional levels of expression because the developmental spectrum of faith is so poorly understood. Without a way for religious adherents to express themselves through higher levels of psychological maturity, large segments of humanity, who have moved beyond traditional levels of religious orientation, will continue to reject religion all together.

Second, a developmental perspective allows each of us to examine our own relationship to religion in a much more personal way. Examining our own sense of meaning, purpose, and significance allows one to see if he or she is sufficiently using all the technologies for happiness that religion can offer. The new model of developmental pluralism and the above personal exercise leave little doubt that every human being alive has a greater opportunity than ever before to find an appropriate path to a greater level of well-being and fulfillment.

Contemplative Teachings

Religion not only serves as a guiding force for behavior and social good but also offers contemplative teachings that can expand the way one perceives reality. Releasing religion across a broad developmental spectrum helps to ensure that religion can maintain a legitimate place in our human landscape. Additionally, a developmental perspective allows religion to continue to evolve to meet the needs of every new level of awareness that might emerge in the future.

Perhaps the biggest tragedy that results from the collective abandonment of religion is that far too often the contemplative teachings at the heart of each tradition are discarded as well. Unbeknownst to the masses who abandon religion, contemplative teachings in each tradition offer techniques and practices with the capacity to change the way one experiences reality. Developmental religious pluralism helps to ensure that the contemplative teachings of the world are preserved.

For those less familiar with spiritual practice in general (as separate from exoteric forms of ritual and other religious commonalities), I highly recommend reading the first volume of this series *Streams of Wisdom*. For now, the following overview supplies a brief introduction:

> The contemplative teachings of each religious tradition offer specific practices (i.e., meditation, centering prayer, etc.) that have the capacity to shift our identity to deeper levels of awareness. In the first volume of the series I refer to these shifts using Wilber's term "state-stage" and Daniel P. Brown's term "vantage point". Changes in vantage point refer to a shift in one's sense of subjectivity. At first, identity moves beyond exclusive identity with an individual egoic personality to identification with an ever-present witness (transcending personal self-structure). Eventually, vantage point development culminates in a radical release into the Absolute ground of being (nondual awareness). These shifts in vantage point occur independently of the stages of development described in this book. *Streams of Wisdom*, Volume 1 of the series in Integral Religion and Spirituality, addresses the details of spiritual development in full.

Vantage point shifts, or what Wilber calls state-stages, are available at every level of religious orientation.[385] This means that a mythic Christian can be living from any vantage point (gross thought, subtle personality, causal witness, or the nondual ground of being). Similarly, a pluralistic Buddhist might be living from a similar gross, subtle, causal or nondual vantage point. Regardless of how one interprets and expresses religion in its exoteric form by way of his or her level of religious orientation, access to increasing vantage points of subjectivity provides a golden thread that runs through all 130 perspectives outlined in this book.

It is ironic that the writer Sam Harris is considered a *New Atheist*. When examining his work in closer detail, his own quotes have the potential to help rejuvenate religion in an integral age through its rational and higher levels of interpretation. Although Harris has certainly abandoned traditional expressions of religion, he most certainly has not abandoned a deep respect for the contemplative teachings that each tradition holds at its core. Harris writes the following:

> Every spiritual tradition rests on the insight that how we use our attention, from moment to moment, largely

determines the quality of our lives. Many of the results of spiritual practice are genuinely desirable, and we owe it to ourselves to seek them out. It is important to note that these changes are not merely emotional but cognitive and conceptual as well. Just as it is possible for us to have insights in fields like mathematics or biology, it is possible for us to have insights about the very nature of our own subjectivity.

It is true that Harris abandons the classic descriptions of God to which traditional levels of consciousness so adamantly cling, but he has certainly not discarded each religion's ability to deliver happiness and fulfillment through specific forms of praxis. He continues:

A variety of techniques, ranging from the practice of meditation to the use of psychedelic drugs, attests to the scope and plasticity of human experience. For millennia, contemplatives have known that ordinary people can divest themselves of the feeling that they call "I" and thereby relinquish the sense that they are separate from the rest of the universe. This phenomenon, which has been reported by practitioners in many spiritual traditions, is supported by a wealth of evidence—neuroscientific, philosophical, and introspective. Such experiences are "spiritual" or "mystical," for want of better words, in that they are relatively rare (unnecessarily so), significant (in that they uncover genuine facts about the world), and personally transformative. They also reveal a far deeper connection between ourselves and the rest of the universe than is suggested by the ordinary confines of our subjectivity....A truly rational approach to this dimension of our lives would allow us to explore the heights of our subjectivity with an open mind, while shedding the provincialism and dogmatism of our religious traditions in favor of free and rigorous inquiry.[386]

The contemplative traditions within our world's great religious traditions reinforce religion's role as a technology for happiness. When religion is allowed to flow through higher lenses of complexity, in the healthiest expressions possible, those that once thought they must abandon religion may find new resources in ancient teachings.

It is important to note that as humanity moves forward on our evolutionary path, we will also develop more sophisticated secular (non-religious) versions of all the teachings offered in our world's contemplative traditions. That is to say that all the shifts in subjectivity offered by our religious traditions will also find practices and techniques stripped of religious language and fit for those who simply have no interest in reintegrating religion into their life. As secular versions of "inner engineering"[387] develop they should and must be incorporated into the larger system of technologies for human happiness. It is only when all human beings have access to the great teachings of the world that we might successfully begin surfing the ever increasing wave of our human potential.

The World We Can Create

Imagine a world wherein religion was translated appropriately for each level of religious orientation. Imagine each of those religions truly serving as a "conveyor belt" for human development. Imagine a world where all levels of religious orientation were honored, and as a result the esoteric teachings and practices of spiritual transformation that lie at the heart of each of our world's contemplative traditions could spread worldwide. Imagine a world wherein the more complex forms of religion, based on reason and open to critical inquiry (rational and higher), were successfully integrated into the other sectors of society (business, politics, etc.).

Because higher expressions of faith are more concerned with this world rather than other-worldliness, this new world would undergo a dramatic shift in the realm of social engagement. Human beings now preoccupied with the afterlife could shift their attention to this world by engaging the evolutionary impulse to create a better and more perfect reality here and now. If the model of developmental religious pluralism were adopted fully and implemented successfully, our world would be guided by leaders who know the truth of our contemplative traditions, who knew from their direct experience that consciousness is not primarily and originally divided into subject and object, me and you, them and us, but rather is one single ocean of interconnectivity.

This is not a mere utopian vision of peace and harmony. The world will always be home to individuals who, for numerous reasons, stop growth along the developmental spectrum. As we honor each developmental stage as a station in life, we recognize that human beings with less developmental maturity, infused with ego-centric and ethno-centric drives, will likely continue to prefer to make war based on notions of ethnic and cultural divide rather than working toward cooperation based on our common fundamental human unity. Yet, even as individuals at magic and mythic levels of development continue to force their limited perspectives on the rest of the world through violence and cohesion, greater levels of cooperation and coordination are inevitable as more human beings move into rational, pluralistic and integral stations of life.

The evolutionary path has proved for millennia that self-organization reaching to higher levels of complexity and organization is the most fundamental impulse at the heart of the creative universe. From atoms to molecules to cells, the drive of Eros, expressed through evolution, will perpetually unfold. And with it the world will move toward higher levels of intelligence, care, and potential resulting in even greater levels of fullness and happiness.

It is up to each of us as to how we engage. Either we let the evolutionary impulse of the universe drag us along unwittingly, or we make the decision, once and for all, to align ourselves with its principles and consciously evolve.

The evidence provided in this book is just the beginning of a practical and pragmatic shift that will help humanity realign with the greatest insights of our many cultures, traditions, and academic disciplines. The fragmented world is on the verge of an integral awakening. Can you feel it?

Appendix 1

A Visual Representation of the Great Conveyor Belt

The Conveyor Belt Transforming our World's Religions into Vehicles of Evolution

ACCORDING TO DUSTIN DIPERNA · RAINBOW OF ENACTMENT
VISUALIZATION BY INTEGRAL INFORMATION ARCHITECTURE

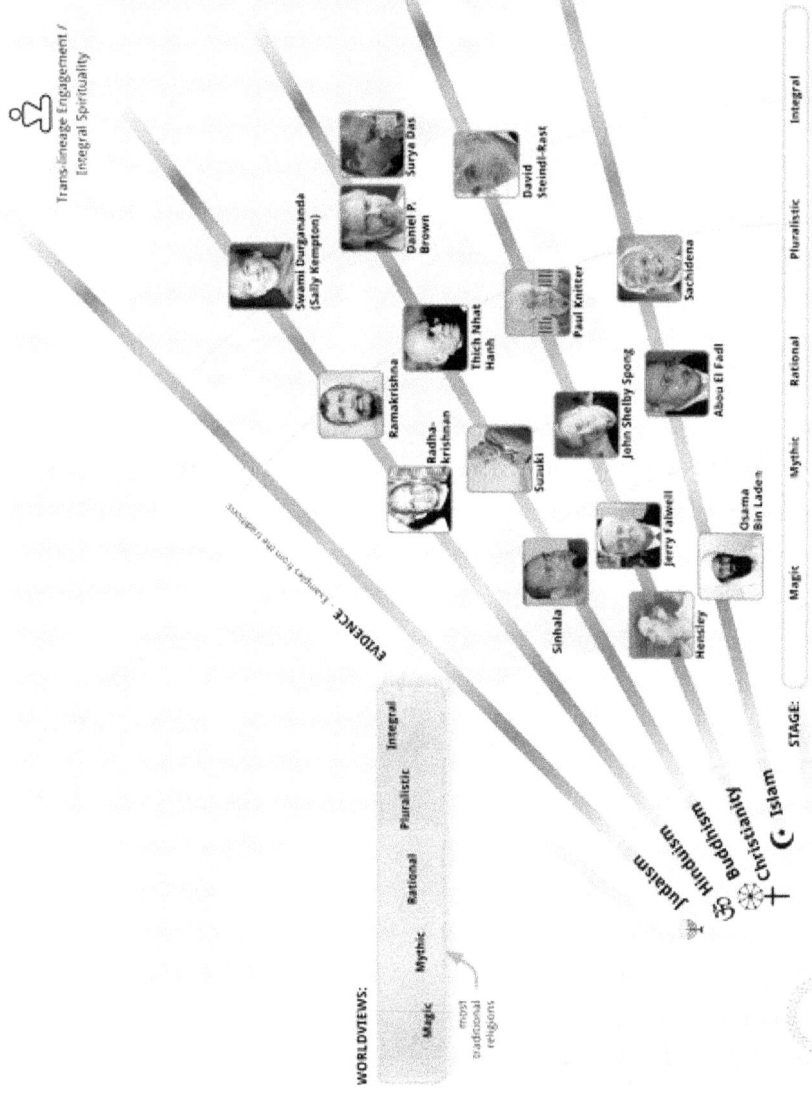

Trans-lineage Engagement /
Integral Spirituality

EVIDENCE · Lessons from the Leaders

WORLDVIEWS:

Magic · Mythic · Rational · Pluralistic · Integral

most traditional religions

Swami Durgananda (Sally Kempton)

Daniel P. Brown

Surya Das

David Steindl-Rast

Ramakrishna

Radha-krishnan

Thich Nhat Hanh

Paul Knitter

Sachidena

Suzuki

John Shelby Spong

Abou El Fadl

Sinhala

Jerry Falwell

Hensley

Osama Bin Laden

Judaism

Hinduism

Buddhism

Christianity

Islam

STAGE: Magic · Mythic · Rational · Pluralistic · Integral

233

Appendix 2
Integral Religious Studies in a Developmental Context

This appendix helps to position the theoretical aims of Integral Religious Studies within the multifaceted streams of inquiry already underway in today's broader examination of religious studies. Here, I begin with a description of how religious studies first emerged in the West, and then historicize the trajectory of the discipline over the past several centuries. Next, after having articulated the early streams of scholarly thought, I examine the limitations of the modern approaches to religion to show how postmodern methodologies in general, and the approach offered in this book in particular, correct for the mistakes of modern scholars. Finally, supporting the important truths uncovered by today's postmodern scholarship, I move on to explore how the model of developmental religious pluralism presented in this book enfolds a culturally sensitive hermeneutic of psychological development into a more holistically oriented, integral version of religious studies.

By way of historicizing Integral Religious Studies and situating the emergence of developmental religious pluralism into the proper moment in time, I hope to account for the fact that all belief, theory, and modes of discourse are dependent upon and conditioned by the particular historical context in which they arise. Such historical illuminations not only create deep reverence for the past but also allow us to consciously create new possibilities for the future.

Historicizing Religious Studies

The history and complexity of religious studies is full of nuance, particularities, and overlapping factors that influence our understanding of and assumptions about religious topics. As with almost any subject it can be problematic to address such complexity with a framework that employs broad generalizations. However, despite the validity of critical arguments against the use of generalizations, it is my contention that providing at least some sort of general historical account of religious studies does have heuristic value in so far as it helps to orient the reader. To this end, the following section seeks to demonstrate, in brief, how the evolution of religious studies has unfolded and how we, as scholars, thinkers, practitioners, and external observers of religion now have the capacity to use a meta-theoretical perspective to observe and integrate all of the practice and scholarship that has come to pass thus far.

A View Through a Western Lens

For the purposes of this outline, leaving open the possibility of multiple paths to modernity,[388] we examine religious studies as it evolved in the cultural context of the West.[389] For means of classification and categorization we begin by looking at two general types of theoretical shifts within the field. I label these two types of shifts "vertical" and "horizontal," respectively. Vertical transformational shifts, or what might be called "paradigm shifts," are those changes in academic inquiry that dramatically revolutionize the way in which the field of study is understood. Most often, vertical shifts result from revolutions in culture, society, and identity that deeply transform collective worldviews.

Vertical shifts in paradigm can be directly contrasted with horizontal shifts that represent changes in theoretical approach within an already existing paradigm. Horizontal shifts use a multitude of orientations to ask a wide variety of questions within a common working model of the world. In other words, despite the new additions to the field that horizontal shifts bring, the general worldview or vertical paradigm within which differences emerge is left unchanged.

Disaggregating these two types of theoretical shifts (horizontal and vertical) in the subsequent pages will provide an initial framework that helps to make sense of the countless recalibrations that have transpired in the field of religious studies over the past centuries. As our shared narrative of religious studies unfolds, I will clarify which categorizations represent vertical shifts in paradigm and which represent horizontal shifts in methodological approach.

The Three Paradigms of Religious Studies

Vertical transformation unfolded within religious studies by way of three broad historical stages: (1) premodern fusion, (2) modern differentiation, and (3) postmodern contextualization. As with most developmental sequences, not only did these three historical stages move from levels of less complexity (premodern) to levels of greater complexity (postmodern), but each new stage of historical unfolding also used relevant characteristics of each previous stage for its foundation. The next few pages explore each of these paradigmatic shifts in greater detail.

Premodern Fusion

In the West, centuries of dominance and obedience gave full reign of power and authority to the Catholic Church. For most of the 1st Millennium and for several centuries into the second millennium, knowledge in general and theological knowledge in particular was trapped in the interpretive framework and filter of the Church. The inerrancy of the Bible dictated cultural and social possibility leaving little room for freedom of thought outside of its narrow lens. In short, the Church was simultaneously researcher, authority, and disseminator of wisdom. As a result of this early fusion of value spheres, the study of religion was not divorced from the rest of knowledge. Religion itself had not yet been made an object of conscious reflection; religious studies as we know it today simply did not exist.

Religious scholars are all too familiar with these early modes of scholarship. University of Chicago professor Bruce Lincoln articulates how we might best view religious studies within the context of premodern fusion: "For insofar as the task of defining anything presumes a discrete object that can be identified in contradistinction to others, this implies a model of 'religion' that emerged only with the Enlightenment. Prior to that time, even in western Europe religion cannot be analytically (or practically) disarticulated from virtually all other aspects of culture."[390] To say it another way, and to reinforce Lincoln's point, in premodern times religion was so completely embedded into culture that it had not yet emerged as a legitimate field of objective inquiry.

Wilber explains premodern fusion along the same lines as Lincoln, emphasizing the fact that "none of the premodern worldviews clearly differentiated art-aesthetics, empirical-science, and religion-morals." It was precisely because these value spheres were undifferentiated in the premodern historical paradigm that "what happened in one sphere could dominate and control what happened in the others." Wilber continues, "thus, a scientist like Galileo could be prevented from pursuing the sphere of science because it clashed with the prevailing sphere of religion-morals. An artist such as Michelangelo was in constant conflict with Pope Julius II about the types of figures he was allowed to represent in his art, because expressive-art and religion-morals were not clearly differentiated, and thus oppression in one sphere was oppression in the other."[391] We'll come back to this idea shortly, but for now it is worth noting that certain elements of this type of oppression and domination created a ruthless reaction in the opposite direction as the next vertical paradigm began to emerge (leading from differentiation to disassociation). As we will discover together, the reaction to years of Church oppression was so strong that, for many, it leads to a direct repression of all forms of lived spirituality.

Modern Differentiation

Beginning with the Renaissance and finally culminating in the Western Enlightenment, a vertical shift in consciousness developed that would forever change the way in which knowledge was pursued.[392] Between the fourteenth and eighteenth centuries, elite thinkers began to individuate away from a type of conformist and mythic-centered knowledge platform. As reason and self-reflexivity gained strength, the Church systematically lost its hold as a single source of authority. These key confluences combined to create a full, vertical, paradigmatic transformation leading from premodern fusion to modern differentiation.

Again, it is perhaps Wilber who offers the most astute articulation of this vital fulcrum in Western social consciousness. Echoing the modern scholar Max Weber and contemporary theorists like Jurgen Habermas, Wilber explains that the modern paradigm of consciousness allowed a new perspective to emerge that consciously differentiated the major value spheres. Intellectuals exploring Plato's spheres of Beauty, Truth, and Goodness, or simply put, art, science, morals, were free from the domination of the Church and able to pursue their own truths independently.

The relative autonomy of value spheres represents a substantial leap forward. Whereas in the premodern paradigm it was simply not possible to pursue any independent truth outside of the confines of the Church, the modern paradigm created the possibility of the independent pursuit of knowledge that placed universal reason as the new centralizing authority. The significance such a shift had for the cultural consciousness of the West cannot be overstated.

One prime example drives the point home. As we learned, in

premodern times Church and State were fused: "If you disagreed with religious authorities, you could be tried for both heresy (a religious crime) and treason (a political crime). For heresy, you could be eternally damned; for treason, temporally tortured and killed..."[393] With a relative degree of differentiation, truth based on reason and science was positioned on a pedestal, replacing the infallibility of scripture. Quite extraordinarily, with the rise of the Enlightenment, the religious and political heretics of yesterday became the intellectual leaders of the new modern cultural revolution.

Despite the positive implications of this differentiation of values, the transition into modernity was not without its own set of problems. Following Wilber's articulation, it becomes clear that the momentum to differentiate each sphere of knowledge as separate and distinct was so strong that each went in a different direction without maintaining connection to the other. Differentiation turned into a pathological form of dissociation. In fact, the dissociation became so extreme, that the sphere of empirical science began to dominate the spheres of art and morality by "denying them any real existence at all."[394] Science became the new king, whilst morals and art suffered the repercussions of being second-class considerations (a phenomenon still existent today). Wilber puts it succinctly, "if differentiation was the dignity of modernity, disassociation was the disaster."[395]

In addition to differentiation of values, modern consciousness also created a rational turn inward toward greater degrees of self-reflexivity, taking the external focus away from the heaven of "other-worldly-ness" and brought the focus into "this world." "Instead of the infinite above," as Wilber puts it, "the West pitched its attention to an infinite ahead."[396] Progress and the promise of an improved future became the new God of those with modern consciousness:

> The standard God of the modern Western world was set. It would become the God of the bourgeois as well as of the dedicated scientist; the God of the materialist as well as the social reformer; the God of the Greens and the "back to nature" movement wherever it appeared; the God of democracy as well as the God of the Marxists and Maoists—what they all have in common is the God of all that is visible, and all that can be seen, and all that can be grasped with the hands ... An "other world" of any sort was thrown over; and the eyes of men and women settled steely on the horizons not above but in front of them, settled coldly on this world, and this world, and this world again. If salvation could not be found on this small earth, it could not be found at all.[397]

At this point in our historical narrative, it is vital that we make a clear distinction between the *practice of* religion and spirituality and the *study of* religion and spirituality. Whereas the practice of spirituality involves a direct relationship to spiritual teachings and personal implication, the study of religion and spirituality requires only an indirect and objective stance. Of course there are those who take both perspectives as well (scholar-practitioners) but for the purposes of this brief outline this distinction between a personal relationship (practitioner) and objective relationship (scholar) to spirituality provides a foundation for a more comprehensive historical understanding. As we shall see, the clear differentiation and eventual integration of each of these approaches play a significant role in the emergence of an integral approach to religious analysis.

Up until and through the beginning of the Renaissance, personal and objective approaches to the study of religion were fused (along with the major value spheres). It was assumed, with a few exceptions, that the study of religion could only be legitimately conducted by those adherents on the inside of the tradition. With the birth of modernity, however, these two spheres were distinguished and seen as independent from one another. For the very first time, one could take religion as an object of study from outside of the tradition itself. Religious belief was no longer a prerequisite for engagement.

However, Wilber observes that as reason and autonomy gained even more momentum, social consciousness confused the whole of spirituality with its premodern variations (an error still rampant today). Alas, the practice of religion became conflated with a premodern level of consciousness, leaving us with what Wilber calls the "level-line fallacy."[398]

With the new distinction between the practice of religion and the study of religion we can add more clarity to our historical account. Even as the personal practice of spirituality became frozen at premodern levels, trumped by the age of reason and scientific inquiry, the study of religion and spirituality as object carried on. This means that while premodern interpretations and personal practice stagnated for the vast majority of spiritual adherents, the study of spirituality as an objective field of inquiry continued to progress through modern and eventually postmodern paradigms of inquiry.

One of the secondary objectives of this book and the particular integral methodology I call developmental religious pluralism is to reunite the practitioner and scholarly orientations toward religion and spirituality. Ultimately, a deeper understanding of religion and spirituality's historical stagnation will open and release spiritual practice from its premodern shackles, allowing its more complex manifestations to flourish in modern, postmodern, and integral engagement. Before moving deeper into how this liberation may happen, let's first consider some of the other ways that the modern study of religion continued beyond premodern paradigm of understanding.

Sensitivity to Methodological Approach

Just as the shift from premodern to modern represents a vertical shift, many horizontal shifts occurred within modern consciousness as well. Following the Enlightenment, a particular type of sensitivity developed with regard to the objective study of religion. This new sensitivity showed scholars that there were multiple horizontal approaches to the same subject. Scholars discovered that the scientific study of religion produced dramatically different but equally valid results depending upon the disciplinary lens used by the researcher. As the centuries unfolded, scholars began to apply specific methodologies from other fields of academic inquiry to examine religion and religious phenomena. Overtime, religion was examined through the lenses of anthropology (Feuerbach)[399], sociology (Weber, Durkheim), psychology (Freud, James, Jung, Frazer, Adler, Otto, Tyler) and phenomenology (Saussaye, Kristensen, van der Leeuw). Although each of the above approaches (sociology, psychology, etc.) were in fact new, representing authentic categorical shifts in terms of their horizontal methodology, they all occurred within the same vertical paradigm of modern differentiation. That is to say, all attempts at theorizing, no matter how diverse, were still articulated (historically) from within the confines of a modern level of consciousness.

Essentializing Religion

In addition to a more particularized approach that understood how different lenses of social science produce different perspectives on religion, an essentialized approach also unfolded with modern consciousness that attempted to position and categorize major religious traditions. In an effort to gain more clarity, modern scholars assumed that they could systematize religion and religious phenomena into broad universal categories. This particular approach, seeking universal essences and broad commonalities, is now emblematic of the modern paradigmatic approach.[400]

The common classification "world religions" stems directly out of this early attempt to find the essence of the great religious traditions around the globe. When speaking of world religions in an academic context, we usually list at least thirteen major systems of praxis: Hinduism, Buddhism, Christianity, Islam, Judaism, Sikhism, Jainism, Taoism, Shintoism, Confucianism, Zoroastrianism, Baha'i, and Indigenous.

Although it can be helpful to use such categories, it is valuable to remember that this type of categorization is limited by the contours of modern consciousness. "The construction of 'world religions' is underpinned by a certain kind of theorizing," explains Gavin Flood, "whose roots are in the Enlightenment and which seeks universals. The ability to abstract the world religions from history and to see them as in some sense equal (though not often equal to Christianity with which they have been set in contrast), might itself be seen as part of the modernist idea of progress towards a clearer future in the academy."[401] As we will see below in our discussion of postmodern contextualization, Flood's comment does not imply that the category "world religions" is problematic in and of itself, but rather it points to the fact that significant issues arise if the generalizations about traditions lack a deeper and more nuanced perspective.

The differentiation of value spheres, the sensitivity to horizontal methodology, and the first attempts to categorize world religions are vital to our understanding of religious studies today. Despite the fact that scholars today correct many of the mistakes made by these early modernists, the value that this initial clarification added cannot be understated. The important distinctions of anthropology of religion and sociology of religion, those initial insights into the origin of religion, psychology of religion, and use of phenomenological methodologies to explain the "sacred" in its various forms, continue to add to our collective knowledge systems and religious sensibilities. Similarly, the categorizations of various systems of faith, despite the misleading sense of homogeneity that they once implied, are still key elements to developing greater religious understanding and religious literacy worldwide. Now, however, we move on to the third turning of the wheel of religious studies to see how even these modern approaches were transcended and enveloped into a new vertical paradigmatic shift.

Postmodern Contextualization

The modern paradigm of differentiation, despite the incredible value that it added, left several substantial problems that would need to be resolved by the next generation of scholars. The next major vertical paradigm shift into postmodernity is usually linked to the second half of the twentieth century, although its roots began to sprout almost a century earlier. Radical critiques of the modern position (from its lack of cultural, historical, and contextual sensitivity to its erroneous assumption about the existence of some sort of objective God's eye view), lead postmodern scholarship to revolutionize the modern paradigm with a new kind of contextualization and an ultra-sensitivity to time, place, identity, language, and interpretation. Let's unpack each of the horizontal categorical shifts at the postmodern paradigm one at a time. Recall that this historical account is provided to remind the reader where we have come from and to where we might head as religious studies blossoms into an integral age.

Sensitivity to Universal Claims

As modern consciousness found itself taken as the object of reflection, its theories were brought into greater suspicion. For starters, as touched upon above with Flood's insight, postmoderns continually bring the term "world religion" under strong scrutiny due to the fact that it emerged from a modern level of consciousness that lacked a certain degree of sophistication and awareness of the social power structures of Western discourse (e.g., Foucault), which inadvertently imposed static categories onto the cultural and religious "other" (e.g., Said's *Orientalism*). Today's scholars claim that any approach to categorize universal characteristics of traditions is naïve at best and based on totalitarian impulses at worst. The claim is made on solid ground, in principle. Each tradition, the postmodern critique explains, is so internally diverse, and so much shaped by regional values and identity that such broad categorizations lose value. Flood continues his point with even greater strength:

> While the academic study of religions has largely moved away from the essentialist understandings that religion has some common, perhaps transcendent, essence it has only begun to take seriously the claim that religion cannot be abstracted from its cultural matrices. Courses on "world religions" still present these constructed entities as if they are in some timeless realm (perhaps a realm of pure doctrine) outside of wider cultural patterns and history (especially colonial history, the relation between religion and capitalism, and recently globalization)... To address this issue the academic study of religion needs to examine religions within their political, cultural, and social contexts.[402]

Postmodern scholar Paul Griffiths takes a more critical approach, although it manages to deliver equal force along similar lines: "the sortal 'world religion' was developed and is still often deployed for the properly theoretical purpose of depicting alien practice as a consumable good accommodatable by late-capitalist appetites."[403] In other words, rather than engaging the uniqueness of each manifestation of religiosity in the world, modern approaches tend to homogenize religion and place it neatly into categories that represent merely a pale reflection of the diverse reality on the ground. It is from this base that, for better or worse, generic categorizations of religion are "consumed" by a privileged (often Western) elite.

Other postmodern scholars, like Jonathan Z. Smith, bring less of a critique to the categorization of religion but take strong positions regarding the study of religion as a whole. Smith explains that "religion is solely the creation of the scholar's study. It is created for the scholar's analytic purposes by his imaginative acts of comparison and generalization. Religion has no independent existence apart from the academy. For this reason, the student of religion, and most particularly the historian of religion, must be relentlessly self-conscious. Indeed, this self-consciousness constitutes his primary expertise, his foremost object of study."[404] Although extreme in nature, Smith's comments set the foundation for almost all postmodern scholarship. Rather than focusing upon a world "out there" of religious practices and beliefs (the modern paradigm's primary object), postmodern scholarship in religion turns the lens onto knowledge itself and its linguistic and cultural modes of expression.

Sensitivity to the Scholar's Point of View

Among the many horizontal realizations of postmodernity, one fundamental discovery was that the postmodern scholar must be self-reflective. He or she must be aware of his or her own position, biases, and subtle conditioning that might bend his or her research project in a particular direction and ideological agenda. Such self-reflective awareness was simply not present in modern scholarship.

Building upon the work of French social scientist Pierre Bourdieu, Flood explains that "reflexivity refers to the ability of a researcher, or indeed as a strategy embedded within method, to become aware of the contexts of research and the presuppositions of the research programme."[405] According to Flood, assumptions are "the inevitable historical contingencies within which we all operate."[406] Therefore, it is not to say that we must avoid assumptions all together, but rather we must seek to uncover and critically reflect upon all those assumptions molding and shaping our particular discourse that might otherwise remain unknown. By bringing our particular assumptions to light and exposing the cultural, linguistic, social, and historical conditioning, we gain a more transparent perspective on his or her own reality. Following the lead of postmodern scholars, the method employed in this book deliberately employs this type of self-reflexive approach.

One example of self-reflexivity is useful to provide you with an understanding of how this postmodern approach shows up in scholarship. As postmodern scholarship deepened, a realization began to emerge that the language used to describe a given subject was equally if not more important than the content of the subject itself. "The importance of contextualism, interpretations, and hermeneutics in general," Wilber explains, "came to the fore with what has been called the linguistic turn in philosophy— the general realization that language is not simply representation of a pre-given world but has a hand in the creation and construction of that world. With the linguistic turn, which began roughly in the nineteenth century, philosophers stopped using language to describe the world and instead started looking at language itself."[407] The self-reflexive mirror had been set in place.

So what does it mean if all research and theory is shaped by language and co-created by the point of view of the researcher? Karl Popper's "myth of the framework"[408] suggests that within the context of religious studies and spiritual praxis "mystics and religious practitioners are prisoners of their conceptual frameworks." Furthermore, Popper explains, "spiritual knowledge must always be shaped by or screened through them."[409] Popper's insight teaches us that our identities and speech are preconditioned by the particular frameworks that lend meaning and social validation to our experience. Even if the insights are valid, whether one is a spiritual practitioner or a religious scholar, each insight can only be accessed by way of "our situated phenomenal awareness of them."[410] Similarly, renowned postmodern scholar and philosopher Paul Ricoeur "has accepted the modern mantle of criticism, to take nothing for granted and to test everything. So far, he is with Descartes," explains Ferrer. "With other postmodernists, however, he has turned his critical eye upon modernity itself, questioning the human capacity to arrive at the Cartesian idea of a single, clear and distinct, God's-eye point of view."[411]

Gavin Flood helps to further fill out the postmodern perspective on "point of view" using a congruent line of thought:

> Research within the many fields which comprise religious studies is in the end conversation with texts and persons. The researcher is entering into a dialogue with a text or person and herself becoming a part of an intersubjective and intertextual matrix in which all understanding—

and explanation—arises. Understanding is always from a place.... and is legitimized by wider social forces. To develop method sensitive to context is to be open to the 'otherness' of the material or persons who are the 'object' of study and to recognize speaking and hearing subjects as the place of meaning.

It is clear that "point of view" is not only subject to language, but also to time, place, and culture. All of which represent fundamental postmodern sensitivities that I employ throughout this book, as far as they go.

Sensitivity to Interpretation

Because there is always an observer, a researcher, or an individuated perspective with all of its relative conditioning, scholarship now understands that the whole of reality is subject to interpretation. This leads to the startling discovery that there is not a single objective world out there that we are all describing. Rather, the world out there is always subject to our own unique perspective; we participate in the creation of the world in each instant of cognition.

In the most general sense, the study of interpretation is called hermeneutics. As intellectual giant Paul Ricoeur points out, "hermeneutics itself puts us on guard against the illusion or pretension of neutrality."[412] There is always a relative vantage point from which one is articulating.

As one of the pillars of the postmodern paradigm, it serves us well to understand interpretation with a more nuanced perspective. Understanding interpretation not only serves the heart of postmodern thought but it too serves as the core foundation of this book. Let's dive deeper following the lead of postmodern scholar and theologian David Tracy. Tracy explains that "any act of interpretation involves at least three realities: some phenomenon to be interpreted, someone interpreting that phenomenon, and some interaction between these first two realities."[413]

It is perhaps easy to underestimate the power and importance of interpretation. "Interpretation seems a minor matter, but it is not." Tracy explains, "every time we act, deliberate, judge, understand, or even experience, we are interpreting. To understand at all is to interpret."[414] Tracy continues, "Interpretation is thus a question as unavoidable, finally, as experience, understanding, deliberation, judgment, decision, and action. To be human is to act reflectively, to decide deliberately, to understand intelligently, to experience fully. Whether we know it or not, to be human is to be a skilled interpreter."[415]

The significance of interpretation is directly linked to the discovery that language creates our day-to-day reality on levels previously unimagined. Modern scholars simply lacked the realization that in every instant we are imprisoned within the confines of our language; we know the world only through representation. Fundamental to this linguistic turn is a more profound understanding that language is composed of what Saussure called "signs and signifiers," representations of reality that do not and cannot refer directly to the thing in itself.

The American Pragmatist philosopher Charles Sanders Peirce, taking a slightly different approach to the significance of signs, explains what it is like to live from within this new linguistic postmodern paradigm of interpretation: "It seems a strange thing, when one comes to ponder over it, that a sign should leave its interpreter to supply a part of its meaning; but the explanation of the phenomenon lies in the fact the entire universe—not merely the universe of existents, but all that wider universe, embracing the universe of existents as part, the universe which we are all accustomed to refer to as 'the truth'—that all this universe is perfused with signs, if it is not composed exclusively of signs"[416] In other words, signs are never neutral with an absolute meaning, but rather they are always, first and foremost, representations and interpretations of ideas.

As religious studies gained clarity and sophistication, scholars began to point out that there are other individual and social factors outside of language that also influence interpretation. Like linguistic differences, such variances create significant differentiation in religious praxis, belief, and behavior. For instance, gender or power differentials drastically influence the way a particular tradition evolves over time. Similarly, interaction with others' value systems create versions of syncretism and accommodation that might seem foreign to a practitioner of the same faith in a different area of the world. Although this book focuses on the role of interpretation from an individual perspective, all arguments are always first and foremost situated in the larger context of culture, social structure, identity, and history (see the section on Integral Religious Studies below for details).

Interpretation, as valuable as it is to recognize, is not in and of itself the ultimate end or goal. Rather scholarship follows a pragmatic imperative that insists that interpretation leads to some form of effective action. "All theory of interpretation—like all theory itself—is an interpretation as good or as bad as its ability to illuminate the problems we discover or invent and its ability to increase the possibilities of good action."[417] The entire thrust of this book is designed to produce more effective action in the world as a result of a better understanding of religious interpretation.

The result of this new contextual understanding, among other things, created a radical shift toward new forms of religious pluralism. (In chapter 1, we looked deeper into some of the new perspectives that arise directly out of the postmodern turn in religious studies). Let's stay the course to see how this postmodern lens might be transcended as well.

Post-Postmodern Participatory Integration

Astute scholars like Flood sense the need for yet a fourth vertical paradigm shift in religious studies. There is a growing need for religious studies to "engage much more with wider debates in social sciences and humanities and to develop a rigorous metatheoretical discourse."[418] However partial it might be, this book begins to fill out Flood's vision of a fourth turning.[419]

According to Wilber, "if the great achievement of the Enlightenment (and 'modernity') was the necessary differentiation of the Big Three [value spheres of Art, Morals, and Science], the great task of 'post modernity' is their integration, overcoming what [Charles] Taylor called 'a monster of arrested development'."[420] It is to this end that the current volume continues the postmodern march toward a more holistic model of religious studies. Although only time will tell if the ideas in this book earn the rights to declare a valid paradigm shift, it is still useful to differentiate this work from the past methodologies by using a new term: Integral Religious Studies.

In this context, the word integral has a specific meaning, best defined as:

> Comprehensive, inclusive, non-marginalizing, embracing. Integral approaches to any field attempt to be exactly that: to include as many perspectives, styles, and methodologies as possible within a coherent view of the topic. In a certain sense, integral approaches are "meta-paradigms," or ways to draw together an already existing number of separate paradigms into an interrelated network of approaches that are mutually enriching.[421]

The following graphic helps to illustrate the course of religious studies over the past thousand years and offers at least one way in which the scholar of Integral Religious Studies might view the current academic inquiry.

Integral Religious Studies in Context

	Vertical Paradigm	Horizontal Approach
Post-postmodern	Participatory Integration	Integral Methodological Pluralism
Postmodern	Contextualization	Hermeneutics; Post-colonialism; Historicization; Identity; etc.
Modern	Differentiation	Anthropology of Religion; Sociology of Religion; Psychology of Religion; etc.
Premodern	Fusion	Religion not yet objectified

(Left vertical axis label: Historical Stages)

Figure A

The graphic above represents both vertical shifts (Fusion, Differentiation, Contextualization, and Participatory Integration) as well as major horizontal shifts at each of those vertical stages. Each new vertical paradigm transcends and includes the important features of the one that preceded it. For example, the postmodern paradigm includes the valuable horizontal methodological approaches that emerged in the modern paradigm. Notice however that there was a major developmental split as religious studies moved from fusion to differentiation or premodernity to modernity. The all-so-valuable process of including the previous paradigm was almost entirely abandoned. The approach taken in this book begins to reunite the value spheres once dissociated from one another at the split into modernity. Joined in dialogue whilst avoiding premodern fusion, domination, and repression of one sphere over the other, the wound of a pathological version of modern differentiation is *finally healed.*

With the first three vertical shifts in paradigm (premodern, modern, postmodern) fully articulated, we now turn to the contours of a post-postmodern version of religious studies. As shown in the figure above, religious studies moved from fusion to differentiation to contextualization. We now turn to the newly emerging paradigm we call participatory integration or simply Integral Religious Studies and the particular horizontal methodological approach at that paradigm called developmental religious pluralism.

Several characteristics place the models presented in this book apart from those earlier paradigms. Whilst including the sensitivities of modern and postmodern consciousness, this book offers several ways that religious studies might leap forward yet again. Although details will be fleshed out over the following chapters in much greater depth, a few initial comments are worth citing here.[422]

The following list offers some of the key features of the post-postmodern approach taken in this book. I demonstrate below only some of the ways in which I transcend and include the important features of the previous paradigmatic methodologies, incorporating them all into an approach Wilber calls integral methodological pluralism. This book:

1. *Corrects for the errors of modern scholarship while still including an evolutionary perspective.* Although developmental in nature, the modern paradigm failed to see cross-cultural contexts and the influence of linguistics and social structures of power. Because it lacked a general sensitivity to these various complexities, the modern level of consciousness posited a world "out there" that was real in and of itself, as if it could be directly known. These basic errors led to universal assertions about the nature of reality, especially in the realm of religion. Not only did these assertions tend to be Western-centric but scholars within the modern paradigm often made arrogant strides to place Christianity in particular, and the monotheistic traditions in general, above and superior to all other religious traditions.[423] As its first point of methodological self-reflexivity, this book skillfully navigates around this modern trap. Although this book does indeed employ a developmental approach, it does so only on careful footing so as to not make similar mistakes as those early modern pioneers like E.B. Tyler and Frazer, who using an evolutionary perspective, failed to bring a critical and sensitive perspective to their approach.

2. *Adds a developmental understanding to postmodern interpretation.* Just as each idea and concept needs to be contextualized into what Flood calls the "intersubjective and intertextual matrix," I use such ideas to also elaborate how we might take seriously the notion that "understanding is always from a place." Each interpreter or researcher is always positioned from a particular perspective. Whether that place of understanding is related to identity (i.e., gender, profession, race) or some broader social, cultural, or historical lineage, perspectives are always conditioned to a certain degree. Furthermore, because no single perspective can be void of a particularized position, this

book pays careful attention to how psychological development changes one's perspective, in conjunction with that of identity role and social-cultural context. Rather than falling back to some sort of modern universal truth claim, pegging tradition against tradition or culture against culture, this book enhances and propels a more nuanced perspective of religious interpretation by basing its claims on cross-cultural studies of how individual human beings grow in terms of psychological complexity.

3. *Uses broad categorizations of "world religions" but does not seek to essentialize each tradition assuming it to be monolithic and homogeneous in structure.* Although the book is indeed divided into four categories according to various traditions (Christianity, Islam, Buddhism, and Hinduism) it does so to further prove the diversity within each of these categories. Not only is this book privy to culturally conditioned differences between traditions, but it also takes this sort of careful scholarship one step further to show how beyond broad identity categorizations (gender, class, etc.) psychological development plays yet another important factor that creates radical diversity and heterogeneity even within traditions embedded in the same cultural-linguistic matrix.

4. *Seeks to include cultural and systemic conditioning whilst avoiding a form of individualistic psychological reductionism.* Although I do indeed focus on psychological factors in this book, I've been careful not to confuse the vertical paradigm shift of Integral Religious Studies as a whole with the specific slice of Integral Religious Studies undertaken here (i.e., developmental religious pluralism). Those readers already familiar with Wilber's Four Quadrant Model as first presented in *Sex, Ecology, Spirituality*, will recognize that despite the fact that all quadrants (interior and exteriors of individual and collective spheres) are taken into careful consideration, the main thrust of this book delivers a careful consideration of the influence of the interior of the individual sphere when considering religious analysis. Just as each historical stage of religious inquiry tended to bring full attention to the new details whilst blinding itself from older important truths, this new form of study needs to be cautious not to reduce everything to a psychological lens, despite how profound these discoveries might be. If we develop tunnel

vision and only see development to the exclusion of the modern contributions of differentiation, and the postmodern contributions of how identity, context, and history shape religious thought we will be embracing the very small-minded paradigm that we are trying to transcend with this more integral and comprehensive approach.

5. *Revitalizes the intellectual currents of pragmatism.* Following in the footsteps of scholars like Charles Sanders Peirce, John Dewey, and William James, the developmental hermeneutic expressed herein shares the understanding that "linguistic behavior is a kind of action and its validity is vouchsafed inasmuch as it achieves desired communicative ends."[424] To echo James, "Grant an idea or belief to be true, what concrete difference will its being true make in any one's actual life?"[425] This book adheres to religious scholar Jorge Ferrer's suggestion that "pragmatist philosophy always begin in the midst of things, colored by sentiments, events, and human needs, a philosophy subject to constant revision and to new demands."[426] To this end, this book and the theory represented is, as Wilber often says, "the first word, not the last word" in what I hope will be an extended and invigorating look at what it means to call a particular approach integral in its orientation to religious studies. May this book's central thesis be judged not only on its accuracy but also by whether or not it can produce effective action in the world.

Although pushing beyond the limitations of postmodern contextualization to transcend yet include its important distinctions is a fairly recent endeavor in religious studies, several scholars are beginning to explore the field of Integral Religious Studies more fully. At the Integral Theory Conference held at JFK University in Pleasant Hill, California, in 2010, Bruce Alderman gave a stunning presentation on the ways in which a post-postmodern view can help religion move beyond its tendencies toward mere inclusivism and pluralism.[427] At the same conference, Geert Drieghe surveyed some of the various problems that religious diversity presents to the average pluralist and how an integral lens can help scholars move beyond their current roadblocks toward a more effective methodological approach.[428] In the *Oxford Handbook of Religion and Science* still other integral scholars find an even broader application. In their timely article, Sean Esbjorn-

Hargen and Ken Wilber use an integral lens to offer a successful and truly impressive proposal for the "comprehensive integration of science and religion."[429]

The integral grassroots movement, outside the realm of academic scholarship, is already applying the methodologies of Integral Religious Studies in a more direct way. Two prime examples come from within the Christian tradition in the United States. The first is represented by the efforts of Reverend Tom Thresher in the state of Washington. Setting his teachings in a developmental context, Thresher follows Wilber's lead and is in sync with the ideas in this book, claiming that churches are uniquely positioned to transform our society.[430] Currently, Thresher heads one of the very first integrally informed churches and is successfully guiding his congregation from a predominately pluralistic religious orientation to one that is fully integral. Thresher's recent book *Reverent Irreverence: Integral Church for the 21ˢᵗ Century* begins to outline what we might hope for from an integral church.

Cindy Wigglesworth's work with Unity Church represents a second powerful example. Recently, Unity Church pledged to become an "explicitly integral church." In her current position as founder and owner of Conscious Pursuits Inc., Wigglesworth plans to use both her knowledge of Integral Theory as well as her Spiritual Intelligence Assessment tool to help transform Unity's entire system into one that employs post-postmodern sensibilities. Although still in its initial phases of transformation, her work with the Unity Church is a harbinger of times to come.[431]

Conclusion

As we have seen, each new development in religious studies includes the insights of the previous stage but then seeks to add powerful correctives and contributions. Just as context became a central focus of postmodern scholarship, inclusion of the psychological development becomes one of the new horizontal methodological approaches to post-postmodern analysis. If we call the postmodern era the emergence of "contextual" sensitivity, the integral age is most certainly an era of "developmental" sensitivity. As psychological maturity increases, so too does the individual's level of complexity, his or her ability to take perspectives and his or her ability for compassionate embrace of the religious or social "other." Such are worthy explorations of both scholars and religious practitioners alike in the coming decades.

Although the rest of this book uses a methodology that focuses on individual development rather than collective development, the content presented in the following sections mirrors the historical considerations outlined in this chapter. Thus, each vertical paradigmatic shift in historical consciousness offered in this chapter is recapitulated in individual human's psychological structures over the course of a single lifetime. That is to say, because humans today stop variously along the spectrum of development, each level or stage of paradigmatic unfolding (premodern, modern, postmodern) is still present and still active in each of the traditions of our world's religions.

For clarity purposes, rather than employ the historical paradigmatic terms premodern, modern, postmodern and post-postmodern used in this chapter to refer to the stages as they unfold in the psychology of an individual, the remainder of this book uses the terms magic, mythic, rational, pluralistic, and integral. Although the collective/historical dimensions do indeed correlate with the psychological stages, this distinction between individual terminology and collective paradigmatic terminology will make it even more obvious when I am speaking of historical stages versus an individual's stage of development. Furthermore, using five stages to define psychological development rather than the four used to describe paradigms allows for a more nuanced and sophisticated approach to developmental interpretation.[432]

Appendix 3
Engage on the Web

If this new model of developmental religious pluralism is to have any future at all, its success will need the help and participation of a much wider audience.

For the latest information regarding developmental religious pluralism, Integral Religious Studies, and the Great Human Tradition in general please visit: www.BrightAlliance.org.

This model can only be perfected with multiple perspectives from around the globe from each culture and every developmental level. Please don't hesitate to offer your comments, suggestions, and critique.

May all beings repose in the infinite love-bliss of *being*.
May the evolutionary and creative impulse of the universe
guide our actions and intentions in the realm of becoming.
May this global initiation into the Great Human Tradition
manifest the whole potential of Earth's destiny.

Bibliography

Alatas, Syed Farid. *An Islamic Perspective on the Commitment to Inter-Religious Dialogue.* Kuala Lumpur: International Institute of Advanced Islamic Studies, 2008.

Aslan, Adnan. *Religious Pluralism in Christian and Islamic Philosophy: The Thought of John Hick and Seyyed Hossein Nasr.* Richmond, England: Curzon, 1998.

Barrett, David B., George Thomas Kurian, and Todd M. Johnson. *World Christian Encyclopedia: A Comparative Survey of Churches and Religions in the Modern World.* Oxford; New York: Oxford University Press, 2001.

Barnett, Thomas P. M. *The Pentagon's New Map: War and Peace in the Twenty-First Century.* New York: G.P. Putnam's Sons, 2004.

———. *Great Powers: America and the World After Bush.* New York: G.P. Putnam's Sons, 2009.

Bartholomeusz, Tessa J, and Silva De, Chandra Richard. *Buddhist Fundamentalism and Minority Identities in Sri Lanka,* Albany, NY: State University of New York Press, 1998.

Banchoff, Thomas F. *Democracy and the New Religious Pluralism.* Oxford; New York: Oxford University Press, 2007.

———. *Religious Pluralism, Globalization, and World Politics.* New York: Oxford University Press, 2008.

Beck, Don, and Christopher C Cowan. *Spiral Dynamics: Mastering Values, Leadership, and Change: Exploring the New Science of Memetics,* Vol. Developmental Management, Cambridge, Mass., USA: Blackwell Business, 1996.

Bender, Courtney., and Pamela E. Klassen. *After Pluralism: Reimagining*

Bibliography

Religious Engagement. New York: Columbia University Press, 2010.

Beneke, Chris. *Beyond Toleration: The Religious Origins of American Pluralism*. Oxford; New York: Oxford University Press, 2006.

Berger, Peter L. *The Social Reality of Religion*. London: Faber, 1969.

―――. *The Desecularization of the World: Resurgent Religion and World Politics*. Washington, D.C. Grand Rapids, Mich.: Ethics and Public Policy Center W.B. Eerdmans Pub. Co., 1999.

Bidmos, M. A. *Inter-Religious Dialogue: The Nigerian Experience*. Lagos: Islamic Publications Bureau, 1993.

Boase, Roger. *Islam and Global Dialogue: Religious Pluralism and the Pursuit of Peace*. Aldershot, Hants, England; Burlington, Vt.: Ashgate, 2005.

Chittick, William C. *Imaginal Worlds: Ibn Al-Arabi and the Problem of Religious Diversity*. Vol. SUNY series in Islam Albany: State University of New York   Press, 1994.

Clayton, Philip, and Zachary R. Simpson. *The Oxford Handbook of Religion and Science*. Vol. Oxford Handbooks Oxford; New York: Oxford University Press, 2006.

Cobb, John B. *Christian Faith and Religious Diversity*. Minneapolis: Fortress Press, 2002.

―――, John B., and Paul F. Knitter. *Transforming Christianity and the World: A Way Beyond Absolutism and Relativism*. Maryknoll, N.Y.: Orbis Books, 1999.

―――, John B., and Ward. McAfee. *The Dialogue Comes of Age: Christian Encounters With Other Traditions*. Minneapolis: Fortress Press, 2010.

Coolsaet, R. *Jihadi Terrorism and the Radicalisation Challenge in Europe*. Aldershot, England; Burlington, Vt.: Ashgate, 2008.

Covington, Dennis. *Salvation on Sand Mountain: Snake Handling and Redemption in Southern Appalachia*, Reading, Mass.: Addison-Wesley, 1995.

Coward, Harold G. *Modern Indian Responses to Religious Pluralism*. Albany: State University of New York Press, 1987.

Cox, Harvey Gallagher. *Fire From Heaven: The Rise of Pentecostal Spirituality and the Reshaping of Religion in the Twenty-First Century.* Reading, Mass.: Addison-Wesley Pub., 1995.

Dean, Thomas. *Religious Pluralism and Truth: Essays on Cross-Cultural Philosophy of Religion.* New York: State University of New York Press, 1995.

Deida, David. *Intimate Communion: Awakening Your Sexual Essence,* Deerfield Beach, Fla: Health Communications, 1995.

———. *Naked Buddhism: 39 Ways to Free Your Heart and Awaken to Now,* Austin, Tex.: PLEXUS, 2002.

DeLong-Bas, Natana J. *Wahhabi Islam: From Revival and Reform to Global Jihad,* Oxford; New York: Oxford University Press, 2004/2007.

Denny, Frederick Mathewson. *An Introduction to Islam.* 3rd ed., Upper Saddle River, N.J.: Pearson Prentice Hall, 2006.

Durkheim, Emile, and Karen E. Fields. *The Elementary Forms of Religious Life.* New York: Free Press, 1995.

Eck, Diana L. *A New Religious America: How a "Christian Country" Has Now Become the World's Most Religiously Diverse Nation.* San Francisco: Harper San Francisco, 2001.

El Fadl, Khaled Abou. *Reasoning With God: Rationality and Thought in Islam.* Oxford: Oneworld, 2002.

———. *The Great Theft: Wrestling Islam From the Extremists,* New York, N.Y.: Harper San Francisco, 2005.

Esbjörn-Hargens, Sean., and Michael E. Zimmerman. *Integral Ecology: Uniting Multiple Perspectives on the Natural World.* 1st ed. ed., Boston: Integral Books, 2009

———., Jonathan Reams, and Olen Gunnlaugson. *Integral Education: New Directions for Higher Learning.* Albany: State University of New York Press, 2010.

Farr, Thomas F. *World of Faith and Freedom: Why International Religious Liberty Is Vital to American National Security.* New York: Oxford University Press, 2008.

Ferrer, Jorge N., and Jacob H. Sherman. *The Participatory Turn: Spirituality, Mysticism, Religious Studies.* Albany, NY: State University of New York Press, 2008.

Feuerstein, Georg. *Yoga: The Technology of Ecstasy*, 1st ed., Los Angeles: J.P. Tarcher, 1989.

—————. *The Yoga Tradition: Its History, Literature, Philosophy, and Practice,* Prescott, Ariz.: Hohm Press, 2001.

Flood, Gavin D. *Beyond Phenomenology: Rethinking the Study of Religion.* London; New York: Cassell, 1999.

Forman, Mark D. *A Guide to Integral Psychotherapy: Complexity, Integration, and Spirituality in Practice.* Albany: State University of New York Press, 2010.

Fowler, James W. *Stages of Faith: The Psychology of Human Development and the Quest for Meaning,* 1st ed., San Francisco: Harper & Row, 1981.

—————. *Weaving the New Creation: Stages of Faith and the Public Church,* [San Francisco]: Harper San Francisco, 1991.

—————, Richard Robert Osmer, and Friedrich Schweitzer. *Developing a Public Faith: New Directions in Practical Theology : Essays in Honor of James W. Fowler.* St. Louis, Mo.: Chalice Press, 2003.

Frazer, James George. *The Golden Bough.* Abridged ed. ed., New York: The Macmillan company, 1940.

Gabbay, Alyssa. *Islamic Tolerance: Amir Khusraw and Pluralism.* Milton Park, Abingdon, Oxon; New York: Routledge, 2010.

Gardner, Howard. *Frames of Mind: The Theory of Multiple Intelligences,* New York: Basic Books, 1983.

Ghose, Aurobindo. *The Synthesis of Yoga,* Lotus Press, 1992.

—————. *On the Veda,* [1st University ed.] ed., Pondicherry: Sri Aurobindo Ashram,1956.

Graves, Clare., and William R. Lee. *Graves: Levels of Human Existence: Transcription of a Seminar at the Washington School of Psychiatry, October 16,*

1971. Santa Barbara, Calif.: ECLET Pub., 2002.

————., and Christopher C. Cowan and Natasha Todorovic. *The Never Ending Quest: Dr. Clare W. Graves Explores Human Nature.* Santa Barbara, Calif.: ECLET Publishing, 2005.

Griffin, David Ray. *Deep Religious Pluralism.* ed., Louisville, Ky.: Westminster John   Knox Press, 2005.

Habermas, Jürgen. *The Philosophical Discourse of Modernity: Twelve Lectures.* Vol. Studies in contemporary German social thought Cambridge, Mass.: MIT Press, 1987.

————, and Eduardo Mendieta. *Religion and Rationality: Essays on Reason, God, and Modernity.* 1st MIT Press ed. ed., Vol. Studies in contemporary German social thought Cambridge, Mass.: MIT Press, 2002.

Hann, C. M. *The Postsocialist Religious Question: Faith and Power in Central Asia and East-Central Europe.* LIT Verlag Münster, 2006.

Hanson, Paul D. *The People Called: The Growth of Community in the Bible.* Louisville, Ky.: Westminster John Knox Press, 2001.

Harding, Susan Friend. *The Book of Jerry Falwell: Fundamentalist Language and Politics.* Princeton, N.J: Princeton University Press, 2000.

Harris, Sam. *End of Faith: Religion, Terror, and the End of Faith.* New York, W.W. Norton and Company, 2005.

Harvey, Peter. *An Introduction to Buddhism: Teachings, History, and Practices.* Cambridge [England]; New York: Cambridge University Press, 1990.

Hick, John. *God Has Many Names: Britain's New Religious Pluralism.* London: Macmillan, 1980.

————. Problems of Religious Pluralism. New York: St. Martin's Press, 1985.

————, and Paul F. Knitter. *The Myth of Christian Uniqueness: Toward a Pluralistic Theology of Religions.* Maryknoll, N.Y.: Orbis Books, 1987.

————. *A Christian Theology of Religions: The Rainbow of Faiths.* 1st American ed., Louisville, Ky.: Westminster John Knox Press, 1995.

————, Dennis L. Okholm, and Timothy R. Phillips. *Four Views on Salvation in a Pluralistic World.* Grand Rapids, Mich.: Zondervan Pub. House, 1996.

Hutchison, William R. *Religious Pluralism in America: The Contentious History of a Founding Ideal.* New Haven: Yale University Press, 2003.

Hoffman, Lois Norma Wladis, Scott G Paris, et al. *Developmental Psychology Today*, 6th ed., New York: McGraw-Hill, 1994.

Hurd, Elizabeth Shakman. *The Politics of Secularism in International Relations.* Princeton: Princeton University Press, 2008.

Ingersoll, Elliott, and David M. Zeitler. *Integral Psychotherapy: Inside Out/ Outside in.* Albany: State University of New York Press, 2010

Isherwood, Christopher. *Ramakrishna and His Disciples,* New York: Simon and Schuster, 1965.

James, William. *The Varieties of Religious Experience,* Garden City, N.Y: Image Books, 1978.

Jenkins, Philip. *The Next Christendom: The Coming of Global Christianity.* Rev. and expanded ed. ed., Oxford; New York: Oxford University Press, 2007.

Johnston, Douglas, and Cynthia Sampson. *Religion, the Missing Dimension of Statecraft,* New York: Oxford University Press, 1994.

Johnston, Douglas. *Faith-Based Diplomacy: Trumping Realpolitik.* Oxford; New York: Oxford University Press, 2008.

Jones, Charles Brewer. *The View From Mars Hill: Christianity in the Landscape of World Religions*, Cambridge, Mass: Cowley Publications, 2005.

Jones, Ken. *The New Social Face of Buddhism: A Call to Action*, Boston: Wisdom Publications, 2003.

Kegan, Robert. *The Evolving Self: Problem and Process in Human Development,* Cambridge, Mass: Harvard University Press, 1982.

————. *In Over Our Heads: The Mental Demands of Modern Life,* Cambridge, Mass: Harvard University Press, 1994.

Keller, Catherine. *Face of the Deep: A Theology of Becoming.* London; New York: Routledge, 2003.

————, and Laurel C. Schneider. *Polydoxy : Theology of Multiplicity and Relation.* New York: Routledge, 2010.

Klostermaier, Klaus. *Hindu Writings*, Oneworld Publications, 2000.

————. *A Survey of Hinduism.* 3rd ed., Albany: State University of New York Press, 2007.

Knitter, Paul F. *Jesus and the Other Names : Christian Mission and Global Responsibility*, Maryknoll, N.Y: Orbis Books, 1996.

Kohlberg, Lawrence. *The Psychology of Moral Development: The Nature and Validity of Moral Stages,* 1st ed ed., San Francisco: Harper & Row, 1984.

Kozinski, Thaddeus J. *The Political Problem of Religious Pluralism: And Why Philosophers Can't Solve It.* Lanham, Md.: Lexington Books, 2010.

Krapohl, Robert H, and Charles H Lippy. *The Evangelicals: A Historical, Thematic, and Biographical Guide,* Westport, Conn.: Greenwood Press, 1999.

Kumar, P. Pratap, *Religious Pluralism in the Diaspora.* Leiden; Boston. Brill, 2006.

Küng, Hans. *A Global Ethic for Global Politics and Economics.* New York: Oxford University Press, 1998.

————. *Christianity and World Religions: Paths of Dialogue with Islam, Hinduism, and Buddhism.* Maryknoll, N.Y.: Orbis Books, 1993.

————. *Islam: Past, Present and Future.* Oxford: Oneworld, 2009.

Lincoln, Bruce. *Holy Terrors: Thinking About Religion After September 11.* 2nd ed., Chicago: University of Chicago Press, 2006.

Loevinger, Jane, and Augusto Blasi. *Ego Development: [Conceptions and Theories],* 1st ed., San Francisco: Jossey-Bass Publishers, 1976.

Lopez, Donald, *Religions of Tibet in Practice,* Princeton, N.J.: Princeton University Press, 1997.

Mahadevan, T. M. P. *Outlines of Hinduism, Rev. ed., Bombay: Chetana, 1961.*

Maslow, Abraham H. *The Farther Reaches of Human Nature.* New York, N.Y., USA: Arkana, 1993.

Milarepa, Kunga Lama, and Brian Cutillo, *Drinking the Mountain Stream: Songs of Tibet's Beloved Saint.* Boston: Wisdom Publications, 1995.

Miller, Melvin E, and Susanne R Cook-Greuter. *Transcendence and Mature Thought in Adulthood: The Further Reaches of Adult Development*, Lanham, Md.: Rowman & Littlefield, 1994.

Moore, Diane L. *Overcoming Religious Illiteracy: A Cultural Studies Approach to the Study of Religion in Secondary Education.* 1st ed. ed., New York: Palgrave Macmillan, 2007.

Netland, Harold A. *Encountering Religious Pluralism: The Challenge to Christian Faith & Mission.* Downers Grove, Ill.: InterVarsity Press, 2001.

Nhãát, Hòanh, and Jennifer Schwamm. Willis. *A Lifetime of Peace: Essential Writings by and about Thich Nhat Hanh*, New York: Marlowe & Co.: Distributed by Publishers Group West, 2003.

Nielsen, Niels Christian. *Religions of the World*, 3rd ed., New York: St. Martin's Press, 1993.

Osmer, Richard Robert. *Teaching for Faith: A Guide for Teachers of Adult Classes.* Louisville, Ky.: Westminster/John Knox Press, 1992.

―――. *The Teaching Ministry of Congregations.* Louisville, Ky.: Westminster John Knox Press, 2005.

Otto, Rudolf. *The Idea of the Holy; an Inquiry Into the Non-Rational Factor in the Idea of the Divine and Its Relation to the Rational.* New York: Oxford University Press, 1958.

Pagels, Elaine H. *The Gnostic Gospels.* 1st Vintage Books ed. ed., New York: Vintage Books, 1981.

Panikkar, Raimundo. *The Intrareligious Dialogue.* ed., New York, N.Y.: Paulist Press, 1999.

Patalon, Miroslaw. *The Philosophical Basis of Inter-Religious Dialogue: The Process Perspective.* Newcastle upon Tyne [England]: Cambridge Scholars Pub., 2009.

Petito, Fabio, and Pavlos Hatzopoulos. *Religion in International Relations: The Return From Exile.* 1st ed., New York: Palgrave Macmillan, 2003.

Piaget, Jean. *The Development of Thought: Equilibration of Cognitive Structures,* New York: Viking Press, 1977.

Peirce, Charles S. *Collected Papers.* Cambridge: Belknap Press of Harvard University Press, 1960.

Popper, Karl R., and Mark Amadeus. Notturno. *The Myth of the Framework : In Defence of Science and Rationality,* London; New York: Routledge, 1994.

Prothero, Stephen R. *A Nation of Religions : The Politics of Pluralism in Multireligious America.* Chapel Hill: University of North Carolina Press, 2006.

―――. *Religious Literacy : What Every American Needs to Know―and Doesn't.* 1st ed., San Francisco: HarperSanFrancisco, 2007.

―――. *God Is Not One: The Eight Rival Religions That Run the World―and Why Their Differences Matter.* 1st ed., New York: HarperOne, 2010.

Queen, Christopher S. *Engaged Buddhism in the West,* Boston, Mass.: Wisdom Publications, 2000.

Quinn, Philip L., and Kevin Meeker. *The Philosophical Challenge of Religious Diversity.* New York: Oxford University Press, 2000.

Radhakrishnan, S. *The Hindu View of Life; Upton Lectures Delivered At Manchester College, Oxford, 1926,* London New York: Urwin Books, 1961

Ramakrishna. *Sayings of Sri Ramakrishna; the Most Exhaustive Collection of Them, Their Number Being 1120,* [10th ed.] ed., Madras: Sri Ramakrishna Math, 1965.

Ricœur, Paul, and John B. Thompson. *Hermeneutics and the Human Sciences: Essays on Language, Action, and Interpretation.* Cambridge [Eng.]; New York Paris: Cambridge University Press Editions de la Maison des sciences de l'homme, 1981.

Bibliography

Sachedina, Abdulaziz Abdulhussein. *The Islamic Roots of Democratic Pluralism*, New York: Oxford University Press, 2001.

Said, Edward W. *Orientalism*. 1st ed. ed., New York: Pantheon Books, 1978.

Schwartz, Scott W. *Faith, Serpents, and Fire: Images of Kentucky Holiness Believers*, Jackson: University Press of Mississippi, 1999.

Sellars, Wilfrid, Richard Rorty, and Robert Brandom. *Empiricism and the Philosophy of Mind*. Cambridge, Mass.: Harvard University Press, 1997.

Sharma, Arvind. *Modern Hindu Thought: An Introduction*, New Delhi; New York: Oxford University Press, 2005.

Sims, Patsy. *Can Somebody Shout Amen!: Inside the Tents and Tabernacles of American Revivalists*, Vol. Religion in the South Lexington:University Press of Kentucky, 1996.

Slee, Nicola. *Women's Faith Development: Patterns and Processes*. Vol. Explorations in practical, pastoral, and empirical theology Aldershot, Hants, England; Burlington, Vt.: Ashgate, 2004.

Smith, David. *Hinduism and Modernity*, Vol. Religion in the modern world, Malden, Mass. Blackwell Pub, 2003.

Smith, Huston, and Huston Smith. *The World's Religions : Our Great Wisdom Traditions*, [San Francisco]: Harper San Francisco, 1991.

Smith, Jane I. *Muslims, Christians, and the Challenge of Interfaith Dialogue*. New York: Oxford University Press, 2007.

Smith, Jonathan Z. *Imagining Religion: From Babylon to Jonestown*. Vol. Chicago studies in the history of Judaism Chicago: University of Chicago Press, 1982.

Smith, Wilfred Cantwell. *Religious Diversity : Essays*. New York: Harper & Row, 1976.

Spong, John Shelby. *Why Christianity Must Change Or Die: A Bishop Speaks to Believers in Exile : A New Reformation of the Church's Faith and Practice*, 1st ed, [San Francisco, Calif.]: HarperSan Francisco, 1998.

————. *Rescuing the Bible From Fundamentalism: A Bishop Rethinks the Meaning of Scripture.* 1st ed., San Francisco, California: Harper San Francisco, 1991.

————. *A New Christianity for a New World : Why Traditional Faith Is Dying and How a New Faith Is Being Born,* San Francisco: Harper San Francisco, 2001.

Suzuki, Daisetz Teitaro. *An Introduction to Zen Buddhism,* 1st Grove Weidenfeld ed ed., New York: Grove Weidenfeld, 1991.

Suzuki, Daisetz Teitaro, Taitetsu Unno, and Daisetz Teitaro Suzuki. *Buddha of Infinite Light,* 1st Shambhala ed., Boston New York: Shambhala Publications in association with the American Buddhist Academy Distributed in the U.S. by Random House, 1997.

Stein, Z. "Myth busting and metric making: Refashioning the discourse about Development". Excursus of Integral Leadership Review. Integral Leadership Review. Vol 8. No. 5, 2008.

Steinbronn, Anthony J. *Worldviews: A Christian Response to Religious Pluralism.* St. Louis, Mo.: Concordia Pub. House, 2007.

Stiver, Dan R. *Theology After Ricoeur : New Directions in Hermeneutical Theology.* 1st ed., Louisville: Westminister John Knox Press, 2001.

Stokes, Kenneth. *Faith Development in the Adult Life Cycle.* New York: W.H. Sadlier, 1982.

Tambiah, Stanley Jeyaraja. *Buddhism Betrayed? : Religion, Politics, and Violence in Sri Lanka,* Vol. A Monograph of the World Institute for Development Economics Research (WIDER) of the United Nations University Chicago: University of Chicago Press, 1992.

Taylor, Mark C. *Critical Terms for Religious Studies,* Chicago: University of ChicagoPress, 1998.

Teresa. *The Interior Castle,* Vol. The Classics of Western spirituality, New York: Paulist Press, 1979.

Thomas, Scott. *The Global Resurgence of Religion and the Transformation of International Relations : The Struggle for the Soul of the Twenty-First Century.* 1st ed., Vol. Culture and religion in international relations New York, N.Y.: Palgrave Macmillan, 2005.

Bibliography

Tillich, Paul. *Dynamics of Faith*, New York: Harper, 1956.

Tracy, David. *Dialogue With the Other : The Inter-Religious Dialogue.* Vol. Louvain theological & pastoral monographs ; 1 Louvain Grand Rapids, Mich.: Peeters   Press W.B. Eerdmans, 1991.

————. *Plurality and Ambiguity : Hermeneutics, Religion, Hope.* Chicago: University of Chicago Press, 1994.

————. *Blessed Rage for Order : The New Pluralism in Theology: With a New Preface*, Chicago: University of Chicago Press, 1996.

Tylor, Edward B. *Primitive Culture; Researches Into the Development of Mythology, Philosophy, Religion, Language, Art, and Custom.* 4th ed. ed., London: J. Murray, 1993.

Varghese, Alexander. *India: History, Religion, Vision and Contribution to the World.* Atlantic Publishers, New Delhi, India, 2008.

Walker, Susan. *Speaking of Silence.* New York: Paulist Press, 1987.

Weber, Max, Peter Baehr, and Gordon C. Wells. *The Protestant Ethic and the "Spirit" of   Capitalism and Other Writings.* Vol. Penguin twentieth-century classics, New York: Penguin Books, 2002.

Wilber, Ken, Jack Engler, and Daniel P Brown. *Transformations of Consciousness: Conventional and Contemplative Perspectives on Development*, 1st ed ed., Boston New York: New Science Library Distributed in the U.S. by Random House, 1986.

————. *Up From Eden. A transpersonal view of human evolution.* Theosophical Publishing House. Wheaton, Ill.—Chennai (madras), India. Quest books, 1996.

————. *Integral Psychology: Consciousness, Spirit, Psychology, Therapy*, 1st pbk. ed., Boston: Shambhala, 2000.

————. *The Marriage of Sense and Soul ; One Taste*, 1st ed ed., Boston: Shambhala,
2000.

————. *Sex, Ecology, Spirituality : The Spirit of Evolution*, 2nd ed., rev ed., Boston: Shambhala, 2000.

————. *A Sociable God : Toward a New Understanding of Religion*, Boston: Shambhala, 2005.

————. *Integral Spirituality : A Startling New Role for Religion in the Modern and Postmodern World*, Boston: Integral Books, 2006.

End Notes

1 See "Wilber" in the bibliography for a list of references.

2 The basic conceptual outline presented in this book was inspired by Wilber's book Integral Spirituality (2006). More specifically, this book builds upon Wilber's notion of the "conveyor belt" (p 214–239). Wilber calls the conveyor belt "the single biggest problem facing the world in the interior quadrants, bar none" (p 179). This book represents an attempt to begin facing this major problem.

3 Wilber, 2006, p 183.

4 Although this presentation focuses mainly on the influence of individual psychological development on religious interpretation, additional companion books to this volume expand their reach to include both social and cultural influences, as well as intricate explorations of the role of spiritual experience and what Wilber calls state-stages. In particular, volume 1 of the series addresses the critical distinction between states of consciousness and vantage points. The author is also currently organizing religious leaders and scholars from around the globe to contribute chapters to tradition-specific volumes in the series.

5 The author is well aware of the stance that "universals" or "broad sweeping cross-cultural claims" are problematic for many within the postmodern academic milieu. These issues are addressed in chapters 1 and 3.

6 This is not to say that lower levels of religious interpretation fail to make a positive impact in the world. They certainly can and do. However, their efforts for social good are necessarily limited to the capacities built in to their particular worldview. However, even if these individuals can generate social good, they are also much more likely to create conflict because of their limited, often ethnocentric perspective. Individuals at higher levels of religious orientation are much less likely to do this, as they have the capacity to take multiple perspectives and to hold the complexity of paradox and apparent difference.

7 These categorizations were originally used by Jean Gebser and were later

adopted by Wilber. It has been brought to my attention that the term "mythic" is sometimes perceived as an arrogant categorization made by "outsiders" (e.g., those at the mythic stage of development do not see their own beliefs as myths but rather as truth). Keeping this in mind, appropriate changes to the names used for each stage will be considered in subsequent publications.

8   Religious orientation is defined at the end of this introduction.

9   The term meta-systemic refers specifically to Michael Commons model of Hierarchical Complexity. See Commons, M. L., Richards, F. A., & Kuhn, D. (1982). "Systematic and Meta-systematic Reasoning: A Case for a Level of Reasoning beyond Piaget's Formal Operations." Child Development, 53, 1058–1069.

10 Wilber was the first to coin the term "orienting generalizations." See Sex, Ecology, Spirituality.

11 Stein, Z., 2008.

12 See the work of Heinz, Day, Rizzuto, McDargh, as presented at the Symposium on Faith Development Theory and the Modern Paradigm. Further work is published here: The International Journal for the Psychology of Religion, 11(3), 2001.

13 See the description of the modern and postmodern paradigm described in appendix 2 for more detail.

14 See chapter 1.

15 Some may claim that the term "spiritual development" includes an area of development more encompassing than one might suspect when using the term "spiritual intelligence" alone (i.e., spiritual development = state-stage access + vantage point + structure-stage development). However, for the purposes of this book we use the terms spiritual development and spiritual intelligence as synonyms. That is, both terms refer to the spiritual line of development as it progresses through structure-stages. Volume 1 of this series focuses on spiritual development as a whole and adds a key role for state experiences and identity shifts (i.e., vantage points) to the conversation.

16 See Esbjörn-Hargens, Sean, and Michael E. Zimmerman. Integral Ecology: Uniting Multiple Perspectives on the Natural World. 1st ed. ed., Boston: Integral Books, 2009; Esbjörn-Hargens, Sean, Jonathan Reams, and Olen Gunnlaugson. Integral Education : New Directions for Higher Learning. Albany: State University of New York Press, 2010; Ingersoll, Elliott, and David M. Zeitler. Integral Psychotherapy : Inside Out/Outside in. Albany: State University of New York Press, 2010; and Forman, Mark D. A Guide to Integral Psychotherapy : Complexity, Integration, and Spirituality in Practice. Albany: State University of New York Press, 2010

17 Postmodern thought forced a massive reexamination of many historical

notions and figures. As David Tracy puts it: "Modernity has been forced to rethink its Enlightenment heritage on both reason and the self in increasingly radical, that is, post-modern, decentering forms. Central here has been the post-modern rereadings of Freud, Marx, and Nietzsche themselves, especially by feminist thinkers. Or consider Walter Benjamin's willingness to rethink the classic traditions he so loved, now guided by the hermeneutical acknowledgement that 'every great work of civilization is at the same time a work of barbarism.' Consider Foucault's noble attempts to rethink and retrieve the 'subjugated' knowledge of our own past. In every case of serious post-modern thought, radical hermeneutical rethinking recurs." (Tracy, 1991, p 3)

18 Eck, Diana L. A New Religious America : How a "Christian Country" Has Now Become the World's Most Religiously Diverse Nation. 1st ed. ed., [San Francisco]: Harper San Francisco, 2001. p 43

19 Certain preliminary forms of pluralism have existed for centuries among leading thinkers and scholars. (See Beneke's Beyond Toleration : The Religious Origins of American Pluralism. Oxford; New York: Oxford University Press, 2006.) However, it wasn't until the 1960s that this form of thinking reached a tipping point in mass culture.

20 Eck, 2001, p 43–4

21 Eck, 2001, p 45

22 Eck, Diane. Prospects for Pluralism: Voice and Vision in the Study of Religion, American Academy of Religions, 2006, Presidential Address, p 745

23 Each faith tradition has faced its own unique problems and has come up with its own novel solutions to issues around religious diversity and religious pluralism. To make matters more complex, issues of religious pluralism are different even within the same tradition depending on the geographic region and culture into which the tradition is embedded (i.e., Islam in the Middle East faces different issues around pluralism than Islam in Indonesia). The four core chapters of this book (chapters 5, 6, 7, and 8) articulate the tradition-specific issues around religious pluralism with regard to Christianity, Islam, Hinduism, and Buddhism, respectively.

24 Although the core of this book focuses primarily on religious pluralism using an individual approach, I expand the analysis in chapters 9 and 10 to look at the collective dimensions as well.

25 For a detailed cross-cultural study on the implications of religious pluralism on the philosophy of religion see Dean, Thomas. Religious Pluralism and Truth: Essays on Cross-Cultural Philosophy of Religion. New York: State University of New York Press, 1995.

26 Competing truth-claims come from multiple angles, from religion to science to any other ideology that seeks to define ultimate reality. However,

some have claimed that the competing truth-claims of other religions pose the biggest threat to legitimacy and deserve the most contemplation. Canon Max Warren, for instance, stated that the influence of agnostic scientific claims on Christian attitudes will be "child's play" in comparison to the challenges that will be brought forward by other religious traditions. (See Smith, Wilfred Cantwell. Religious Diversity: Essays. 1st ed. ed., New York: Harper & Row, 1976. p 7)

27 Most Western scholarship considers the problems of religious diversity and competing truth-claims from a Christian perspective. See Netland, Harold A. Encountering Religious Pluralism: The Challenge to Christian Faith & Mission. Downers Grove, Ill.: InterVarsity Press, 2001.; and Cobb, John B. Christian Faith and Religious Diversity. Minneapolis: Fortress Press, 2002. More recently, however, perspectives from other faiths have become more prominent. See Chittick, William C. Imaginal Worlds: Ibn Al-Arabi and the Problem of Religious Diversity. Vol. SUNY series in Islam Albany: State University of New York Press, 1994; and Aslan, Adnan. Religious Pluralism in Christian and Islamic Philosophy: The Thought of John Hick and Seyyed Hossein Nasr. Richmond, England: Curzon, 1998. For instance, scholar Adnan Aslan, a Muslim, explains his own confrontation with competing truth-claims as follows: "As a person who was brought up and educated in a traditional Muslim society and who feels strongly about the truth of Islam, I have always considered the question of salvation as one of the vital existential questions in my own life. When I came to England to carry out postgraduate study in religious studies, and consequently met several people from very different traditions, the question which came immediately to my mind was whether or not they would be saved. If they are excluded from salvation simply because they were not born to the society to which I was born, then how could I justify the soteriological claims of my religion?" (Aslan, 1998. p ix)

28 Banchoff, Thomas F. Religious Pluralism, Globalization, and World Politics. New York: Oxford University Press, 2008. p 4

29 Hick, John. A Christian Theology of Religions: The Rainbow of Faiths. 1st American ed. ed., Louisville, Ky.: Westminster John Knox Press, 1995. p 18

30 Hick explains that in a Christian context, pluralism means that if we are to "make sense of the idea that the great world religions are all inspired and made salvific by the same historical transcendent influence we have to go beyond the historical figure of Jesus to a universal Source of all salvific transformations. Christians may call this the cosmic Christ or the eternal Logos; Hindus and Buddhist may call it the Dharma; Muslims may call it Allah; Taoists may call it the Tao; and so on." (Hick, 1995, p 23). See also Hick, John, Dennis L. Okholm, and Timothy R. Phillips. Four Views on Salvation in a Pluralistic World. Grand Rapids, Mich.: Zondervan Pub. House, 1996.

31 Hick openly recognizes that with such an open view it is "difficult, if not

impossible, to avoid giving offense to conservative believers and to appear to be undermining faith…"(Hick, 1996, p 31). Here Hick also recounts his own developmental process using a more individualistic lens, as he recounts his progression from a "fundamentalist" to a "pluralist." p 31–40

32 See Cobb, John B., and Paul F. Knitter. Transforming Christianity and the World: A Way Beyond Absolutism and Relativism. Maryknoll, N.Y.: Orbis Books, 1999.; and Heim, S. Mark. Salvations: Truth and Difference in Religion. Vol. Faith meets faith Maryknoll, N.Y.: Orbis Books, 1995.

33 A similar approach is taken by Prothero in his recent book God Is Not One. See Prothero, Stephen R. God Is Not One: The Eight Rival Religions That Run the World—and Why Their Differences Matter. 1st ed. ed., New York: HarperOne, 2010.

34 Cobb, John B., and Paul F. Knitter. Transforming Christianity and the World : A Way Beyond Absolutism and Relativism. Maryknoll, N.Y.: Orbis Books, 1999; "How odd I find it to be writing for a collection of essays in criticism of theologies espousing religious pluralism! Yet I have agreed to do so because of the very narrow way—indeed an erroneous way, I think—in which pluralism has come to be defined. By that definition of pluralism, I am against pluralism. But I am against pluralism for the sake of a fuller and more genuine pluralism." p 62

35 Griffin, David Ray. Deep Religious Pluralism. 1st ed. ed., Louisville, Ky.: Westminster John Knox Press, 2005. p 35

36 Cobb, 1999, p 6

37 For further insight into process philosophy, pluralism, and theology see also the work of Catherine Keller. Keller, Catherine. Face of the Deep: A Theology of Becoming. London; New York: Routledge, 2003. And Keller, Catherine, and Laurel C. Schneider. Polydoxy: Theology of Multiplicity and Relation. New York: Routledge, 2010.

38 Cheng, Chung-ying. Toward an Integrative Religious Pluralism, in Griffin, 2005. p 212

39 Our approaches are different in that I take a generally individualistic orientation to pluralism in introducing the key role of psychological development, whereas Cheng elegantly finds integration through the work of Cobb, Whitehead, and Chinese Yijing using a more systemic theological orientation based on the integration of truth-claims.

40 Cheng, Chung-ying. Toward an Integrative Religious Pluralism, in Griffin, 2005. p 213

41 ibid.

42 For a discussion of all three in relation to religious pluralism see Kozinski, Thaddeus J. The Political Problem of Religious Pluralism: And Why

Philosophers Can't Solve It. Lanham, Md.: Lexington Books, 2010.

43 Banchoff, 2008, p 5

44 Banchoff, Thomas F. Democracy and the New Religious Pluralism. Oxford; New York: Oxford University Press, 2007. p 5–6; Although Banchoff takes a predominately collective approach, he does leave room for individual attitude and belief: "The new religious pluralism, then, is not just about demographics. It is also about more diverse patterns of individual belief." (Banchoff, 2007, p 6)

45 Others like Christopher Beneke focus less on international dynamics and look more specifically at specific social dynamics within particular nations. Beneke points out that in America, religious pluralism was built into its founding principles. See Beneke, 2006, p 157).

46 Kumar, P. Pratap. Religious Pluralism in the Diaspora. Leiden; Boston: Brill, 2006.

47 See Gabbay, Alyssa. Islamic Tolerance: Amir Khusraw and Pluralism. Milton Park, Abingdon, Oxon; New York: Routledge, 2010.

48 See Hutchison, William R. Religious Pluralism in America: The Contentious History of a Founding Ideal. New Haven: Yale University Press, 2003.

49 When public declarations of inequality are declared, they are usually met with disapproval. In September of 2010, for example, when Rev. Terry Jones, a pastor in Florida, threatened to burn the Qur'an in public demonstration, his low level of religious orientations was met with a hostile response from the majority of America's postmodern culture.

50 Some researchers are, however, more careful with how they use the term extremist. For instance, in the United Nations Development report on Arab Knowledge the authors make the important distinction between extreme loyalty and extremism: "A distinction should be made between extreme loyalty (Ta'asub) and extremism (Tataruf). Extreme loyalty may remain merely excessive zeal for a particular idea or affiliation. When this goes too far, it falls into the snare of extremism, which in turn leads to obscurantist, inward looking positions incapable of discrimination. This brings us up against extremism in forms that generate its counterpart of counter-extremism, this preventing the dialogue and outreach that are the foundations for recognition, mutual understanding, and eventual cooperation and partnership." UNDP, Arab Knowledge Report 2009: Towards Productive Intercommunication for Knowledge, p 16. Accessed October 2, 2010, http://www.arabstates.undp.org/contents/file/newfiles/AKR09_E/Intro.pdf

51 Eck, 2001, p 24

52 Eck, 2001, p 23

53 Ferrer, 2008, p 29–30

54 It is true that both Eck and Ferrer bring a strong degree of sophistication to their argument. Certainly, both include cultural and contextual nuance to their individual categorizations. However, they both miss the developmental nature of their attitudinal categories. In the model of developmental religious pluralism introduced in the second half of this chapter, I take the individually oriented approach of Eck and Ferrer, one step further.

In most cases the continuum itself, particularly when it ranges from less inclusive to more inclusive, is a direct result of a developmental process. That is to say, most postmodern scholarship fails to take into account that over time, when given the proper conditions for growth, adherents generally move from exclusionary to more pluralistic views. We will come back to more detailed analysis of exlusivism, inclusivism, and pluralism using a vertical approach in chapter 4. (As we will see, it is more accurate to use the attitudinal continuum of exclusivists, inclusivists, and pluralists as it correlates with developmental levels rather than a horizontal typology. Exclusivist, inclusivist, and pluralist categories tend to align with mythic, rational, and pluralistic levels respectively.) For now, let's focus on the typological spectrum ranging from extremist to moderate to show how an integral perspective brings an even more sophisticated model.

55 See McBrien in Hann's The Postsocialist Religious Question: "This discourse is careful to distinguish between 'good Muslims,' who practise moderate forms of Islam (references are sometimes made to prayer, but mostly to ethical and moral norms of Islam), and 'bad extremists.' The discourse gives little indication, however, of how members of extremist groups can be identified…The vagueness of the terms employed in the discourse allows governments to manipulate the categories in order to label nearly any threat to the nation or state as one of religious extremism." Hann, C. M.. The Postsocialist Religious Question: Faith and Power in Central Asia and East-Central Europe. LIT Verlag Münster, 2006. p 58

56 In later chapters (particularly chapter 5) we will explore the fact that religious extremism is sometimes the direct result of a low level of moral development combined with some sort of motivation (often political) that serves as a catalyst for action.

57 It is important to mention the multiple ways that "complexity" shows up in religious orientation. There is an important distinction between horizontal complexity (building a greater knowledge base of information) and vertical complexity (as represented and established through transformative reorientations in worldview). When using the term complexity in this book, I refer strictly to vertical complexity unless otherwise noted. Understanding the difference between horizontal complexity and vertical helps to explain why some individuals at lower levels of structural development (vertical complexity)

can and do still develop radically in-depth arguments (horizontal complexity) to support their claims.

58 This book is situated in and informed by a Wilberian Four Quadrant analysis. I focus, however, the majority of the book on individuals and their interior psychological workings. My focus on this particular aspect is best understood when held with the understanding that individuals are always embedded in cultural contexts, inter-subjective relationships, and social systems. Furthermore, although I don't engage it here other than in brief passing, various psychodynamic elements such as shadow and other more severe forms of psychopathology are also relevant. These issues ought to also be held implicitly for a correct understanding to be taken from this book. In volume 1 of the series in The Great Human Tradition, I touch upon some of these psychodynamic and shadow elements a bit more.

59 These names are borrowed from a combination of two sources. First, credit goes to Jean Gebser. Gebser's structures of consciousness ranged from archaic to magic to mythic to mental to integral. Second, credit goes to Ken Wilber for his beautiful ideas outlined in Integral Spirituality, in his chapter "The Conveyor Belt." In this chapter, Wilber introduces both the stages ranging from archaic to magic to mythic to rational to pluralistic to integral as well as the vertical concept of "altitude." As a result, the basic concepts of this book draw heavily upon Wilber's ideas.

60 Using the older model, restricted to only one axis of typology, it is easy to erroneously assume that there exist only two types of individuals within each religious tradition. In our common parlance we often refer to Islamic extremists and Islamic moderates but seldom hear anything that offers any other optional categorizations. With the new and more accurate model offered using an integral approach, a whole new dimension of analysis emerges that allows us to more accurately describe the diversity of religious actors in the world.

61 It is clear that even if deep structures are indeed the same, their surface features will vary according to religion, identity, and sociocultural context. Just as we all share the same human brain and basic biology, so too do we share the same psychological potentials. The most important research to date in this area considers carefully cross-cultural differences. It is vital that future scholarship continues to correct for portions of developmental models that might be unconsciously biased toward Western/Colonial/Christian-centric hierarchies. Unconscious prejudices were the common mistake of the modernists that post-modernity tries so hard to correct. Any successful post-postmodern scholar must be careful to include the sophistication of the postmodernist while simultaneously resurrecting developmental and evolutionary hierarchies.

62 Although it is not without its controversy, research into several lines of development (i.e., Kohlberg's moral development) has been conducted cross-

culturally, supporting the theory that such development is common to all human beings and not limited to any one particular religion or culture (i.e., Westerners).

63 The stage of religious orientation that this book dubs "magic" is a conflation of what Don Beck and Chris Cowen call purple and red. Although some early readers of this volume protested this conflation (demanding that purple is its own significant stage in religious orientation), I made the final decision to merge the two levels together in order to keep the presentation concise. Furthermore, our research and presentation is intended for an adult audience. Qualities of Beck and Cowen's purple and red memes are more common in younger individuals and only sparingly appear in adults embedded in our four religious traditions.

64 Hoffman, Lois Norma Wladis, Scott G Paris, et al. Developmental Psychology Today, 6th ed., New York: McGraw-Hill, 1994.

65 Although development is indeed directional, rarely does it unfold in a nice and neat linear progression.

66 Other scholars like Goldberg and Fowler have proposed similar ideas in the past.

67 Although Fowler's work did indeed take both Piaget's cognitive development model and Kohlberg's moral development model into consideration and analysis, we argue that keeping each line of development separate and distinct allows for a clearer and more direct analysis.

68 The work of Clare Graves is not limited to simply one single line of development, rather their research is in fact a complete bio-psycho-social system. To date, however, Graves' research still holds the most significant contribution into values development. Although we must be careful to avoid reducing Graves' work to values alone, his contributions are much too important to leave out of our discussion. To this end, we include both Graves' research and the work of Spiral Dynamics but do our best to make clear to the reader that their work involving the psychological development of values is only a small part of a much larger system of human emergence.

69 Gardner, Howard. Frames of Mind : The Theory of Multiple Intelligences, New York: Basic Books, 1983.

70 Wilber, Ken. Integral Psychology: Consciousness, Spirit, Psychology, Therapy, 1st ed., Boston: Shambhala, 2000.

71 To be specific, Wilber's spectrum of altitude begins with infrared and magenta. These levels of religious orientation are often inherent in infants and only arise in adults with debilitating life circumstances. These levels of development correspond to primal faith development on Fowler's scale and the survival meme on Graves' values scale. The psychograph above is slightly

different than the one depicted by Wilber. For simplicity purposes this book conflates magenta and red altitudes.

72 Other theories (e.g. Kurt Fishcer's Skill Theory) claim that development might be more like a "web" of particular skill sets rather than clean and separate areas of linear intelligence. This book agrees with this notion to a certain extent in that our articulation of Religious Orientation is indeed itself a particular "web" (or as we call it a bundle) of various intelligences.

73 See Piaget, J. The development of thought : equilibration of cognitive structures. New York: Viking Press. 1977; Also see Kegan, R. In over our heads : the mental demands of modern life. Cambridge, Mass.: Harvard University Press. 1994.

74 Wilber, 2006.

75 Wilber makes this point several times in Integral Spirituality.

76 Wilber, 2006, p 194–5

77 Much of the foundation laid in the previous pages, such as the "Integral Psychograph," "lines of development," and "altitude," have all been reiterations of ideas first explored by Wilber. In the rest of this chapter and the chapters that follow, I press beyond any already existing application of Integral Theory to offer one of the first attempts to explore an integral approach to religious orientation.

78 There are at least five ways to determine an individual's level of religious orientation: (1) multiple developmental assessment tests (all lines); (2) a single faith-development assessment test; (3) a developmental assessment test of secondary lines; (4) inferred observation of faith development; and (5) inferred observation of secondary lines. Although this book does not go into each of these in great detail, in order to maintain its scope it does its best to hint at the most relevant methods for assessment in various circumstances.

79 Assessment tests are the standard way developmental research is conducted. One example of an assessment test is Susanne-cook Greuter's "Sentence Completion Test" used to determine ego development. A second example is that provided by the Developmental Testing Service founded by Theo Dawson.

80 One might ask: Is faith development (as articulated by Fowler) and religious orientation (as described in this book) the same thing? Or to pose it another way: Does Fowler's line of development determine one's level of religious orientation in total? The answer is "yes" and "no." Yes, Fowler's system is equal to religious orientation if the particular context is one in which ultimate concern is the driving factor and force behind behavior, action, or interpretation. However, as many of us know and have seen repeatedly, religion plays a significant role in cultural and social settings that might not

be related to issues of ultimate concern. There are times in which religion is a background noise influencing behaviors and choices. Because ultimate concern is not always the driving force in every single context, Fowler's system alone is not sufficient to offer a fully integral or comprehensive analysis. Only after we have considered the general characteristics of all the other relevant lines at a particular altitude can we gain a more holistic view of religious orientation and the way it might influence a practice or interpretation of a religious tradition. That is to say, we should draw conclusions about religious orientation only once we have secured as much information as possible.

81 Expressions and signs do not always equal one's capacity for spiritual intelligence. Expression may be higher than religious capacity (e.g., a conformist expressing pluralistic values of his or her family or society). Expression can be lower than capacity (e.g., a neuroscientist who has stunted faith development at a low level of intelligence). This distinction between expression and capacity is similar in nature to the content vs. structure debates that have been ongoing in developmental psychology communities for decades.

82 Fowler, James. Stages of Faith: The Psychology of Human Development and the Quest for Meaning, 1st ed ed., San Francisco: Harper & Row, 1981. p 4

83 Ultimate concern and fulfillment have been viewed, in the context of a larger socio-historical perspective, through at least three different lenses. First, ultimate fulfillment is centered on this world, the visible tangible world in front of us now. This worldly concern involves some of the items listed above— power, sex, prestige, wealth, etc. Second, ultimate concern moves to the realm of the other-worldly. Perhaps here God enters into the picture. Individuals are willing to set aside "this-worldly" desires if in exchange they believe they will obtain something in the afterlife (heaven) or as in some Eastern cultures if they have hope for a better rebirth in the next life, or even liberation. In many traditions, otherworldly incentives become even more attractive if the reward is eternal, like an everlasting paradise. Third, in its final resting place, ultimate fulfillment returns again to focus on this world, however this move is emergent from an entirely new perspective in which one has transcended his own ego and drive for personal gain. One now rests either in complete identification with the Divine (Higher Self) or as a clear channel through which the Divine can work. This third stage takes all of the brilliant and imaginative insights of otherworldly salvation and brings them into this world. There is no difference between samsara and nirvana or heaven and earth. This third stage fulfillment literally feels like living in and creating a heaven here on earth. "The Kingdom of Heaven is here and now"—literally.

To contrast this third stage with the first two is rather stark. In the first stage of ultimate concern the individual is completely unaware of any possibility of ultimate fulfillment or unity. The search for fulfillment is limited to this world. In the second stage the individual decides to immerse him or herself in the Divine, either in communion with or union as; either way the direction is otherworldly and often results in a denial of this world (monkhood, hermitage, etc.). In the third stage, one recognizes that this world and the divine "other" world, are not separate. Both are right here, available in the present moment, for all those who have eyes to see. For I once heard, "God can only see God with God's own eyes."

84 Tillich, Paul. Dynamics of Faith, [1st ed.] ed., New York: Harper, 1956.

85 Fowler, 1981. All summaries are composed using Fowler's book the Stages of Faith. Without affecting the accuracy of each stage description, liberty is taken in this book's definitions to ensure they point to religious undertones whenever possible.

86 Fowler's work is supported by parallel research of Swiss theorist Richard Osmer. See Osmer, Richard Robert. Teaching for Faith: A Guide for Teachers of Adult Classes. 1st ed. ed., Louisville, Ky.: Westminster/John Knox Press, 1992; and Osmer, Richard Robert. The Teaching Ministry of Congregations. 1st ed. ed., Louisville, Ky.: Westminster John Knox Press, 2005.

87 Fowler, James. "Stages of Faith Consciousness", New Directions for Child and Adolescent Development. Volume 1991, Issue 52. p 41

88 Streib, "Faith development research revisited: Accounting for diversity in structure, content, and narratives of faith", 2005.

89 Fowler's work has also been applied to Women's Faith Development. See Slee, Nicola. Women's Faith Development: Patterns and Processes. Vol. Explorations in practical, pastoral, and empirical theology. Aldershot, Hants, England; Burlington, VT: Ashgate, 2004.

90 Streib, Heinz, Variety and Complexity of Religious Development: Perspectives for the 21st Century, p 130-2 (in press).

91 Ibid.

92 Streib, Heinz, 2005. p 114-15

93 Rizzuto, Religious Development Beyond the Modern Paradigm Discussion: The Psychoanalytic Point of View, 2001

94 McDargh, Faith Development Theory and the Postmodern Problem of Foundations, 2001

95 Day, From Structuralism to Eternity? Re-Imagining the Psychology of Religious Development After the Cognitive-Developmental Paradigm, 2001

96 Additional discussion and critique of Fowler's work can be found in: Fowler, James W., Richard Robert Osmer, and Friedrich Schweitzer. Developing a Public Faith: New Directions in Practical Theology: Essays in Honor of James W. Fowler. St. Louis, Mo.: Chalice Press, 2003.

97 Fowler, Faith Development Theory and the Postmodern Challenges, 2001.

98 Ibid.

99 See Wilber, Integral Spirituality.

100   Piaget, Jean. The Development of Thought: Equilibration of Cognitive Structures, New York: Viking Press, 1977; Ethnocentric worldviews are impossible at this stage of development; one does not have the ability to take the perspective of other.

101   Piaget, Jean. 1977.

102   "Hierarchical complexity" is a term first coined by Harvard professor Michael Commons; although used outside of his particular model here in the text, the term offers a beautifully descriptive way to highlight vertical growth.

103   Piaget, Jean. 1977.

104   Wilber, Integral Psychology, 2000; It is also important to note that viewing cognitive development as the driving force of growth is a point of contention within the faith development community. See Day, McDargh, and Heinz for more details. Even with these counter arguments, this book follows Wilber's lead, placing cognitive development as "necessary but not sufficient" for growth in other lines.

105   Loevinger, Jane, and Augusto Blasi. Ego Development: Conceptions and Theories, 1st ed., San Francisco: Jossey-Bass Publishers, 1976.

106   Cook-Greuter, S. Ego Development: Nine Levels of Increasing Embrace, accessed June 23, 2006, http://www.cook-greuter.com.

107   Graves, Clare, Christopher C. Cowan, and Natasha Todorovic. The Never Ending Quest: Dr. Clare W. Graves Explores Human Nature, Santa Barbara, CA: ECLET Publishing, 2005. p 29

108   Ibid.

109   In this quote I have replaced the word "state" with the word "stage." The terms state and stage each have specific meaning in an integral context and by specifying here I am able to keep inherent consistency within the manuscript and the series of Integral Religious Studies at large.

110   Beck, Don, and Christopher C Cowan. Spiral Dynamics: Mastering Values, Leadership, and Change: Exploring the New Science of Memetics, Vol. Developmental Management Cambridge, Mass., USA: Blackwell Business, 1996.

111   See Graves 2005 and Beck 1996.

112   Graves, 2005. p 283

113   Kohlberg, Lawrence. The Psychology of Moral Development: The Nature and Validity of Moral Stages, 1st ed., San Francisco: Harper & Row, 1984.

114   Wilber, 2006.

115   This point of view is represented by a classic case of scientific reductionism. Psychologists like Freud, social theorists like Marx, and even contemporary writers like Richard Dawkins and Sam Harris, promote the "end of faith." This stance is directly due to the fact that they lack sufficient understanding of faith development. We cannot rid ourselves of mythic religion any more than we can get rid of the developmental process as a whole. We are all twelve years old at some point. Religion is here to stay whether we like it or not. As a result, we must find skillful ways to interact with it for the benefit of all.

116   It is important to note here again that development is a messy process. In our examples above we explain each altitude as if various lines develop neatly and more or less in sync—this is done for heuristic purposes and for simplicity of explanation as we introduce this concept. Examples showing the reality of uneven development are given as we proceed.

117   Sachedina, Abdulaziz Abdulhussein. The Islamic Roots of Democratic Pluralism, New York: Oxford University Press, 2001. p 12

118   One analogy that is often used is that of a mountain. Religious traditions all begin at different sides at the base of the mountain. As a result, all the paths up the mountain look different. However, all paths culminate at the top of the mountain at their one goal: God/Godhead.

119   Wilber, 2006. Although Wilber does not appropriate the emergence of this skill to the pluralistic altitude per se, he does indeed make many important clarifications regarding surface structures and deep structures in books like Integral Spirituality and Transformations of Consciousness.

120   Hanson, Paul D. The People Called: The Growth of Community in the Bible. Louisville, Ky.: Westminster John Knox Press, 2001. p 527

121   A lack of understanding of growth hierarchies and a resistance to making value judgments mean that everything is seen and judged as equal. Such a tendency leaves individuals at this level in somewhat of a quagmire, unable to make distinctions, judgments, or improvements.

122   There are many different forms of post-postmodern thinking and not all are integral. See Zak Stein's powerful article, "On the Use of the Term Integral: Vision-logic, Meta-theory, and the Growth-to-Goodness Assumptions" (in press). Therefore, I use the term integral in this context to be normative; to refer to those post-postmodern configurations of religious orientation that are preferable. Such a move prevents us from making the

common mistake to say "higher is better, because it is integral." As Stein points out, higher forms might be just as fragmented and reductionistic as lower levels of development; complexity doesn't automatically equal holistic, integral, whole.

123   Wilber's contribution here is unparalleled. The reader is strongly urged to consult Wilber's work for a detailed description of each of the "three faces of God."

124   "Consent" is a term developed by Brian Robertson at Ternary Software. It is a unique form of integral/"second-tier" decision-making. Often this form of decision-making is associated with a governing system called Holacracy (information discussed in a personal conversation).

125   Wilber, Sex, Ecology, Spirituality, 2000.

126   Cook-Greuter, S. Ego Development: Nine Levels of Increasing Embrace, accessed: June 26, 2006, http://www.cook-greuter.com

127   Wilber, 2006.

128   See more on this integration of religion and spirituality into the other spheres of knowledge in chapter 9.

129   http://www.adherents.com

130   Pagels, Elaine H. The Gnostic Gospels. 1st Vintage Books ed. ed., New York: Vintage Books, 1981. p xxxv

131   Pagels, 1981. p xxiii

132   Barrett, David B., George Thomas Kurian, and Todd M. Johnson. World Christian Encyclopedia: A Comparative Survey of Churches and Religions in the Modern World. 2nd ed. ed., Oxford; New York: Oxford University Press, 2001. Table 1–5, vol 1, p 16

133   Jenkins, Philip. The Next Christendom: The Coming of Global Christianity. Oxford ; New York: Oxford University Press, 2007. p 2

134   Ibid.

135   Jenkins, 2007. p 6

136   Ibid.

137   As we will see, this all changes at an integral level of development.

138   Schwartz, Scott W. Faith, Serpents, and Fire: Images of Kentucky Holiness Believers, Jackson: University Press of Mississippi, 1999.

139   Ibid.

140   Ibid.

141   Covington, Dennis. Salvation on Sand Mountain: Snake Handling

and Redemption in Southern Appalachia, Reading, Mass.: Addison-Wesley, 1995.

142   Covington, 1995.

143   Sims, Patsy. Can Somebody Shout Amen! Inside the Tents and Tabernacles of American Revivalists, Vol. Religion in the South Lexington: University Press of Kentucky, 1996.

144   Cox, Harvey Gallagher. Fire from Heaven: The Rise of Pentecostal Spirituality and the Reshaping of Religion in the Twenty-First Century. Reading, Mass.: Addison-Wesley Pub. 2001. (Originally published in 1995.) p 310–11

145   Covington, 1995.

146   Bartholomeusz, Tessa J, and Chandra Richard Silva De. Buddhist Fundamentalism and Minority Identities in Sri Lanka, Albany, N.Y.: State University of New York Press, 1998. p 2

147   Krapohl, Robert H, and Charles H Lippy. The Evangelicals: A Historical, Thematic, and Biographical Guide, Westport, Conn.: Greenwood Press, 1999. p 42

148   Harding, Susan Friend. The Book of Jerry Falwell: Fundamentalist Language and Politics, Princeton, N.J.: Princeton University Press, 2000. p 88

149   Krapohl, 1999. p 41

150   Krapohl, 1999. p 41

151   Harding, 2000. p 88

152   Sometimes these individuals turn toward religions of the East. In Buddhism, for example, many Westerners find a logical and rational philosophy for living. To make the transition even smoother, many versions of Buddhism were imported to the West at a rational orange altitude, stripped of the myths and superstitions that Westerners were ready to abandon in their own Christian religion. These same individuals are often shocked when they realize that the same types of myths and superstitions abound in the magic and mythical versions of Buddhism practiced in its various cultural contexts abroad.

153   Krapohl, 1999. p 41

154   Obama, Barack. Speech: "Untitled", Sojourners/Call to Renewal-sponsored Pentecost conference, June, 2006.

155   Spong, John Shelby. A New Christianity for a New World: Why Traditional Faith Is Dying and How a New Faith Is Being Born, San Francisco: Harper San Francisco, 2001. p 2

156   Spong, 2001

157   Others like Templeton prize-winning scholar Arthur Peacocke fight similar battles. "Peacocke has urged that the church abandon the 'incomprehensible and unbelievable' teachings of supernaturalism, and present the faith in 'credible' manner." It is interesting to note that Peacocke, like Spong, is also a senior cleric of the Anglican Communion. (Jenkins, 2007, p 9)

158   Spong, 2001, p 137

159   Knitter, Paul F. One Earth, Many Religions: Multifaith Dialogue and Global Responsibility. Maryknoll, N.Y.: Orbis Books, 1995. p 3

160   Knitter, Paul F. Jesus and the Other Names: Christian Mission and Global Responsibility, Maryknoll, N.Y: Orbis Books, 1996. p 4

161   Knitter, 1996, p 5

162   Knitter, 1996, p 5

163   Knitter, 1996, p 7

164   Ibid.

165   Knitter, 1996, p 8

166   Knitter, 1996, p 9

167   Knitter, 1996, p 39

168   Knitter, 1996, p 106

169   Knitter, 1996, p 3

170   Knitter, 1996. p 106: "If there is any truth to James Fowler's stages of faith, I think it is found in the recognition that the more one matures in faith, so much the more will one happily, if somewhat fearfully, embrace the mystery, the expansiveness, the pluriformity of truth."

171   Knitter, 1996, p 17

172   Rudolph Peters in Coolsaet, Jihadi Terrorism and the Radicalization Challenge, p 115

173   pbuh is a common phrase used each time the Prophet Mohammed's name is mentioned in order to show respect. It stands for "peace be upon him."

174   DeLong-Bas, Natana J. Wahhabi Islam: From Revival and Reform to Global Jihad, Oxford; New York: Oxford University Press, 2007.

175   Moghissi, Haideh. Muslim Diaspora: Gender, Culture, and Identity. New York: Routledge, 2006.

176   Denny, Frederick Mathewson. An Introduction to Islam. 3rd ed. ed., Upper Saddle River, N.J.: Pearson Prentice Hall, 2006. p 134

177   Denny, p 135

178   Rudolph Peters in Coolsaet, Jihadi Terrorism and the Radicalization Challenge, 2008. p 115

179   On one side of the street, the current situation in the Middle East parallels (with clear differences) the circumstances during the Western Renaissance between Christian adherents and the strong leadership of the Catholic Church. That is, an extreme mythic form of Islam dominates culture, preventing anything that looks like a rational Islam from emerging. On the other side of the street, the present situation faces brand-new challenges. Unlike evolving forms of Christianity in the 1500s that could rebel against the Catholic Church, there is not a single governing body within the Islamic faith against which more advanced intellectuals can rebel. This exacerbates the problem. Instead of focusing an orange rebellion on an institution (as did the rational Christians), Islamic rationalists are accused of rebelling against the Qur'an, or worse, against Allah. Our integral awareness uncovers that in actuality, rational adherents are rebelling against only mythic forms of the religion and not the faith itself. In extreme cases, those in the Middle East interested in a more rational expression of Islam are often forced to move to the West, or retreat to small, more liberal pockets within neighboring countries; remaining under the radar and more tolerant in their beliefs. Regardless of the challenges facing Islam today, the vertical spectrum of stages is entirely visible. We begin with magic orientation, then work our way up the spiral.

180   More extreme versions of mythic Islam strictly enforce the status quo, repressing versions of Islam (red) of less complexity and resisting all versions of Islam of greater complexity (orange, pluralistic, integral).

181   "No Title", accessed May, 15, 2007, http://www.islamalways.com/en/modules.php?name=News&file=article&sid=89

182   Ibid.

183   "Islam Awareness Home Page," accessed May 15, 2007, http://www.islamawareness.net/

184   "Our Dialogue," accessed May 15, 2007, http://islamicvoice.com/November2004/OurDialogue/

185   This list of five pillars is summarized and taken from several sources, most notably: El Fadl, Khaled Abou, The Great Theft: Wrestling Islam from the Extremists, New York, N.Y.: Harper San Francisco, 2005.

186   El Fadl, 2005. p 121

187   El Fadl, 2005. p 119

188   El Fadl, 2005.

189   Delong-Bas, 2007. p 288

190   Delong-Bas, 2007. p 289

191   Delong-Bas, 2004.

192   Delong-Bas, 2004.

193   Delong-Bas, 2007. p 288

194   Delong-Bas, 2007. p 289

195   Ibid.

196   Ibid.

197   El Fadl, 2005. p 18

198   Ibid.

199   Delong-Bas, 2007. p 288

200   El Fadl, 2005. p 13

201   Wilber, 2006.

202   El Fadl provides an additional account of rational Muslim thought in his book Reasoning with God. See Al Fadl, Khaled Abou. Reasoning With God : Rationality and Thought in Islam. Oxford: Oneworld, 2002.

203   El Fadl, 2005. p 109

204   El Fadl, 2005. p 13

205   El Fadl, 2005. p 14

206   El Fadl, 2005. p 187

207   El Fadl, 2005. p 194

208   El Fadl, 2005.

209   El Fadl, 2005. p 13

210   El Fadl, 2005. p 133

211   El Fadl, 2005. p 134

212   Sachedina, 2001. p 7

213   Sachedina, 2001. p 11

214   Sachedina, 2001. p 13

215   For another fine example of an exploration into the roots of pluralistic attitudes within Islam see Chittick, William C. Imaginal Worlds: Ibn Al-Arabi and the Problem of Religious Diversity. Vol. SUNY series in Islam Albany: State University of New York Press, 1994.

216   Sachedina, 2001.

217   Sachedina, 2001. p 25

218   Sachedina, 2001. p 39

219   Ibid.

220   Wilber, The Marriage of Sense and Soul, 2000, p 194–5

221   No discussion on the stages of development within Islam can leave out at least a brief mention of its mystical branch, Sufism. Like many mystical branches in other traditions, the Sufis developed a set of teachings that place the emphasis on personal experience rather than external dogma. It would not however be accurate to say that all Sufis are beyond a mythic orientation; additionally, one cannot claim (as some readers suggested during their revision of the first draft of this manuscript) that Sufism is an integral version of Islam. Although Sufis do indeed access non-dual states of consciousness (what I shall call vantage-point shifts in subsequent volumes of this series) in which the individual self dissolves into Allah, these experiences are available at every stage of religious orientation. Although these state-stage shifts can be profound, all Sufis (like those in every religious system) must start at square one and then develop up the chain of psychological maturity.

222   "Major Religions of the World Ranked by Number of Adherents," accessed July 15, 2009, http://www.adherents.com/Religions_By_Adherents. html

223   Kung, Hans. Christianity and World Religions: Paths of Dialogue with Islam, Hinduism, and Buddhism. Maryknoll, N.Y.: Orbis Books, 1993. p 139

224   Kung, 1993. p 143–4

225   Knott, Kim. Hinduism: A Very Short Introduction. Oxford University Press, 2000. p 27

226   Monius, Anne. September 25, 2007. Comparative Religious Ethics Lecture. Harvard University.

227   Knott, 2000. p 20

228   Parish, Steven. Moral Knowing in a Hindu Sacred City. Columbia University Press, 1994. p 274

229   This distinction of faith development (structure-stages) is not to be confused with what Wilber calls state-stage development. The term "liberation" used by Hindus is a type of spiritual realization available to all beings at any level of structural complexity. As explained in the footnote in chapter 5 regarding Sufism, state-stages (and vantage-point shifts) must not be confused with the highest rung on the developmental ladder, but rather a second distinct category of development. Volume 1 of this series looks at these distinctions in detail.

230   Smith, Huston, and Huston Smith. The Worlds Religions: Our

Great Wisdom Traditions, [San Francisco]: Harper San Francisco, 1991.. p 20

231   Smith, 1991. p 21

232   Varghese, Alexander. India: History, Religion, Vision and Contribution to the World, Atlantic Publishers, New Delhi, India, 2008. p 206

233   Although structural development may very well have been at a magic level, state-stage development and/or vantage-point development likely came from a place of subtle, causal, or even nondual realization. All of this is to say that a low level of structural development does not jeopardize the profound spiritual status of these early stages.

234   Feuerstein, Georg. Yoga: The Technology of Ecstasy, 1st ed., Los Angeles: J.P. Tarcher, 1989. p 101

235   It is not to say that these rituals are necessarily abandoned by higher levels of development; it may be the case that they are preserved. However, it is certain that all such actions will be held in a larger and more sophisticated context that focuses on pragmatic action rather than manipulation of the external world through spells and incantations. With that said, it is quite clear that the mysteries of the world and our potential as spiritual beings are yet to be fully uncovered; multiple possibilities for future discoveries abound.

236   Feuerstein, 1989. p 102

237   Feuerstein, 1989. p 103

238   It should be noted that both levitation and invisibility could refer to experiences of the subtle body and not the gross physical body. In the case of the subtle body, both siddhis are very much legitimate (i.e., intentionally induced out of body experiences).

239   Feuerstein, 1989. p 43

240   Sharma, Arvind. Modern Hindu Thought: An Introduction. New Delhi; New York: Oxford University Press, 2005. p 25

241   Smith, David. Hinduism and Modernity, Vol. Religion in the Modern World, Malden, MA: Blackwell Pub, 2003.

242   Klostermaier, Klaus K. A Survey of Hinduism. 3rd ed., Albany: State University of New York Press, 2007. p 420

243   The caste system is comprised of a strict social structure that is determined by birth. In the past, the caste system was so strictly enforced that dining, marriage, or even touching members of other castes was forbidden.

244   Ghose, Aurobindo, On the Veda, 1st University ed., Pondicherry: Sri Aurobindo Ashram, 1956. p 370

245   The Upanishads form the philosophical basis for the most popular school of Hinduism called Vedanta (or, literally, the culmination of the Veda).

Although each sect of Hinduism can be interpreted and expressed through every level of development, the teachings of Vedanta often attract a rational form of Hindu expression. Although the following example of Vedanta is in no way exhaustive, it provides the reader with a solid example of the way Hindusim is often expressed through a rational lens.

When viewed at a rational level of orientation, the teaching of Vedanta explains that reality consists of two natures, absolute and relative. Most individuals are only aware of relative existence. Relative existence consists of a world of boundaries and divisions. This is the world as it is commonly understood. We see tables, chairs, windows, doors. We have emotions of happiness and anger. We divide and create boundaries in all aspects of our life giving almost every form that arises a name or description. Even the people in our life we divide into categories; some are friends and family, others enemies. Objects in the relative realm are impermanent and relationships between relative forms are forever changing. As long as one focuses his or her attention on the relative realm, as we saw with pursuits of pleasure, success, and duty, one will never find true happiness. One will never gain ultimate fulfillment.

Vedanta maintains that the key to fulfillment cannot be found in the relative alone but in discovering the second aspect of reality called the Absolute. A gold bracelet, gold earrings, and a gold necklace all have different forms, yet all three are made of the same substance. In the same way, the world is made of thousands of different forms but is inherently all of the same nature. This inherent nature, the unchanging Absolute, the Hindus call Nirguna Brahman (God without attributes). If individuals gain the capability to see and feel beyond the limits of relative nature into the absolute unchanging nature of all things, they hold the single key to liberation. Seeing through the illusion of separateness is the cornerstone of Hinduism. Upon seeing beyond the relative nature of the world, all boundaries of forms and names are lifted. With proper awareness of the Absolute in the external world, one can turn the lens inward and begin examining the 'thing" they call "self."

Vedantists assert that when an individual asks the question "Who am I?" he slowly discovers that the "thing" he once called "I" is not in fact him at all, but simply an object in his awareness. This process is generally described to proceed in a series of realizations that can be given as follows: This thing I call "I" is not my body, because the "I" is aware of my body. Who is this "I"? "I" cannot be my emotions, for I am aware of my emotions. "I" am not my thoughts, I am aware of my thoughts. "Who am I?" the questioning continues. "From where does this sense of I-am-ness come?" Ultimately, there comes a startling recognition that the sense of I-am-ness can only be identified with the unchanging Absolute itself, the only constant in the entire universe. For although everything else in awareness has changed (the body has changed, emotions have changed, thoughts have changed, even the individual soul has changed), one thing has always remained: I-am-ness. This recognition results in what the Hindus call Self-realization or God-realization. One recognizes that Atman (true Self) and Brahman (God/Absolute) are identical. The identification of "I" within the individual, once unaware of its source as it floated around in the lower self (personality), suddenly shifts to realize its natural resting place in the higher Self (Atman-Brahman).

In this re-identification comes the simultaneous recognition that because this very Self is the absolute (or because this Self is actually the gold that makes up all bracelets and necklaces), it is the same Self of all of existence. Once an individual has identified his sense of I-am-ness with the higher Self (and therefore also with the whole of existence) he is said to be liberated from the suffering caused by samsara (the cycles of birth and death)—liberated from the limited unfulfilling existence of chasing after ever-changing relative forms. An individual who has recognized the Self during this lifetime is called a jivamukti, (freed-soul). Hinduism claims that in recognition of the absolute Self, one discovers ultimate fulfillment, or moksha. The Absolute, by its very nature, is the only thing in existence that can provide infinite being, consciousness, and bliss, the three qualities that the individual truly seeks.

246   Sharma, 2005. p 34

247   Sharma, 2005. p 182

248   Radhakrishnan, S. "The Hindu View of Life", Upton Lectures Delivered At Manchester College, Oxford, 1926, London New York: Urwin Books,1961. p 16

249   Feuerstein, 2001. p 93

250   Sharma, 2005. p 184

251   Ramakrishna, 1965. Here Ramakrishna paraphrases the classic Hindu idiom.

252   "Shape" of religion is discussed further in forthcoming volumes. Because pluralism is embedded into the fabric of Hinduism, adherents often express pluralistic values despite the fact that they might only have capacity for mythic or magic levels of orientation; an individual conforming to pluralistic values before such distinctions are earned authentically through growth is an example in which one's expression is greater than his or her capacity.

253   For example, the popular phrase, "Truth is one. Sages call it by many names" comes from the Rig Veda.

254   Ramakrishnan, Ram. Many Paths, One Destination: Love, Peace, Compassion, Tolerance, and Understanding Through World Religions. Tucson: Wheatmark, 2010. p 188

255   Ramakrishna. Sayings of Sri Ramakrishna; the Most Exhaustive Collection of Them, Their Number Being 1120, 10th ed., Madras: Sri Ramakrishna Math, 1965. p 151.

256   Isherwood, Christopher. Ramakrishna and His Disciples, New York: Simon and Schuster, 1965. p 124

257   Beck, 1996. p 287

258   Ghose, 1992. p 261

259   There is a vital distinction that needs to be made here between ego development and state-stage or vantage-point development. Neither should be reduced to the other. Ego development is always part of the individual self-structure and not to be confused with vantage points associated with the witness or nondual. Although it may be true that a certain degree of state-stage/vantage-point development is necessary for higher structural development in certain lines like faith and ego development, the two areas are distinct. More of these elements are explored in volume 1 of this series.

260   Ghose, 1992. p 257

261   Ghose, 1992. p. 263

262   "Major Religions of the World Ranked by Number of Adherents," accessed June 19, 2008, http://www.adherents.com/Religions_By_Adherents. html

263   I acknowledge that there is clear political and spiritual dispute around the proper recognition of the 17th Karmapa – with Thaye Dorje carrying the same title – and quoting Ogyen Trinley here is not my endorsement of one or the other.

264   Interview with the 17th Karmapa conducted by the Global Oneness Movement, "Is the Spiritual Consciousness of the World Changing?," video accessed on June 17, 2010, http://www.youtube.com/watch?v=V9lFQAtV960&feature=channel

265   Eck, 2001. p 153

266   Eck, 2001. p 153

267   Eck, 2001. p 153

268   Eck, 2001. p 153

269   Eck, 2001. p.181

270   Eck, 2001. p. 182

271   Keown, Damien. Buddhism: A Very Short Introduction. Oxford; New York: Oxford University Press, 1996. p 64

272   Milarepa, Kunga Lama, and Brian Cutillo. Drinking the Mountain Stream: Songs of Tibet's Beloved Saint. Boston: Wisdom Publications, 1995.

273   Jackson, Roger. "A Fasting Ritual," in Religions of Tibet in Practice, ed. Lopez, Donald S., Princeton, N.J.: Princeton University Press, 1997. p 271

274   Because Tibetan Buddhism is based within a Mahayana and Vajrayana context, it is likely that all practicing Buddhists will take the Bodhisattva vow, not only the monks.

275   Sa-skya, Paònòdi-ta Kun-dga-rgyal-mtshan, Jared Rhoton, and Victoria R. M Scott. A Clear Differentiation of the Three Codes: Essential Distinctions Among the Individual Liberation, Great Vehicle, and Tantric Systems: The Sdom Gsum Rab Dbye and Six Letters. Vol. SUNY series in Buddhist studies, Albany: State University of New York Press, 2002. p 25; Some of these vows are taken by lay Tibetans as well.

276   Gyatso, Janet. "An Avalokiteshvara Sadhana," in Religions of Tibet in Practice, ed. Lopez, Donald S., Princeton, N.J.: Princeton University Press, 1997. p 266

277   Ibid.

278   Nalanda Translation Committee. "The Life of Tilopa," in Religions of Tibet in Practice, ed. Lopez, Donald S., Princeton, N.J.: Princeton University Press, 1997. p 137

279   Ibid.

280   Ibid.

281   Rinpoche, Thrangu. Songs of Naropa: Commentaries on Songs of Realization. Hong Kong: Rangjung Yeshe Publications, Boudhanath, Honk Kong & Esby, 1997. p 50

282   Keown, 1996. p 86

283   Lobsang P. Lhalungpa explains in his book The Life of Milarepa, "The miraculous powers that Milarepa openly demonstrated were the by-product of his absolute dedication to and mastery of meditation and yoga practice, and especially his achievement of integrating the transparency of awareness with all the subtle energies of the human organism..." See Lhalungpa, Lobsang Phuntshok. The Life of Milarepa. New York: Dutton, 1977. p xxix

284   In addition, each founder had a particular level of state-stage development or what I will call in subsequent work "vantage-point development."

285   For more details see Maslow, Abraham H. The Farther Reaches of Human Nature. New York, N.Y., U.S.A.: Arkana, 1993.

286   Wilber makes a similar point in his book Integral Spirituality. Overall, it is important not to confuse stage complexity (altitude) with depth of vantage point. Although not discussed in this book in detail, these are at least two very distinct forms of spiritual development (as discussed so far in several footnotes). Stages range along a vertical spectrum from magic to mythic to

rational to pluralistic to integral. Vantage points of awareness range along a spectrum of self-reflexivity from (1) an awareness fused with thought, to (2) an awareness fused with personal identity, to (3) an awareness fused with the individual consciousness, to the highest level of awareness, (4) awakened mind (vis a vis the seminal work of Daniel P. Brown). Each vantage point transcends and includes the previous vantage point. This idea is brought up here to avoid any confusion. Although Buddha had reached the highest vantage point (i.e., awakened mind), he still only possessed a rational stage of structural development at best. (For more on this, see my other work on the 3D Wilber-Combs Matrix and vantage points.)

287   Although deities were (and still are) used as teaching aids and skillful means at higher levels of development, those at magic and mythic levels of development tend reifying them and make them the primary points of focus.

288   Harvey, Peter. An Introduction to Buddhism: Teachings, History, and Practices, Cambridge, England; New York: Cambridge University Press, 1990. p 129

289   Harvey, 1990.

290   Suzuki, 1997. p 15

291   Harvey, 1990. p 129

292   Harvey, 1990. p 130

293   Ibid.

294   Bartholomeusz, 1998. p 2

295   Bartholomeusz, 1998. p 5

296   Bartholomeusz, 1998. p 3

297   Ibid.

298   The shape of a religious tradition is usually the direct result of its scripture and when relevant, the level of development of the religious founder.

299   See Sharf, Robert, "Experience," in Taylor's Critical Terms for Religious Studies, p 100

300   Suzuki, 1991. p 39

301   Alan Watts and D.T. Suzuki both note that from a higher level one realizes that simply reciting the name of Amitabha or more specifically "Namu-Amida-Butsu" is not calling on an external being to save you, but rather calls forth one's own Buddha nature; that pure "I-am-ness." The moment one recognizes that pure Buddha nature within, one is reborn into a "Pure Land" free from suffering. Although we entirely agree with this statement, we reemphasize that Watts' and Suzuki's view of Pure Land Buddhism and Amitabha Buddhism is a higher rational altitude interpreting a system that

originated to meet the needs of a magic level of orientation. In its original context, as described above in the section on "magic Buddhism," the meaning of Amitabha was certainly from a lower level: literal salvation from an external being and rebirth in an actual different place called the Pure Land.

302   See Sharf, Robert, "Experience," in Taylor's Critical Terms for Religious Studies, p 100

303   To use the term ethnocentric here may be a little harsh. After all, the West owes more to Suzuki and his explanations on Zen than perhaps any other teacher. The example does, however, help to show that regardless of uneven lines of development, religious orientation can still be determined.

304   Jones, Ken. The New Social Face of Buddhism: A Call to Action, Boston: Wisdom Publications, 2003.. p 92

305   As with any level of orientation there are moderate versions and extreme versions. As seen in previous chapters, some of the extreme versions of religious orientation can turn pathological before too long. One version of extreme pluralistic Buddhism or as we could say pathological pluralistic Buddhism is what Wilber calls "Boomeritus Buddhism." This form of extreme Buddhism takes relativism to its limits. Because everything is seen relativistically through the lens of "equality," at times those at this orientation excuse their own selfish and narcissistic behaviors. "To each his own" relativists at this level declare in order to explain away their own ego-centered actions. Using our newly found integral language, one could describe a person of this orientation as having green cognitive and faith development yet red, egocentric ego development often mixed with pre-conventional moral development; needless to say, psychograph produces a deadly combination with the ability to wreak havoc on the world. Further details regarding "boomeritus" can be found in Wilber's book Integral Spirituality. Ken Jones also goes on to give some of the dangers of extreme relativism in his book The New Social Face of Buddhism.

306   Jones, 2003. p173

307   Jones, 2003. p 179

308   In Integral Spirituality, Wilber claims that things like ecosystems do not arise in awareness until cognitive development has reached turquoise. The reader might ask, "How then could an individual at pluralistic religious orientation (i.e., a socially engaged Buddhist) be fighting for the environment and for protecting ecosystems? Are they fighting for something that doesn't even exist in their awareness?" We must remember that lines of development mature at different rates with cognitive development leading the way. An individual with a green altitude religious orientation might have the cognitive capacity to "see" ecosystems but their other lines of development might very well still rest near pluralistic levels or lower. This difference between lines of development marks a lower level of religious orientation despite turquoise

cognition.

309   Jones, 2003. p 78

310   Jones, 2003. p 92

311   Nhãát, Hòanh, and Jennifer Schwamm Willis. A Lifetime of Peace: Essential Writings by and about Thich Nhat Hanh. New York: Marlowe & Co.: Distributed by Publishers Group West, 2003. p 274

312   Tracy, 1991. p 95

313   Kung, Hans, Islam: Past, Present and Future. Oxford: Oneworld, 2009. p xxiii

314   Flood, 1999. p 35

315   Kung, 2009. p 630

316   Kung, 1993. p xii

317   The Journal of Inter-Religious Dialogue provides a consistent space for scholarly articles and discussion regarding religious exchange. Some of the articles published have led to exciting new breakthroughs. For instance, the first issue of the journal published an article that sought to find common ground between Buddhist and Christians both committed to environmental change. See Hastings, Steven. "Common Ground in EcoChristianity and EcoBuddhism." Journal of Inter-religious Dialogue, Issue 1, 2009.

318   "United Nations Information Service," accessed April, 2010,

http://www.unis.unvienna.org/unis/pressrels/2000/sg2639.html

319   "The Madrid Declaration," accessed April 10, 2010,

http://www.world-dialogue.org/Madrid/english/events/final.htm

320   "The World Conference for Dialogue Guide," accessed April 10, 2010,

http://www.world-dialogue.org/Madrid/english/Guide.pdf

321   "The Madrid Declaration", accessed April 10, 2010,

http://www.world-dialogue.org/Madrid/english/events/final.htm

322   When we include the stages of spiritual orientation into a model of religious understanding, we notice that even if dialogue is initiated by higher levels (i.e., rational, pluralistic, and integral), many people involved on the periphery may still hold lower levels (i.e., mythic and magic) of orientation that have not developed true respect for the religious other. Knowing that the international community smiles upon efforts at dialogue, some individuals at lower levels of development engage in religious dialogue merely to improve their own self-image or to project a positive image of their particular tradition out to the world. To say the least, these types of selfishly motivated individuals

defeat the whole thrust behind religious dialogue.

323   "What Works? Evaluating Interfaith Dialogue Programs," accessed April, 2010, http://www.usip.org/files/resources/sr123.pdf

324   Powerful examples and further explanation of this type of dialogue are provided in several books. See Tracy, David. Dialogue with the Other: The Inter-Religious Dialogue. Vol. Louvain theological & pastoral monographs; 1 Louvain Grand Rapids, Mich.: Peeters Press W.B. Eerdmans, 1991.; Patalon, Miroslaw. The Philosophical Basis of Inter-Religious Dialogue: The Process Perspective. Newcastle upon Tyne [England]: Cambridge Scholars Pub., 2009.; Bidmos, M. A. Inter-Religious Dialogue: The Nigerian Experience. Lagos: Islamic Publications Bureau, 1993.; Alatas, Syed Farid. An Islamic Perspective on the Commitment to Inter-Religious Dialogue. Kuala Lumpur: International Institute of Advanced Islamic Studies, 2008.

325   According to Harold Coward, inter-religious dialogue plays an important historical role. In the context of pluralism, dialogue has helped to significantly catalyze the development of many religious traditions. See Coward's article "Religious Pluralism and the Future of Religions" in Dean's Religious Pluralism and Truth, 1995.

326   Many more examples could be listed to support the efforts toward inter-religious dialogue. One prime example not outlined below is the open letter titled "A Common Word between Us and You" sent from 138 Muslim leaders to Christian leaders in an attempt to find common moral ground between the two traditions.

327   "Second Hindu-Jewish Leadership Summit Declaration," accessed April 10, 2010, http://www.millenniumpeacesummit.com/2nd_Hindu-Jewish_Leadership_Summit_Declaration.pdf

328   "Second Hindu-Jewish Summit Report," accessed April 10, 2010, http://www.millenniumpeacesummit.com/2nd-Hindu-Jewish_Summit_Report-Final.pdf

329   Wayne Teasdale, "Interreligious Dialogue Since Vatican II: The Monastic Contemplative Dimension", Spirituality Today, Summer 1991, Vol.43 No. 2, p 119–33

330   Walker, Susan. Speaking of Silence. New York: Paulist Press, 1987. p 127–8

331   It is also the case that those at a rational level of development might make the same mistakes as early scholars during the modern paradigm and may end up "essentializing religion." Jane Smith, echoing Marcia Hermansen's article "Muslims in the Performative Mode," makes a similar point. Smith writes, "Hermansen, herself Muslim, points out that we often look at our partner in dialogue as an 'essential' Muslim or Christian, as if one person

cold somehow represent all of those who share the same religious affiliation. Hermansen's observation serves to remind us how important it is that we try to discover the real nature of our dialogue partner." Smith, 2007. p 99

332   This might be loosely compared to John Cobb's "complementary pluralism." As Griffin puts it, one type of pluralism "sees a central task of theological dialogue to be the discovery of how these various doctrines are complementary rather than contradictory." (Griffin, 2005. p 39)

333   Although not always related to low levels of development, Smith outlines "one of the major problems of dialogue is the tendency to talk about one's own faith in its ideal form, and to assess the faith of another in terms of the way it is seen to be manifested in everyday life..." (See Smith, Jane I. Muslims, Christians, and the Challenge of Interfaith Dialogue. New York: Oxford University Press, 2007.) It is easy to see how this sort of idealization of one's own faith and concretization of the other persons faith could serve as a true barrier to dialogue if members are at an ethnocentric level of religious orientation, consciously or unconsciously looking for faults in the religious "other."

334   Sachedina, 2001. p 7

335   "The World Conference on Dialogue: Its Promise and Challenges—A Reflection by Shanta Premawardhana," accessed April 10, 2010, http://www.oikoumene.org/resources/documents/wcc-programmes/interreligious-dialogue-and-cooperation/interreligious-trust-and-respect/the-world-conference-on-dialogue-a-reflexion.html

336   Sullivan, Maureen. 101 Questions and Answers on Vatican II. New York: Paulist Press, 2002. p 17

337   Wayne Teasdale, "Interreligious Dialogue Since Vatican II: The Monastic Contemplative Dimension", Spirituality Today, Summer 1991, Vol.43 No. 2. p 119-133

338   Wayne Teasdale, 1991; Organizations like the World Council of Religious Leaders are already on track with just this sort of integrally informed mission.

339   To be even more precise, one could call this type of communication: inter-altitude, intra-religious dialogue.

340   Jones, 2005. p xii

341   This could also be called inter-altitude, inter-religious dialogue.

342   This process follows Wilber's basic outline of "kosmic address" as put forward in his book Integral Spirituality.

343   The terms I, WE, and IT refer to a simplification of Wilber's Four Quadrant model: I (Upper Right), WE (Lower Left), and IT(s) (Upper Right

and Lower Right). See Wilber's Sex, Ecology, Spirituality for more details.

344   Wilber, 2006.

345   "Integral Spiritual Center," accessed April 10, 2010, http://isc.integralinstitute.org

346   Ibid.

347   See Wilber's book Integral Spirituality.

348   Hurd, Elizabeth Shakman. The Politics of Secularism in International Relations. Princeton: Princeton University Press, 2008. p 6

349   Berger, Peter L. The Social Reality of Religion. London: Faber, 1969. p 113

350   Thomas, Scott. The Global Resurgence of Religion and the Transformation of International Relations: The Struggle for the Soul of the Twenty-First Century. 1st ed. ed., Vol. Culture and religion in international relations New York, N.Y.: Palgrave Macmillan, 2005. p 58

351   Thomas, 2005. p 77

352   Johnston, Douglas, and Cynthia Sampson. Religion, the Missing Dimension of Statecraft, New York: Oxford University Press, 1994. p 9–10

353   Berger, Peter L. The Desecularization of the World: Resurgent Religion and World Politics. Washington D.C., Grand Rapids, Mich.: Ethics and Public Policy Center W.B. Eerdmans Pub. Co. 1999. p 2–3

354   Brooks, David, Kicking the Secularist Habit, Atlantic Monthly, March 2003, p 27–8

355   Thomas, 2005. p 11

356   Robert Wuthnow, "Understanding Religion and Politics," Daedalus, Vol. 120, No. 3, Religion and Politics, Summer, 1991. p 11

357   Thomas, 2005. p 56

358   Hurd. 2008. p 3

359   Eisenstadt, 2000.

360   Thomas, 2005. p 60

361   Thomas, 2005. p 9

362   Thomas, 2005. p 9

363   Harris, Sam. End of Faith: Religion, Terror, and the End of Faith. New York, W.W. Norton and Company, 2005. p 26

364   Quoted from: Petito, Fabio and Pavlos Hatzopoulos. Religion in International Relations: The Return from Exile. New York: Palgrave

Macmillan, 2003.; The entire UNESCO constitution can be found online at

http://www.unesco.org/education/information/nfsunesco/pdf/
UNESCO_E.PDF

365   Thomas, 2005. p 51

366   Thomas, 2005. p 13

367   Thomas, 2005. p 13–14

368   Thomas, 2005. p 14

369   See Douglas Johnston's book Faith Based Diplomacy for details.

370   Johnston, 1994. p 17

371   Particularly those insights that create a global ethic and the technologies that train the mind through practices like meditation.

372   Secularization theory assumes that as countries modernize, there will be an increasing diminishment of the influence of religion. Today, even the theory's original creators suggest that their initial thoughts were incorrect. See Perter Berger's The Desecularization of the World.

373   Douglas Johnston books Religion: The Missing Dimension of Statecraft and Faith Based Diplomacy offer a wealth of insight as to how religion might be properly integrated into international relations.

374   Harris, 2005. p 48. Italics are mine.

375   Petitio, 2003. p 102

376   These ideas are borrowed from a forthcoming manuscript titled Inter-group Leadership by Bawa Jain, Secretary General of the World Council of Religious Leaders.

377   In other arguments, the author suggests that one functional and practical format for economic, political, and religious coordination is via a properly established World Federation.

378   Fowler, James. "Faith Development at 30: Naming the Challenges of Faith in a New Millennium," Religious Education Vol. 99, No. 4, Fall 2004.

379   Extreme typologies at lower levels of development tend to suffocate opportunities for true religious freedom and an authentic exploration of knowledge. The UNDP's Arab Knowledge Report in 2009 states: "Knowledge can only flourish in an atmosphere of freedom, and the knowledge society can have no foundation as long as extremism remains in play. Extremism which threatens freedom or bans it—whether through the behavior of certain groups or the tyranny of regimes that practise extremism through the suppression of freedoms—has a negative effect on the enabling environments of the knowledge society....Extremist trends oppose both the acknowledgment of

the Other, and dialogue and outreach. For the most part they rely on calls and conceptions which they formulate with a private logic that tolerates no dissent." UNDP, Arab Knowledge Report 2009: Towards Productive Intercommunication for Knowledge, p 16. Accessed October 2, 2010, http://www.arabstates.undp.org/contents/file/newfiles/AKR09_E/Intro.pdf

380   Farr, Thomas F. World of Faith and Freedom: Why International Religious Liberty Is Vital to American National Security. New York: Oxford University Press, 2008. p 22

381   As Wilber points out in Integral Spirituality, every human being has the right to stop development anywhere along the spectrum he or she chooses. This protection must extend to those at magic and mythic levels alike. In part, protection of lower levels is especially important due to the fact that higher forms of development can only unfold if they are given the opportunity (even if only briefly) to pass through each subsequent stage along the way.

Although it is necessary to give freedom to lower levels, we must also ensure that their potentially divisive beliefs are quickly exposed to higher levels of expression. In part, this will be accomplished by breaking the mold that assumes the fundamentalist's literal version of the tradition the only correct and acceptable view.

382   Knox, Noelle. "Religion Takes a Back Seat in Western Europe," USA Today, August 10, 2005, http://www.usatoday.com/news/world/2005-08-10-europe-religion-cover_x.htm

383   It is worth noting here that as Western Europe continues to become less religious, the rest of the world is experiencing a drastic increase in religiosity. In part, this is due to the fact that as globalization increases and countries are exposed to cultures and worldviews outside of their own, individuals are more likely to cling to the traditions that are most familiar until they have adjusted to the new globalized geo-political-cultural system. Thomas PM Barnett speaks of this phenomenon brilliantly in his book Great Powers. See Barnett, Thomas P. M., Great Powers: America and the World After Bush. New York: G.P. Putnam's Sons, 2009.

384   The author is currently working on a database of religious and spiritual leaders from every tradition and from all levels of development. This database will serve as a resource for all those looking for teachers and teachings at specific developmental levels. If you are interested in contributing to the database or would like to suggest specific religious figures to add, please contact the author directly at ddiperna@drpi.org.

385   Although comparative details need to be worked-out, vantage points are similar to Wilber's state-stages when the term "state stage" refers to subjectivity permanent abiding from a gross, subtle, causal, witnessing, or nondual awareness. Vantage points make up one of at least three key

elements of spiritual development: structure-stage development (i.e., religious orientation), state access (trained access to states/realms/objects) and vantage points (permanent shift in awareness ranging from subjectivity identified with personality to witness to non-duality). I used the term "liberations of consciousness" to describe a similar phenomenon in the first two drafts of this book and published similar ideas in an article on Visser's Integral World website in 2007. I have since adopted the term "vantage point" as used by Harvard professor and meditation teacher Daniel P. Brown. For a more detailed analysis of this topic, please see volume 1 wherein I present a three dimensional Wilber-Combs Matrix.

386   Harris, 2005. p 40–1

387   The term "inner engineering" was first coined by Indian spiritual teacher Satguru Vasudev. Burgess-Smith's T and Me: Journey into Discovery, iuniverse, 2008. p 106

388   Eisenstadt, S. N., "Multiple Modernities," Daedalus, Vol. 129, No. 1, Winter, 2000, p 1-29

389   Even a statement like "the West" is problematic if it is reified. The West, like all other regional blocks of culture, is not monolithic. It is not accurate to say that all of Western culture is a result of Greek thought any more than we can say that it is all Christian. Both statements have partial truths (the West was certainly influenced by Christianity and Greek thought). For the purposes of this opening chapter however, there is heuristic value in telling the narrative of "the West" as if it is a simple entity, as long as we don't assume that its homogeneity is the case in any sort of absolute sense.

390   Lincoln, 2006, p 1–2

391   Wilber, Marriage of Sense and Soul, 2000, p 126

392   Technically the shift was the result of changes in all Four Quadrants and not just consciousness.

393   Wilber, Marriage of Sense and Soul, 2000, p 126

394   Wilber, Marriage of Sense and Soul, 2000, p 132

395   Wilber, Marriage of Sense and Soul, 2000, p 132

396   Wilber, Sex, Ecology, Spirituality, 2000, p 410

397   Wilber, Sex, Ecology, Spirituality, 2000, p 410

398   Here Wilber uses the term "level" to refer to the stage of consciousness (e.g., premodern, modern, postmodern). The term "line" refers to the specific area of intelligence (e.g., spiritual, cognitive, emotional). The term "level-line fallacy" refers to the fact that a particular line of development (spiritual), was

confused with a level of development (premodern), and consequently the entire line of spiritual development was repressed and abandoned to lower levels of development (mythic/premodern). We discuss Wilber's use of both levels and lines in the coming chapters. For further details on the level-line fallacy, see Wilber's Integral Spirituality.

399   One of the first anthropological accounts of religion outside of the West comes from the Persian scholar Abu Rayhan Biruni in the eleventh century.

400   Both Eliade and Geertz are two prime examples of transition scholars, between modernity and postmodernity, who were largely critiqued for "essentailizing" religion.

401   Flood, Gavin D. Beyond Phenomenology: Rethinking the Study of Religion. London ; New York: Cassell, 1999. p 3

402   Flood, 1999, p 2–3

403   Griffiths, Paul. "On the Future of the Study of Religion in the Academy," Journal of the American Academy of Religion 74.1, 2006, 66-74. p 72

404   Smith, Jonathan Z. Imagining Religion : From Babylon to Jonestown. Vol. Chicago studies in the history of Judaism Chicago: University of Chicago Press, 1982. p xi

405   Flood, 1999, p 35

406   Flood, 1999, p 7

407   Wilber, Marriage of Sense and Soul, 2000, p 189

408   See Popper, Karl R., and Mark Amadeus Notturno. The Myth of the Framework : In Defence of Science and Rationality. London ; New York: Routledge, 1994.

409   Ferrer, Jorge N., and Jacob H. Sherman. The Participatory Turn : Spirituality, Mysticism, Religious Studies. Albany, N.Y.: State University of New York Press, 2008. p 27

410   Ferrer, 2008, p 27

411   Stiver, Dan R. Theology after Ricoeur : New Directions in Hermeneutical Theology. 1st ed. ed., Louisville: Westminister John Knox Press, 2001. p 137

412   Ricœur, Paul., and John B. Thompson. Hermeneutics and the Human Sciences : Essays on Language, Action, and Interpretation. Cambridge [Eng.]; New York Paris: Cambridge University Press Editions de la Maison des sciences de l'homme, 1981. p 43

413   Tracy, David. Plurality and Ambiguity : Hermeneutics, Religion,

Hope. Chicago: University of Chicago Press, 1994. p 10

414   Tracy, 1994, p 9

415   Tracy, 1994, p 9

416   See Collected Papers of Charles Sanders Pierce, ed Charles Hawthorn and Paul Weiss, p 5:448n.

417   Tracy, 1994, p 9

418   Flood, 1999, p 3

419   See also the work of David Lawrence and Jorge Ferrer for hints at this new sort of approach.

420   Wilber, Sex, Ecology, Spirituality, 2000, p 148-9

421   From Ken Wilber's "Foreword" in Frank Visser's book, Ken Wilber: Thought as Passion, 2003), pp. xii-xiii.

422   The levels of development represented by the historical time periods are broad generalizations of the average mode of discourse around religious studies at the time. There were both individual exegetes as well as pockets of scholars who, although living in a premodern historical period, were cutting kosmic grooves and functioning at a postmodern, or higher level of development. As such, although living within an earlier historical paradigm, these individuals could have been enacting horizontal approaches from a post-modern or higher structure-stage (e.g., advanced hermeneutics). The Hindu sage Abhinavagupta is a perfect example. There are certainly others.

423   Over the last century the discovery of "myth of the given" has crippled these early beliefs. The myth of the given has been unpacked and explained forcefully by scholars such as Wilfrid Sellars and most recently by Wilber. See Wilfrid Sellars, Empiricism and the Philosophy of the Mind; also see Ken Wilber, Integral Spirituality.

424   Ferrer, 2008, p 4

425   Ferrer, 2008, p 14

426   Ferrer, 2008, p 14

427   For his article: See Alderman, Bruce, "Kingdom Come: Beyond Inclusivism and Pluralism, An Integral Postmetaphysical Invitation," 2010. Published Online at http://www.integraltheoryconference.org/talks

428   For his article see Drieghe, Geert, "Integral Pluralism and the Problem of Religious Diversity," Integral Theory conference papers, 2010. Published online at http://www.integraltheoryconference.org/talks

429   See Esbjörn-Hargens, S., & Wilber, K. (2006). "Toward a Comprehensive Integration of Science and Religion: A Post-metaphysical

Approach." In P. C. Z. Simpson (Ed.), The Oxford Handbook of Religion and Science (pp. 523–46). Oxford: Oxford University.

430   Thresher, Tom, Reverent Irreverence: Integral Church for the 21st Century, 2010, Integral Publishers.

431   In addition to the efforts toward forms of Integral Christianity, other traditions are also beginning to use Integral Theory to update their teachings. Communities are beginning to form around Integral Judaism, Integral Buddhism, Integral Hinduism, all of which are likely to continue as developmental sensitivity continues to grow

432   For a deeper connection to the idea of recapitulation and how it unfolds in various domains of existence, the reader is urged to consult Sex, Ecology, Spiritually, whverein Wilber aptly explains the process of recapitulation in both the interior domains (psychological and cultural) and in exterior domains (biology/behavior and socio-technological systems).

Also available from Dustin DiPerna:

Books

Streams of Wisdom (Integral Religion and Spirituality Volume 1)
Evolution's Ally (Integral Religion and Spirituality Volume 2)
Earth is Eden (Integral Religion and Spirituality Volume 3)
The Coming Waves: Evolution, Transformation, and Action in an Integral Age

iPhone App

Enhance: Meditation for Modern Life

Audio

The Great Human Tradition (Available on iTunes and on Amazon)

www.ingramcontent.com/pod-product-compliance
Lightning Source LLC
Chambersburg PA
CBHW062043080426
42734CB00012B/2550